The Lancashire Giant

Sir David Shackleton
Geo. Lord, St Annes-on-Sea: SP.

The Lancashire Giant

David Shackleton
Labour Leader and Civil Servant

ROSS M. MARTIN

LIVERPOOL UNIVERSITY PRESS

First published 2000 by
LIVERPOOL UNIVERSITY PRESS
4 Cambridge Street
Liverpool L69 7ZU

British Library Cataloguing-in-Publication Data
A British Library CIP record is available

ISBN 0 85323 934 7 *cased*
0 85323 944 4 *paper*

Typeset by Northern Phototypesetting Co. Ltd, Bolton
Printed and bound in the European Union by
Antony Rowe Ltd, Chippenham, Wilts.

To the memory of
Hugh Armstrong Clegg,
true scholar and friend

Contents

List of Illustrations

Preface

I first learnt of David Shackleton, and something of his career, in the course of writing a book on the history of the Trades Union Congress. That encounter left me puzzled about the way most writings dealing with the early Labour party ignore the weighty part he plainly played in its formative years, both as a trade unionist and as a parliamentarian. It also left me curious about his later career, outside the labour movement. For at the age of 47, while still at the pinnacle of the movement, he suddenly joined the Home Office when Winston Churchill beckoned; and then six years later won the ultimate bureaucratic prize, the permanent secretaryship of a ministry. I thus had two principal aims in mind when I started work on this book. One was to remedy the neglect of Shackleton's role in the establishment of the Labour party. The other was to throw what light I could on the question of how an ill-educated, working-class man coped with life at the summit of the early twentieth-century civil service.

Initially, too, I thought of the book as a plain 'political' biography, a straightforward account of the public doings of a public man. I assumed that Shackleton would follow the standard working-class pattern of an obscure childhood and youth, with no diaries or personal correspondence extant, and with little on the public record of a personal nature. In the event, while he did largely follow this pattern, some unexpectedly rich sources were also uncovered. First, there were limited personal papers (cited below as SP) held by his descendants. These consist of a large, disorganized scrapbook of mostly unsourced and/or undated newspaper clippings interleaved with a number of loose letters and other documents, together with a diary Shackleton kept during a visit to the United States in 1902. Second, I was able to interview four people who knew him personally – a granddaughter, Nancy Smith, who was 18 years of age when he died in 1938; a grandson, David Catlow, who was 25 then; a nephew, Ernest Wilkinson, who was 40 in 1938; and Sir Frederick Leggett who, in his thirties and early forties, was a senior official at the Ministry of Labour throughout Shackleton's time there. Third, there was the provincial press, and especially the little weeklies published in the cotton towns of north-east Lancashire – with their gossipy columnists, their varying editorial allegiances, their detailed reportage of local politics and meetings, and their parasitical snippings from the London press. Fourth, there were unanticipated aspects of both the Ministry of Labour's records and the minutes of Lloyd George's War Cabinet.

The insights afforded by these sources (while still, I presume, inadequate for a genuine 'psycho-biography', for which I have neither the skills nor the interest) added a new dimension with two consequences. First, it enabled me to depict in some detail the style and attitudes of a man who was certainly more typical of the trade unionists and union officials of his time than those, further to the left, who have generally hogged the limelight in works on the Edwardian labour movement. Second, it forced the division of the book into two parts: 'The Life' and 'The Man'. It is to be emphasised that Part II ('The Man') seeks simply to assemble the pieces of a personality, so far as these are discernible in what Shackleton wrote or was reported as saying, and in what others have said or written about him. There is no attempt, in other words, to explain *why* he was the kind of person he was.

I have had a great deal of help. The late Ernest Wilkinson hugely enriched the personal side of the biography with his detailed adult and near-adult memories of an uncle he admired, and with his meticulous researches into the family's early history. It is a matter of deep regret that Ernest died without having read the first complete draft of this book, though it was by his side at the time. The youthful memories of Nancy Smith and the late David Catlow were also an invaluable source. It was the initiative of the late Mary and Harold Miller, of Sheffield, which led me – via Mick Bacon, of Lytham St Anne's – first to Ernest Wilkinson, and eventually to David Catlow, Nancy Smith and the Shackleton papers.

Rodney Lowe was the soul of generosity in the details he provided of relevant file categories in the Ministry of Labour's labyrinthine archives in the Public Record Office, and greatly eased my task there, as well as directing me towards some other sources. I had notable archival pointers from Stephen Bird, Labour Party Archives; J. B. Darbyshire, Blackburn District Library; S. E. Barclay, Darwen District Library; S. Halstead, Rawtenstall District Library; and Janet Claridge, University of Birmingham Library. The staff of the Borchardt Library, La Trobe University, were as always marvellously helpful, but Brita Daly made a singular contribution by imprisoning essential microfilms for me.

In the belief that there is no substitute for grappling with the raw material oneself, I did not use a research assistant in researching this book. On the other hand, John Dunleavy, Vivienne Martin and John Whiteoak furnished me with substantial information on specific topics. In addition, Keith Abbott, Leitha Martin Bevilacqua, Vivienne Martin and Michael Ross each generously checked some references in London for an author on the other side of the globe. Marilu Espacio typed the early drafts with the same consummate skill and patience she displayed throughout the 22 years that our professional partnership lasted. Liz Byrne and Michael O'Keefe helped a computer novice grapple with later drafts. Alex Bevilacqua masterminded the crucial initial scanning of the book's illustrations.

John Miller, Talis Polis and Cameron Hazlehurst each put a fine tooth-comb through a draft of the book, to its particular benefit. Valued comments on it were also provided by Judith Brett, Leitha Martin Bevilacqua, Annemarie Flanders, Angus McIntyre, Lena Martin, Vivienne Martin and Nancy Smith. Lena Martin endured the long silences that go with writing, and I am immeasurably grateful for that.

R. M. M.
October 1998
Melbourne

Introduction

In 1956 the *Manchester Guardian* published a fifty-year-old photograph of a group of nine solemn men standing in a wide doorway. The caption beneath, noting that the photograph was taken on the terrace of the House of Commons in 1906, describes the men as the 'leaders of the first Parliamentary Labour Party'.[1] Four of them stand well to the fore, as befits senior office-holders. Three of these have names (Keir Hardie, Ramsay MacDonald, Arthur Henderson) which are invariably prominent in writings about the beginnings of the British Labour party; and each of them has been the subject of at least four full biographies.[2] The fourth man was David James Shackleton.

Physically big by today's standards, Shackleton was mountainous by the standards of those inhabiting Lancashire factory towns at the start of the twentieth century. He was further distinguished by a career with two sharply differentiated and almost equally remarkable phases. In the first, he cast a towering shadow across the Edwardian labour movement. In the second, he scaled the austere heights of the British civil service.

His working life began at the age of nine, in a cotton mill. Thirty years later, in 1902, as a trade union official endorsed by the Labour Representation Committee (LRC), he won a parliamentary by-election which proved to be a turning-point in the history of the Labour party-to-come. From that point, he rose swiftly in the councils of both the LRC/Labour party and the Trades Union Congress (TUC); and, for five years from the start of 1906 to the end of 1910, straddled the political and industrial wings of the labour movement in a way unmatched even by a later Ernest Bevin. For most of 1906 and 1907, he was the effective leader of the new parliamentary Labour party despite losing (by one vote) the caucus election for its formal leadership, which Keir Hardie won. In 1907 he was elected chairman of the TUC's executive; and a little while later astonished observers, both inside and outside the labour movement, by declining an armchair ride into the parliamentary party's leadership. Subsequently, he had the high distinction of being the only TUC chairman in a century, and more, to be granted a second term of office. Then abruptly, in 1910, he abandoned the lofty, public heights

---

1 *Manchester Guardian*, 14 February 1956.
2 In the case of both Hardie and MacDonald, the total is seven.

of the labour movement for a middle-ranking appointment in the bowels of the civil service. Six years later, just as abruptly, he surfaced again as permanent secretary of the new Ministry of Labour. Shortly after that he became, as the press of the day put it, 'the first Labour knight'.

These are the bones of a notable career. Yet Shackleton has rarely figured – in a substantial, studied way – in the historiography of the British labour movement.[3] Nor do the many published biographies and autobiographies of his labour contemporaries give much idea of his achievements as either a parliamentary or a trade union leader. This pattern of neglect is not easily explained.

Part of the explanation may well be the fact that he was not a writer and left no significant body of personal papers. But the same can be said of Arthur Henderson, whose style and early career closely parallel Shackleton's. On the other hand, Henderson had longevity on his side: he was a national figure in the labour movement for some thirty years, whereas Shackleton was similarly prominent for, at most, eight years. Against this, the case of Victor Grayson suggests that the brevity of this kind of prominence, in itself, is no deterrent to labour biographers.[4] What seems to have weighed heavily in Grayson's favour was a reputation as a rebel and a spellbinding speaker, combined with the fact that he was also (in Barbara Tuchman's phrase) 'a raving Socialist'.[5] Shackleton, in contrast, was not only no rebel in the romantic sense and lacked a flair for oratory, but consistently disclaimed Socialism as a political faith.[6] Those disclaimers, especially, probably told against him. H. A. Turner has argued that the frequently Socialist leanings of British labour historians were at least partly responsible for a longstanding literary neglect of the cotton unions, 'an unsympathetic subject' because of their conservatism.[7] If Turner is right, then the manner of

3   There are three clear exceptions: Bealey and Pelling, *Labour and Politics* (1958), based especially on Bealey's 1957 article, 'The Northern Weavers'; Clegg et al., *History of British Trade Unions*, vol. 1 (1964); and Martin, *TUC* (1980). As for the civil service phase of his career, it is done something like justice in *Adjusting to Democracy* (1986), and a number of articles, by Rodney Lowe.

4   Grayson, a national figure for just 30 months after winning the Colne Valley by-election in 1907, is celebrated in three full biographies and in a five-page profile in Kenneth Morgan's *Labour People*. The profile is one of seven in a section on 'The Founding Fathers' of the Labour party which also includes Hardie, MacDonald, Henderson, the Webbs and two others – but not Shackleton.

5   *Proud Tower*, p. 379. 'A former theological student with a gift for oratory and a fondness for drink, he preached Socialism as the deliverance of the poor with a fervour that swept through the mill towns like fire.'

6   Henderson (though he did not formally join a Socialist organization, the Fabian Society, until 1912) had by 1906 publicly 'embraced the [Socialist] doctrines ... from which he had recoiled in 1903'. Leventhal, *Arthur Henderson*, p. 28.

7   *Trade Union Growth, Structure and Policy*, p. 30. A similar tendency to focus on radical, at the expense of conservative, facets of the labour movement has been suggested in the case of American labour historiography. See Greene, '"Strike at the Ballot Box"', p. 166.

Shackleton's departure from the labour movement could only have reinforced any such lack of sympathy. Many on the left called it desertion – and renegades, as Royden Harrison once remarked, are among the firmly 'non-approved subjects' of labour history.[8]

Nevertheless, unfashionable though he might be among labour historians, Shackleton had qualities that make him more representative of the Edwardian labour movement than those of his contemporaries – like Tom Mann and Ben Tillett – who have attracted much greater literary attention. For his broad outlook, unlike theirs, more nearly characterised the general run of British trade union officials and members. It was an outlook embodying what John Saville described as 'the ideology of labourism'.[9] This entailed a belief in the efficacy of three things above all: social change by constitutional means; self-help rather than state assistance; and (given the existence of independent trade unions) fair dealing between capital and labour. Labour historians, as Saville pointed out elsewhere, have often badly underestimated the 'tenacity and persistence of [this] labourist tradition'.[10] It is a tradition which goes a long way towards explaining Socialism's limited penetration of the British working class before the First World War.[11]

Shackleton was a product of this tradition. He shared the values of the bulk of the trade union officials and activists who had to be won over if the LRC, the infant form of the Labour party, was to take root. That meant he shared their initial commitment to one or other of the traditional parties – in most cases, as for him, to the 'radical', reformist wing of the Liberal party. On the other hand, he also seems to have embraced earlier than many of his colleagues the idea ('what was new in turn-of-the-century "labourism"') of independent political action.[12] And circumstances enabled him to play the major role in an event, the Clitheroe by-election of 1902, which guaranteed the LRC/Labour party a future by at once bringing the powerful cotton unions onside and persuading the Liberal party leadership to enter into a secret electoral-sharing agreement with Labour. Thereafter, he consistently defended the Labour party as an admittedly uneasy alliance of Socialists and non-Socialist trade unionists, and he fought doggedly to protect the ideological flexibility (that 'spacious concept of unity', in McKibbin's phrase)[13] which distinguished the party from its more doctrinaire counterparts on the

8 'Labour Party History', p. 12.
9 Saville in Benewick et al., *Knowledge and Belief in Politics*, pp. 215–16.
10 Saville, 'Notes on Ideology and the Miners before World War I', pp. 25–6.
11 See Joyce, *Visions of the People*, p. 84; McKibbin, *Ideologies of Class*, pp. 296–7.
12 Joyce, *Visions of the People*, p. 76.
13 *Evolution of the Labour Party*, p. xvii. What this entailed, above all, was the absence of any constitutional commitment to Socialism. This feature of the British Labour party created a problem for the Second Socialist International, which eventually managed to admit it in 1908 on the reasoning (Karl Kautsky drafted the resolution) that it was at least 'organised independently of the bourgeois parties'. Quoted in Cliff and Gluckstein, *The Labour Party*, p. 56n. See also Elliott, *Labourism and the English Genius*, pp. 3, 25.

Continent.[14] At the same time, true to his labourist roots, he also fought to protect the trade unions' right to deal independently with government ministers, and repeatedly repulsed the party's attempts to strip the TUC of its political functions.

The trade union phase of Shackleton's career has two key elements. One is his typicality in terms of the origins and outlooks of those who chiefly surrounded him. The other is the great authority he enjoyed among them during the five years from 1906 to 1910. Strikingly, neither of these elements figure in the second, civil service phase. As the administrative head of the Ministry of Labour, his working-class origins and lack of a formal education made him a spectacularly odd man out. As for his authority among those who surrounded him in the years following his appointment to the permanent secretaryship, there was evidently a great deal of affection, but nothing like the clear respect and deference he had enjoyed in the labour movement. And his leap into the senior rank of the civil service, unlike his breakthrough in the matter of royal honours,[15] established no precedent.

---

14   During Shackleton's time, too, the British party was distinguished by the social class from which its leadership was drawn – as Keir Hardie boasted in the course of proposing a toast to Shackleton, the guest of honour at a dinner celebrating the achievement of the Trade Disputes Act in 1906: 'while there [on the Continent] the movement depended almost entirely upon the middle-class educated leaders, in this country the working-class leaders were the only recognised leaders of labour'. *Blackburn Times*, 22 December 1906.

15   His knighthood, as McKibbin puts it, made 'the path to honours ... broad and rosy' for working-class candidates. *Ideologies of Class*, p. 19. But not, it has to said, quite as quickly or as munificently as McKibbin's phrase implies.

Part I

The Life

1

Beginnings, 1863–1893

David Shackleton, like so many raised in the valleys of north-east Lancashire in the 1860s, seemed destined for a life of labour in a cotton mill. That was the implication of his parentage and birthplace.

Number 20 Alma Terrace was part of a grim, cramped row of stone houses known locally as the Alma Cottages. They stood in Cloughfold, slanting across a hillside overlooking the river Irwell. Cloughfold was one of a close-knit cluster of villages populating the Rossendale valley and tributaries, which were collectively defined by their centre, Rawtenstall. Rawtenstall was a cotton town: by 1867 it boasted 145 mills.[1] One of them crowned the hill at Cloughfold. The huge Hall Carr mill loomed over the Alma Cottages like the castle of a feudal lord over the huts of his serfs.

David Shackleton was born in 20 Alma Terrace on Saturday 21 November 1863. It was a desperately hard time. The mills of Lancashire had been cut off from the American South, their main source of raw cotton, by the Civil War. The great 'cotton famine' was at its height, and north-east Lancashire had been 'the area to suffer first and extremely harshly'.[2] Shackleton's family was wholly dependent on cotton. His father, William, and his mother, Margaret, were listed as power-loom weavers in the census of 1861. William's older sister was a weaver, his younger brother a 'roller maker',[3] and his parents both cotton-mule spinners. They all lived in the Alma Cottages.

It was also a perilous time for the children of cotton operatives. Shackleton, the second of four born to his parents, was the only one to live past infancy. The first-born, a boy, died early in the year of Shackleton's birth, aged six months. The others, both girls (aged four months and two years), died in 1868 of scarlet fever in the epidemic which killed their mother: she was no more than 24 years old. Shackleton, as an adult, had no recollection of her other than the memory of playing with a toy horse and cart she had given him. He did, however, have a vivid memory of an uncle (presumably Abraham, his father's brother) carrying him, 'pick-a-back', away from the house of his birth in which his mother and sisters lay, to the safety of his grandparents' home.[4]

1. Pevsner, *Buildings of England*, p. 205.
2. Ellison, *Support for Secession*, p. 20.
3. This refers to the rollers involved in cotton-spinning machinery.
4. *M.A.P.*, 26 January 1907, p. 110.

Shackleton was four at the time of his mother's death.[5] Almost exactly a year later, his father remarried. Mary Jane Holt, the new wife, was some two years older than the father. She was also an unmarried mother. Her daughter, Ellen Ann, was Shackleton's junior by just eight months. Ellen Ann's birth certificate shows no father. Although brought up as Shackleton's stepsister, she was almost certainly his half-sister, conceived while William's first wife was carrying Shackleton. Ellen Ann's mother, late in life, appears to have told her that William was in fact her natural father. Ellen Ann, as a married woman with her own children, gave her maiden name as Holt when registering the birth of the first three, but changed it to Shackleton when the fourth was born.[6] Between 1871 and 1882, Shackleton's stepmother gave him five sisters in addition to Ellen Ann. All of them survived to adulthood.

The father, William, plainly had ambition for himself. In his late teens, before his first marriage, he attended evening classes at the Rawtenstall Mechanics' Institute.[7] By the time of the 1871 census he had graduated from weaver to 'grocer and roller coverer'.[8]

His ambitions for his only son are less clear. He sent him to a dame school at the age of five; and then, after a year, to the Longholme Wesleyan Day School in Rawtenstall. He sent Ellen Ann there too. All of this cost good money: the Longholme 'school pence' was twopence a week for each child. At that time, he was not legally required to provide either with an education.[9] But as soon as Shackleton turned nine, William put him to work as a 'half-time' weaver.[10] The nine-year-old David probably started at the Hall Carr mill, on the hill at Cloughfold, above the Alma Cottages. William worked there himself at this time. Shortly afterwards, during 1873 it seems, the family left Rawtenstall for Haslingden. There, the father realized his evident ambition. He left the mill altogether, and set up as a watchmaker. The son,

---

5.   The loss, very early in the child's life, of one parent through death (John Burns, Arthur Henderson, Tom Mann, Will Thorne, Ben Tillett) or other causes (Keir Hardie, Ramsay MacDonald) was, it seems, almost de rigueur among the more prominent labour leaders of Shackleton's generation.

6.   I am indebted for the detailed evidence on which the conclusions in this paragraph are based to the researches and the memory of the late Ernest Wilkinson, the son of Ellen Ann.

7.   I am indebted to John Dunleavy for this information.

8.   A 'roller coverer' was concerned with refitting spinning rollers (see note 3 above). Becoming a 'grocer' was one way, involving the use of a home front room, initially low capital, and part-time work (with a wife's help), in which ambitious nineteenth-century working men sought – sometimes successfully – to claw themselves up the ladder. See, e.g., Roberts, *The Classic Slum*, pp. 3, 6.

9.   The Education Act of 1870 did not make education compulsory but permitted local school boards to compel attendance, if they chose. Few seem to have done so before the end of 1872 (even by 1876 only 50 per cent of the population of England was subject to compulsion). But as soon as Shackleton entered employment, he and his parents were subject to a compulsory education requirement under the Factory Act of 1844. See Barnard, *Short History of English Education*, pp. 196–7.

10.   William himself was sent to work as a half-timer in a weaving mill at the age of seven. *Nelson Leader*, 14 November 1919.

however, remained a half-time weaver, and was taken on at the Laneside mill, where parochial tradition mistakenly had him first learning his trade.[11]

The life of a young weaver in the 1870s was far from easy. 'Half-time', as Shackleton recalled, meant a working-week that was 'nominally thirty hours ... but in practice ... thirty-six hours'.[12] In other words, on six days a week he began in the mill at 6 a.m., worked for six hours; and, on weekday afternoons, then went to school.[13] This arrangement initially put 2s a week into his father's pocket.[14]

Shackleton was later to boast about this stage of his life: 'by the time I was twelve I had two looms, which ... was a unique achievement for a half-timer, and before I was thirteen I had three looms, as a half-timer, which certainly is, and I dare say always will be, a record in the weaving industry'.[15] In what he described as 'my "spare" time', he was 'employed' in his father's watch-making business. But, nevertheless, there was still valued time to play cricket and football, and to become, in his own estimation, 'something of a champion at them'.[16]

In Haslingden, Shackleton at first went to the Wesleyan Day School, but soon transferred to the Church of England Day School. It would have been cheaper for his father.[17] Shackleton recalled his schooldays with satisfaction. 'At school I did well. At least I presume so, for during my last year of schooling I was a monitor and taught the smaller boys.'[18] Certainly, the schoolmaster of the Church school, a Mr Jump, took an interest in Shackleton, and apparently urged his parents to allow him to look to a career in teaching.[19] But Mr Jump's advice was not taken.

Shackleton was put to full-time weaving as soon as he reached the legal age of 13. That was not quite the end of his formal education. He attended night-classes at the Haslingden Mechanics' Institute, though not at the secondary

11. *Haslingden Gazette*, 9 August 1902.

12. *M.A.P.*, 26 January 1907, p. 110.

13. He may, on the other hand, have worked mornings and afternoons in alternate weeks, on weekdays, a common practice towards the end of the century.

14. But it could have been a crucial 2s, as was often the case among Lancashire working-class families. See Anderson, *Family Structure in Nineteenth Century Lancashire*, p. 33; Liddington and Norris, *One Hand Tied Behind Us*, p. 34.

15. *M.A.P.*, 26 January 1907, p. 110. At that time, an *adult* who was a 'four-loom weaver' was regarded as exceptional. See Joyce, *Work, Society and Politics*, p. 114.

16. *M.A.P.*, 26 January 1907, p. 110. Later, speaking in support of a Daylight Saving Bill, he gave some indication of his enthusiasm for sport. 'I take myself back about 30 years, when as a young fellow I wanted to do a little cricket. I spent all my day in a cotton factory in humidity averaging 70 to 80 degrees ... It was only a few weeks – not more than two months – that I would get from home to the cricket field a mile away to get some cricket ... I had to walk two miles every night ... and sometimes I could not get a turn of the bat.' *Parl. Debs.*, 5 March 1909, vol. 1, col. 1772.

17. See Adamson, *English Education*, p. 363.

18. *M.A.P.*, 26 January 1907, p. 110.

19. *Rechabite and Temperance Magazine*, November 1900, p. 25; unknown newspaper, 27 February 1904: SP.

level. But by his own account, he once again fell victim to the monitorial system.[20]

> Education was just being placed within the reach of the working-classes, and the night schools were full of grown, even middle-aged men, with here and there a greybeard. I was a good elementary scholar, and so nearly all my time as a pupil was spent as a teacher, instructing men old enough to be my father, in the 'three R.'s'. This was all very well, and I enjoyed the work, but it meant that I myself never got beyond the elementary stage.[21]

He also taught, as a teenager, at Sunday school.

The family moved again in January 1878, this time to Accrington, a larger and industrially more diverse town than Haslingden. William had evidently acquired more capital, and advertised himself in the *Accrington Directory* as a watchmaker and jeweller who dealt also in bicycles and musical instruments. Shackleton, now 14, found work as a weaver. For a time, too, he continued to attend night school at Haslingden, walking the four miles each way.

A few weeks after the family arrived in Accrington, north-east Lancashire became the site of what Sidney and Beatrice Webb were later to describe as 'one of the greatest industrial struggles on record'.[22] The cotton strike of 1878, opposing a 10 per cent cut in wage rates, lasted more than two months and ended in total victory for the mill owners. It was marked by considerable violence.[23] In Accrington, the violence did not reach the levels experienced in some other weaving towns, but during one tumultuous May evening mobs stoned two houses, and a number of people – civilians and police – were hurt. Before the week ended, after other stone-throwing episodes, a number of young men were charged with riot, police reinforcements arrived, 118 special constables were sworn in, and a 40-man cavalry troop (from the 5th Dragoons) was stationed in the town.[24] Crowds continued to throng the town centre, but now it was to admire the dragoons and their horses; and when these were replaced by an infantry detachment early in June, 'the excitement in the town' quickly faded.[25]

The nature of the young Shackleton's involvement in these events is uncertain. It is known, however, that he did not yet belong to the weavers' union. This was not unusual for a lad of his age. Even so, he would still have

---

20.   This system of teaching, associated with the names of Andrew Bell and Joseph Lancaster, was widely employed in Shackleton's time. It involved systematic use of abler or more advanced students (monitors) to teach other students. Effectively a system of 'mass production in education', its great advantage was its cheapness. Barnard, *Short History of English Education*, p. 64. One of its disadvantages, as illustrated in Shackleton's case, was the way it could reduce the educational opportunities of the monitors. See Vincent, *Bread, Knowledge and Freedom*, p. 97. Nowadays, this system of teaching tends to be described as 'peer tutoring'.

21.   *M.A.P.*, 26 January 1907, p. 111.

22.   Webb, *History of Trade Unionism*, p. 344.

23.   See King, '"We Could Eat the Police!"', pp. 439–71.

24.   *Blackburn Times*, 18 May 1878; *Blackburn Standard*, 25 May 1878.

25.   *Blackburn Times*, 8 June 1878.

been parted from his looms, probably for the duration of the strike – but possibly for only the last six weeks if he was at a mill which remained working, on the basis of an independent workplace agreement, until a general lockout was imposed in May. In either case, his father's home and occupation would have given him a security that most of his workmates lacked.

As he later recalled, he was 'particularly impressed' by two aspects of the strike: 'the one, the employment of English soldiers against Englishmen, the other, the poor organisation and feeble resources of the strikers'.[26] He recalled it as leading him – a youth with an early interest in public affairs, stimulated by shared readings and discussions with his paternal grandfather, an ardent Liberal – 'to study still more closely industrial questions and problems'.[27] Pursuing this interest required planning. 'I used to eat my dinner whilst at my work, so as to be able to spend the dinner hour in a reading-room, where I eagerly devoured the *Manchester Guardian* and the *Manchester Examiner*.'[28] He confessed to getting 'very excited over the General Election of 1880'[29] when he was 17 years of age; and he was said to have joined a Liberal club in the same year.[30] He later told the House of Commons that he 'had the honour to carry a banner ... in a campaign against the House of Lords' in 1884.[31]

Strangely, on the other hand, the two books that, in recollection, 'greatly influenced this period of [his] life' were not directly political works.[32] One was William Cobbett's *Advice to Young Men*.[33] The other was *Hugh Wellwood's Success*, by Anne Jane Cupples, which the young Shackleton used in his Sunday-school teaching, and particularly valued for its 'practical wisdom'.[34]

His father and stepmother were total abstainers, and enrolled him in a Band of Hope at an early age. 'I have never touched strong drink in my life',

26. *M.A.P.*, 26 January 1907, p. 111.
27. Ibid.
28. *Pearson's Weekly*, 15 March 1906.
29. *M.A.P.*, 26 January 1907, p. 111.
30. *Cotton Factory Times*, 11 July 1902.
31. *Parl. Debs.*, 24 June 1907, vol. 176, col. 946.
32. *M.A.P.*, 26 January 1907, p. 111.
33. It is to be noted, however, that Cobbett's 'Young Men' did not include a mere millhand – as the book's full title makes clear: *Advice to Young Men, and (incidentally) to Young Women, in the Middle and Higher Ranks of Life*.
34. *M.A.P.*, 26 January 1907, p. 111. The full title of the Cupples book is *Hugh Wellwood's Success; or, Where There's a Will There's a Way*. First published in 1869, it presents the instructive story of a curate's two sons. Hugh, the elder by two years, and a hard-working prize-winning student at school, was 'by nature as merry-hearted a boy as his brother, and ... as fond of play ... but he never allowed his amusement to interfere with his lessons or any duty he had to perform'. In contrast, the younger Maurice, though 'a remarkably clever boy' with a much 'better head for learning', was 'so fond of play that he neglected his lessons'. But then finally, after vicissitudes and with the help of his elder brother, Maurice's attitude improves. Discovering that 'real pleasure came from doing his duty', he ceases to be 'a lazy tom-noodle'. Hugh, needless to say, 'grew up to manhood, spreading sunshine wherever he went, and beloved by all who knew him'. Cupple, *Hugh Wellwood's Success*, pp. 6, 27, 29, 48.

he was to claim in his forties.[35] On the other hand, he did smoke when he was 18; but found it too expensive, and never tried it again.

The only published reference he made to his relations with his parents is notable for its warmth: 'I had the best of parents, my boyhood was altogether happy and comfortable.'[36] And most things point to a dutiful son. Yet, as a youth, he defied them in one thing at least – and that a matter of the gravest domestic significance. He married without his father's consent. This would have taken determination and courage. For the father was cast in the classical Victorian mould (see Chapter 9), and Shackleton would have been drilled in biblical standards of parental authority and filial obligation. On this occasion, moreover, he not only disobeyed his father but lied – about his age. Nineteen at the time of his marriage on 3 August 1883,[37] his father's consent was required by law. The age entered in the marriage register is 21.[38]

Sarah Broadbent, his bride, was 18. Her parents, too, withheld consent; and she also registered her age as 21. Parental opposition was probably inevitable. Sarah, like Shackleton, worked in the mill. The convention of the time and the class was that working children living in the parental home handed their weekly pay to their mother or father who, in return, gave them a spending allowance.[39] This meant, other considerations aside, that their marriage cost each of their families the better part of the income of a full-time weaver.

The father's reaction to the son's resolve is reflected in Shackleton's possessions at the moment of his marriage. All he had then, apart from the clothes he wore, was 'wrapped in one of those large red handkerchiefs which were common in Lancashire' at the time.[40] And the marriage ceremony was conducted in the Wesleyan Methodist Chapel at Antley, well away from both families, who had three other Wesleyan chapels closer to their homes.[41] There was still a defensive edge 23 years later in Shackleton's reference to his marriage. 'When I was twenty [*sic*] I did what no doubt many wise people would consider a very foolish thing, but what nevertheless proved to be the best stroke I ever made in my life. In short, I married, my wife, like myself, being employed in the mills.'[42] Ironically enough, William, the father, had also first married at about the same age. But his bride, unlike his son's, was pregnant.[43]

35. *M.A.P.*, 26 January 1907, p. 111.
36. *Pearson's Weekly*, 15 March 1906.
37. He later recalled his age at that time, incorrectly, as 20. *M.A.P.*, 26 January 1907, p. 111. His wife, speaking to a reporter about their golden wedding, got it right – and also mentioned that she was 18 when she married. Unknown newspaper, n.d. [4 August 1933]: SP.
38. I am indebted to Ernest Wilkinson for evidence of this.
39. Older children might be dealt with a little differently in some cases. See Liddington and Norris, *One Hand Tied Behind Us*, p. 32. But the Shackleton practice, as Ernest Wilkinson experienced it, was firmly in the traditional mould. Letter to author, 2 January 1989.
40. Letter from Ernest Wilkinson to author, 17 July 1979.
41. Again, I am indebted to Ernest Wilkinson for these details.
42. *M.A.P.*, 26 January 1907, p. 111.
43. The evidence, again, is from Ernest Wilkinson. In this respect, however, the father's marriage, not the son's, was probably more typical of the time and the class. See Rule, *Labouring Classes in Early Industrial England*, pp. 196–7.

The Union Man

Shortly after his marriage, 'in view of [his] new responsibilities', Shackleton joined the local weavers' union.[44] The Accrington Power Loom Weavers' Friendly Association, founded in 1858, was the largest union in the town. In 1886 its membership was 3,522,[45] and probably accounted for something like three-quarters of the town's weavers.[46] Of these members, 2,576 paid a basic contribution of 1d a week; the remaining 946 chose to pay 2d a week in order to qualify for funeral benefit.[47] The funeral benefit of £5 represented the friendly-society aspect of the union.[48] The union was financially healthy.[49]

Shackleton, reportedly prompted by his wife and father-in-law, a tinplate worker, took an active interest in the union's affairs from the start.[50] He was elected to its management committee within 15 months of becoming a member, attending his first committee meeting a few days short of his twenty-first birthday. His true career had begun, though he was not yet aware of that. His ambitions still centred on the mill. He wanted to become an 'overlooker'.[51]

Shortly after his election, Shackleton was sacked – ostensibly for a reason other than his union involvement.[52] He then found that he had also been blacklisted. 'I wore my boots out, trying to get work, but every gate was shut against me.'[53] His wife, however, was still in work and, at her urging, he eventually gave up the hunt for a while, allowing her to 'keep the home together, till things [came] right'. It was to be a disheartening 17 weeks before things came right. In the meantime, he did the housework, 'read a great deal', and 'more than once … thought seriously of becoming either a policeman or an insurance canvasser'.[54]

44. *M.A.P.*, 26 January 1907, p.111.
45. *Cotton Factory Times*, 25 June 1886.
46. A slightly smaller membership of 3,230 in 1892 amounted to 75 per cent of all weavers in the town. Ibid., 5 June 1892.
47. Ibid., 25 June 1886.
48. The outgoings on this account, for the half-year ending 31 May 1886, amounted to £110. In the same period, £130 had been paid in 'levies' to the Weavers' Amalgamation; and a little over £50 was expended from an 'emergency fund' (amounting originally to more than £300, invested at 2 per cent) in connection with four strikes, only one of which involved an Accrington mill.
49. It had recently acquired (at a cost of £1,640) a row of ten houses, on which £105 had been spent in renovations. On 'real receipts' during the half-year of over £573, 'we have saved' almost £151, so that the 'total worth' of the union, including office stock, amounted to £2,173.
50. Unknown newspaper, 27 February 1904: SP.
51. The role of the overlooker, or 'tackler', was part foreman but mainly mechanic.
52. The formal ground, as he later told the House of Commons, was trivial: 'He had occasion to be up nearly all night owing to sickness at home. He should have been at his work at 6 a.m.; he was a quarter of an hour late, and was informed that his services were no longer required. He had been an active member in the trades union movement … but his employer did not tell him that that was the reason why he was discharged.' *Parl. Debs.*, 8 May 1903, vol. 122, cols. 208–9.
53. *M.A.P.*, 26 January 1907, p. 111.
54. Ibid.

He finally obtained work, through a friendly overlooker, in a mill with an owner who lived outside Accrington. His new employer tolerated Shackleton's union activities to the extent of giving him time off, 'provided I left a capable substitute behind me', to attend to union business.[55] Despite an oft-repeated story that his blacklisting led to continual harassment until he left Accrington,[56] Shackleton seems to have stayed with this employer up to his departure from the town in 1893. During this time, too, he must have been promoted to the position of overlooker. For, as he proudly told a meeting of Lloyd George's War Cabinet years later, he had 'worked both in the position of a workman and a foreman'.[57]

He soon made his mark in the Accrington weavers' union. By 1885 he was one of its delegates to the Northern Counties Amalgamated Weavers' Association (Weavers' Amalgamation). In 1887 he was elected its auditor, and in 1890 to its presidency, which he retained until he left the town. During the same period, he also established a significant presence in the Weavers' Amalgamation itself. He spoke at the first meeting he attended; and 50 years afterwards, Tom Shaw could still recall the way Shackleton's 'common sense and striking appearance made a tremendous impression on those present'.[58] In 1889 he was elected a trustee, but the following year failed to win selection as one of four delegates to the annual meeting of the TUC. In 1892, however, he won not only a TUC delegate's position but also (from a field of ten candidates) the auditorship of the amalgamation.

The Accrington period saw other achievements as well. He was secretary, 'for several years', of the Liberal Association for the town's North-east Ward.[59] His standing in the temperance and friendly society movement is reflected in his election as auditor for the Blackburn District of the Independent Order of Rechabites (see Chapter 4) in 1892. But in December the same year, a much weightier prize came his way. He was appointed a Justice of the Peace (JP). This, in its time, was a signal honour for a man of his class.[60] The first working-class magistrates had been created as recently as 1885, by the third Gladstone government.[61] Another Accrington man, Thomas Birtwistle, then secretary of the Weavers' Amalgamation, had been one of them. Shackleton's appointment came when the Liberals again won government, and was part of a much larger burst (seventy as against six) of working-class JPs.[62] Officially, the appointment was linked to his presidency of the weavers' union, but some suspected that his political connections

55. Ibid.
56. See, e.g., *Cotton Factory Times*, 11 September 1908.
57. *War Cabinet*, 523, 31 January 1919: CAB 23/9, p. 38.
58. *Manchester Guardian*, 2 August 1938.
59. *Colne & Nelson Times*, 11 July 1902.
60. Moreover, he was reputedly 'the first operative actually working at the mill elected to a position of this kind'. *Cotton Factory Times*, 18 November 1910.
61. See Martin, *TUC*, p. 31.
62. Ibid., p. 61.

might have been more significant.[63] Accrington Conservatives, while grudgingly acknowledging Birtwistle's competence on the bench, opposed Shackleton's appointment on general grounds.

> Of Mr David Shackleton we know but little ... If, however, the weavers are entitled to a representative, what about the miners, and other working men ... ? And why stop there? Why should not the chimney sweepers and the scavengers and the lamplighters also have their representatives on the Bench? ... It is tending towards making a burlesque of the Bench.[64]

In terms of Shackleton's future career, however, his most significant achievement by far during the Accrington period had to do with learning, not position. For it was in Accrington that he mastered the procedures involved in calculating weavers' wages. The pay of both weavers and spinners in the cotton industry depended on a system of piecework rates set out in lists that had to take account of a wide range of variables. The extraordinary complexity of the system demanded an unusual skill on the part of their full-time officials.[65] Their unions, as a result, came (from 1861) to rely on a process of selecting officials which centred on a formal examination testing ability in calculating 'sorts' (see Chapter 2).[66]

Shackleton evidently taught himself this skill. Ellen Ann, his eldest half-sister, told her son that his uncle 'always had a text book rigged up over one of the looms' in the mill where they both worked.[67] Others recalled that 'it was common to find a book open in his weft-can at the mill, for he took his meals to the factory so that he might have time to practice [*sic*] working out sorts'.[68] His skill in quantitative calculation received early recognition, as we have seen, when he was made auditor of the Accrington weavers' union at the age of 24. By the winter of 1890–91, he was conducting evening classes in calculation sponsored by his union. The classes were attended 'by about 18 or 20 young men', whom he taught 'how to work the standard list for weaving, so that the weavers will know all the sooner whether the employers are

63. See *Colne & Nelson Times*, 11 July 1902.

64. *Accrington Division Gazette*, 3 December 1892.

65. 'For although the lists are elaborately worked out in detail ... the intricacy of the calculations is such as to be beyond the comprehension not only of the ordinary operative or manufacturer, but even of the investigating mathematician without a very minute knowledge of the technical detail. Yet the week's earnings of every one of the tens of thousands of operatives are computed by an exact and often separate calculation under these lists. And when an alteration of the list is in question, the standard wage of a whole district may depend upon the quickness and accuracy with which the operatives' negotiator apprehends the precise effect of each projected change in any of the numerous factors in the calculation.' Webb, *History of Trade Unionism*, p. 308.

66. The outcome, in the Webbs' words, was 'a combination, in the Trade Union world, of the accountant and the lawyer'. Ibid., p. 309. H.A. Turner later preferred 'trade union technicians'. *Trade Union Growth, Structure and Policy*, p. 129.

67. Ernest Wilkinson to author, 17 July 1979.

68. Unknown newspaper, 27 February 1904: SP.

paying up to the standard list or not'.[69] He conducted a similar series of classes a year later. It was this specific demonstration of his abilities on which he placed most weight in the letter he wrote when he applied, in January 1893, for the secretaryship of the Ramsbottom Weavers' Association.[70]

69. *Cotton Factory Times*, 3 July 1891.
70. 'I may say, as to calculating prices, I have been teacher of two classes & have been appointed for a third time, for the purpose of learning the young men of our society the system of calculation, & I think I shall be able to do the work required of me as a secretary.' Shackleton to Ramsbottom Weavers' Association, 12 January 1893.

2

The Local Union Official, 1893–1902

There were 24 applications for the vacant position of secretary to the Ramsbottom Weavers, Winders and Warpers' Association. Five of the applicants, chosen by the union's executive committee, then took an examination set by W. H. Wilkinson of Haslingden, and Ernest Holmes of Burnley. The result was a shortlist of two: Shackleton and John Farron, a former president of the Ramsbottom union. The committee selected Shackleton.[1] In March 1893, he moved himself into the union's office and his family into the house connected with it.

His departure from Accrington was marked by a formal farewell at the Liberal Club, and the presentation of a couch from the weavers' union. He retained one formal link with the town, his seat on the Accrington magistrates' bench. Some were sceptical of his ability to combine this role with that of a full-time union official in Ramsbottom,[2] but he appears to have had no problem in doing so.

Shackleton's new union was much less well endowed than the one he left. With a little over a thousand members, it was one-third the size. In the half-year to 31 May 1893, its income was £226; and its balance sheet (his first) showed a loss of £59.[3] In addition to the union's financial problems, he had to cope in his first few months with at least one major employer who paid below the union-approved 'list prices', refused to talk to him, and intimidated employees who sought to attend a union meeting.[4] Outside the union, he

1. *Cotton Factory Times*, 20 January 1893. Farron, who regained the union's presidency early in 1894 while Shackleton was still secretary, subsequently became secretary of the Rossendale Weavers' Association.
2. '[H]ow he will be able to manage [all] this ... remains to be seen.' *Ramsbottom Observer*, 27 January 1893. Yet the distance between the two towns was, by rail, only about 14 miles.
3. *Cotton Factory Times*, 16 June 1893. The loss was 'caused chiefly by the exceptionally heavy expenditure [£113] in breakdown and stoppage pay' (a benefit relating to machinery breakdowns). Shortly after his arrival, Shackleton narrowly won the agreement of a special general meeting to a ruling that such payments would in future be made only in the case of stoppages of three days or more, instead of the old minimum of one day. Ibid., 28 April 1893.
4. '[I]t was, to say the least of it, rather a singular coincidence that a representative of the firm should, upon that particular night, be standing within a few yards of the meeting place ... Naturally enough, the weavers seeing the person named within such close proximity at such a time, fought shy of the meeting, with the result that there was not a single one attended.' Ibid., 3 November 1893.

became sufficiently prominent in the Ramsbottom Liberal Club to be recorded as presiding over 'the first social party of the session', chairing a political lecture, and seconding a vote of thanks to Miss Caroline Fothergill for a talk on 'Rambles in Yorkshire'.[5] But Ramsbottom was no place for an able man with ambition. In little more than a year, Darwen beckoned.

The Darwen Weavers, Winders and Warpers' Association, formed in 1857, was an altogether more imposing union. It had over 5,000 members, more than the combined membership of the Ramsbottom and Accrington unions. Its founding secretary, improbably named Entwistle Entwistle, was appointed before the days of formal examinations and held office for 35 years until his death in 1892. For most of those years, he was a part-time secretary, and had to supplement his salary by selling 'caps etc' from a market stall.[6] Entwistle's immediate successor, Joseph Cross – one of the new, examined breed – stayed barely two years before moving to the secretaryship of the even larger (with almost 11,000 members) Blackburn Weavers' Association.

The Darwen selection procedure differed significantly from Ramsbottom's: there was no formal examination. Each of the four men on the shortlist, drawn from an initial list of around 40 applicants, was already the secretary of a weavers' union.[7] That meant they had passed an examination testing their technical competence. They were required only to address a special general meeting of the union's members. In the ballot held after all four had spoken, Shackleton won 148 of the 206 votes cast.[8]

The difference in the status of the Darwen and Ramsbottom unions is also reflected in the secretary's salary. At Ramsbottom, Shackleton was paid £1 10s a week, a most superior wage for a weaver at the time.[9] His starting salary at Darwen was £2, later increased to £2 5s.[10]

---

5. *Ramsbottom Observer*, 27 October 1893; 19 January 1894; 16 February 1894.

6. Darwen Weavers' Association, *Souvenir of Celebrations*.

7. *Cotton Factory Times*, 11 May 1894.

8. DWA, *Minutes* (GM), 7 May 1894. When the Ramsbottom union chose Shackleton's replacement, the successful applicant (not already a union secretary) won selection only after passing an examination taken by all of the four shortlisted candidates. Once again, W. H. Wilkinson was one of the examiners. The other was Shackleton. *Cotton Factory Times*, 25 May 1894.

9. Weavers then earned from 14s to 20s (£1) a week; but warpers, also pieceworkers and members of the Darwen and Ramsbottom unions, made from 20s to 30s. See Webb, *Industrial Democracy*, p. 105.

10. The secretary of the umbrella organization, the Weavers' Amalgamation, was at this time paid £3 a week. There were also occasional supplements to Shackleton's salary, apart from payments relating to conferences and deputations outside Darwen. Thus, on one occasion, he was paid 2s 6d for attending to a legal settlement 'out of office hours' and, on another, 7s 6d for work in connection with the union's annual tea party, ball and concert. DWA, *Minutes* (Ctee), 5 October 1896; 11 December 1899.

The Darwen Weaver's Secretary

It was late in May 1894 when the Shackletons moved to Darwen with their three children – a girl (Margaret Jane) and a boy (Ernest), both born in Accrington, and a boy (Fred) born in Ramsbottom. Once again, they occupied a house, owned by the union, which was next door to its office.

For the next eight years, Darwen was the focus of Shackleton's life. It was a tragic time for the family. Fred died in 1898, aged four, of appendicitis; and Ernest in 1901, shortly before his twelfth birthday, of pneumonia. But there were no matching misfortunes in Shackleton's public life.

His timing was good. When he went to Darwen, the Lancashire cotton industry was on the verge of an economically buoyant and industrially calmer 12 years, following a long period of resisted wage cuts and union recognition battles. Between 1894 and 1902, his union's membership rose from a little over 5,000 to 7,000, and its accumulated funds from about £9,000 to more than £13,000.[11] Industrially, the union was 'recognised by every employer in the town, full list prices are paid in every mill, and little trouble is experienced ... in ... negotiations with employers'.[12] In the town at large, it was the biggest of the local unions and an investor, to the tune of £2,000 (at 2¾ per cent), in the Darwen corporation.[13]

As secretary, Shackleton had many responsibilities, but one was central, and drew on the expertise tested in the examination he sat before winning the Ramsbottom secretaryship. This was the task of checking 'sorts' – that is, employers' calculations relating to the cloth woven by a particular weaver and the 'price' the weaver was paid, as set out on a ticket or a tally-board. Both the dimensions of this task and its importance to his members are illustrated in the fact that, during 1899-1901, Shackleton recalculated a total of 3,237 sorts brought to his office and established that underpayment was involved in 1,290 (40 per cent) of them.[14] Such a high rate of error was partly a function of the complexity of the system, but typically owed something to sharp practice ('nibbling', it was called in union circles) on the part of employers.[15]

---

11. *Colne & Nelson Times*, 11 July 1902. Its financial returns for the first three years of the new century, moreover, showed a profit ('a gain') ranging from £110 to £553, for every quarter except the second of 1901, when there was 'a loss of £90 ... brought about by [machinery] breakdowns and a heavy death roll', entailing payments of stoppage and funeral benefits. *Cotton Factory Times*, 16 January 1903.

12. Ibid.

13. DWA, *Minutes* (Ctee), 15 August 1898.

14. DWA, *Report ... for Quarter Ending Dec. 31st, 1899; 1900; 1901*. In all cases, the procedure was that both the weaver and the employer concerned were informed of the results of his calculation. Millowners appear to have invariably accepted his corrections.

15. See DWA, *Report ... for Quarter ending March 31st, 1899*. Shackleton once said as much in a public speech, but most diplomatically: 'He did not say that they [the underpayments] had all been intentional. Quite a number of them had been mistakes by the clerk who had the work to do.' *Cotton Factory Times*, 23 January 1903.

A secondary aspect of this core function was the calculation of limited benefits relating mainly to funeral costs and to compensation for working time lost through machinery breakdowns. These, as a comment in one of Shackleton's annual reports implies, were thought important as a means of attracting new members: 'Our terms are easy and our benefits are equal, if not better, than any other trade society in Lancashire, in proportion to the payments made.'[16] Non-unionists were also the target when – with particular reference to the union's strike fund – he warned them that in the event of a strike or lockout ('a resort to war'), they would be 'left to shift for themselves'.[17] Recruitment was a constant concern and membership drives were frequent, Shackleton attending numerous meetings for this purpose.

Weaving was a predominantly female occupation. The cotton unions, 'the only [unions] to organize women effectively', accounted for more than 80 per cent of England's female unionists;[18] and the Weavers' Amalgamation, to which Shackleton's union belonged, claimed 45,000 women in a membership of 80,000.[19] Nevertheless, in comparison with their numbers, women and girl weavers were heavily under-represented in the membership of the weavers' unions. Shackleton frequently complained that much of the blame for this lay with men, themselves unionists, who did not accept a similar 'necessity for their wives and children becoming connected with our Society'.[20]

As union secretary, he was also required to play a social role. An 'annual tea party, concert and ball' was the climax. On this occasion, in 1899, after some 540 people had 'sat down to tea', and finished, 'the cloths were removed [and] the secretary, Mr Shackleton, occupied the chair' to oversee dancing in the Co-operative Hall and a concert in the Industrial Hall.[21]

There is no indication that his position as secretary was anything other than secure. But he had his critics and, more significantly, he was not always

16.   DWA, *Annual Report*, 1895. In the year he wrote this comment, the Darwen union decided (or, as he later put it, 'he persuaded his committee') to award 10 scholarships annually to help members improve their skills by attending Technical School weaving classes, the union paying the class fee and, for those passing the examination, 'a book prize' worth 5s. *Cotton Factory Times*, 24 September 1897; 9 December 1904. These scholarships, later increased to 20, appear for many years to have remained singular to Darwen, among local weavers' unions. They are an early reflection of Shackleton's lifelong obsession with education. See, especially, Chapter 10.
17.   *Cotton Factory Times*, 30 April 1897.
18.   Turner, *Trade Union Growth, Structure and Policy*, pp. 24–5.
19.   *Cotton Factory Times*, 2 February 1894.
20.   DWA, *Report … for Quarter ending September 30th, 1899*. His differences with local craft unions extended to the effect of their exclusionary policies on the job prospects of the sons of weavers, which at least once roused him to threaten reprisals. 'We do not believe in this protective system [restricting access to apprenticeships], but we recognise that the time has arrived for us to defend ourselves, and let the members of protected trades know that, if their doors are closed to our boys, we shall not assist them in finding work for their girls, and shall refuse to learn them our trade.' Ibid., 30 June, 1897.
21.   *Cotton Factory Times*, 8 December 1899.

able to win his way. One source of criticism which surfaced publicly had to do with the practice of 'bating' (fining) weavers for defective cloth. Shortly after arriving in Darwen, he won much praise for resolving a longstanding dispute on this issue.[22] Five years further on, however, one of his members wrote a letter to the editor (under the intriguing *nom de plume*, 'Sniff') claiming to have informed the union about bating at a particular mill, 'but nothing has been done for us'.[23] 'Another Weaver' wrote in support of 'Sniff', saying 'there is not a union in England that does less for its members than Darwen' – and citing other cases of alleged obstructionism before waspishly concluding: 'They are getting their salaries risen very nicely.'[24] This remark presumably referred to an occasion, eight months before, when Shackleton was given a pay rise. That occasion, as it happened, was also one on which his critics flexed their muscles. For while the executive had proposed an increase of 10s, to £2 10s a week, the union's general meeting (by 45 votes to 25) reduced the rise to 5s.[25]

Earlier, too, Shackleton had been involved in a lengthy struggle over the union's representation at the annual Trades Union Congress.[26] Prior to Darwen, he had been the Accrington union's sole Congress delegate in 1890 and 1891, and represented the Weavers' Amalgamation in 1892, but was absent the following year when the impoverished Ramsbottom union, of which he was then secretary, sent nobody. The Darwen union, in contrast, sent two delegates to the 1894 Congress. But its new secretary was not one of them. The signs of intense struggle were evident from that point on. The first quarterly general meeting of 1895, after 'long discussion', decided against sending anyone to Congress for 'the next five years'.[27] Another general meeting rescinded that decision six months later, and a two-man delegation attended the 1895 Congress.[28] But, again, it did not include Shackleton. Nor was he one of the delegates that the union executive chose for the 1896 Congress, although the anomaly was formally acknowledged this time in an agreement that 'the question of the Secretary attending Trades Congresses' should be put on the agenda of the October (post-Congress) general meeting.[29] The executive subsequently recommended to the October meeting that future Congress delegations should consist of the chairman and the secretary, but the meeting (by 35 votes to 10) decided to specify only the secretary and

22. Ibid., 22 June 1894.
23. Ibid., 29 September 1899.
24. Ibid., 6 October 1899.
25. DWA, *Minutes* (GM), 23 January 1899.
26. The following account is derived wholly from the union's minutes, which give little or no idea of the lines of division.
27. DWA, *Minutes* (GM), 28 January 1895.
28. Ibid., 29 July 1895.
29. Ibid. (Ctee), 10 August 1896.

one other executive member.[30] Shackleton accordingly attended the Congress of 1897, his first in five years, and thereafter every Congress for the next 13 years – sometimes representing the Weavers' Amalgamation, but mostly as a delegate from the Darwen union.

The Wider Union World

Shackleton's secretaryship gave him access to a range of inter-union bodies. Four were of particular significance: the Darwen Trades Council; the Northern Counties Amalgamated Weavers' Association (Weavers' Amalgamation);[31] the United Textile Factory Workers' Association (Textile Factory Workers' Association); and the Trades Union Congress (TUC).

The Trades Council was concerned principally with local industrial and municipal matters. Shackleton's union was its largest affiliate. On taking up his secretaryship, he was appointed one of the weavers' delegates to the council which, in turn, promptly put him on its executive committee.[32] The council provided him with a ready, and ostensibly 'non-political' channel into local politics.

The Weavers' Amalgamation has been labelled the 'Second Weavers' Amalgamation'.[33] The First Amalgamation, the North-east Lancashire Amalgamated Weavers' Association, had been formed in 1858. The Second Amalgamation was founded in 1884.[34] Established on a broader geographic basis and with a more centralised administrative structure than its older competitor, it was also the first British union to institute a formalized, industry-wide structure of collective bargaining by agreement with employers.[35] Its affiliated membership soon overtook that of the First, but some overlap remained, and for close to 20 years – until the First disbanded – they 'maintained a curious co-existence, part competitive, part co-operative'.[36]

---

30.   Ibid., 28 September 1896; ibid. (GM), 19 October 1896. That was not quite the end of the matter. In March 1897, on the application of one Thomas Turner, the executive put a motion rescinding the October decision to a ballot of members at a general meeting. It was defeated by 74 votes to 45. Then, in January 1898, a second motion to rescind the October decision was put to a similar membership ballot. Again it was defeated, if by a slimmer 39 votes to 32.

31.   Its formal title, as given here, was briefly its first, and that most commonly found in published sources. But its true formal title, throughout Shackleton's association with it, was the Northern Counties Amalgamated Associations of Weavers.

32.   *Cotton Factory Times*, 29 June 1894.

33.   See Turner, *Trade Union Growth, Structure and Policy*, pp. 132–5.

34.   But it had its genesis in a Northern Counties Central Weavers' Committee formed four years earlier. See Bullen, *Lancashire Weavers' Union*, pp. 13–17.

35.   See Clegg, *History of British Trade Unions*, vol. III, p. 413.

36.   Turner, *Trade Union Growth, Structure and Policy*, p. 135. In 1886, of the unions Shackleton was to lead, Ramsbottom was still affiliated to the First Amalgamation, but Darwen and Accrington had left – though only Accrington had actually joined the Second Amalgamation. *Cotton Factory Times*, 21 May 1886. Nine years later, when Shackleton was in Darwen and the Second Amalgamation covered 32 unions with a total of 83,195 members, both Darwen and Ramsbottom were also affiliated. Weavers' Amalgamation, *Minutes*, 14 December 1895.

The Darwen union, as it happened, moved to affiliate to the Weavers' Amalgamation only a few days before Shackleton took over as secretary.[37] He was promptly appointed one of its delegates to the amalgamation's plenary body, the General Council, of which he had been a member continuously since 1885 on behalf of either the Accrington union or the Ramsbottom union. The following year, on the nomination of the Darwen executive, he won election to the amalgamation's Central Committee.[38] In 1898, he defeated Joseph Cross, his predecessor at Darwen, in a contest for the vice-presidency. He was then in his mid-thirties, and much younger than both the president and the secretary.[39] But his dominance was evident from the start, in 1899, of a long campaign for restoration of the 10 per cent wage cut that had sparked the great strike of 1878. For it was Shackleton who acted as the amalgamation's principal spokesman, both in negotiations with employers and in reporting back to the unions.[40]

The third body was the Textile Factory Workers' Association. This emerged, in a strangely halting and indecisive fashion,[41] from a Factory Acts Reform Committee which had been formed in 1871 to bring all the cotton unions together for the purpose of lobbying ministers and parliamentarians. Shackleton attended its general meetings in 1894 as the Darwen weavers' delegate, and the next year as a delegate from the Weavers' Amalgamation. The association disbanded in 1896, 'over political differences',[42] and was not 're-organized' until 1899,[43] when Shackleton was elected to its executive, the Legislative Council. During the next three years, apart from arranging to have certain questions put to Lancashire candidates in the general election of 1900, the association was primarily concerned with mounting parliamentary deputations.

The Congress of the TUC, held annually since 1868, was the most comprehensive gathering of British trade union leaders. Once the Darwen weavers' union stopped dithering and allowed Shackleton to return to Congress, it was immediately evident that he was not to be one of the myriad whose names figure only in the published list of delegates. At the 1897

---

37.   In May 1894, its quarterly general meeting, dealing with an affiliation motion that had been deferred two years before, voted 47 to 5 in favour. The executive committee subsequently accepted the amalgamation's formal offer of affiliation at the third of its weekly meetings to be recorded in Shackleton's hand.

38.   Darwen was one of the largest affiliates: only Blackburn, Burnley and Nelson were bigger.

39.   The president, David Holmes, was in his mid-fifties; the secretary, W. H. Wilkinson, in his late forties. Both had held office since the foundation of the amalgamation.

40.   See Weavers' Amalgamation, *Minutes*, 15 April 1899; 6 May 1899; *Cotton Factory Times*, 11 July 1902; *Colne & Nelson Times*, 11 July 1902. He played a similar role in other trade disputes involving the amalgamation. See *Cotton Factory Times*, 22 June 1900; 15 February 1901; 19 April 1901.

41.   See Turner, *Trade Union Growth, Structure and Policy*, p. 127.

42.   Bullen, *Lancashire Weavers' Union*, p. 22.

43.   *Cotton Factory Times*, 10 August 1900.

Congress, he moved two resolutions.[44] In 1898, he was elected one of six tellers, moved a resolution,[45] seconded another, and spoke in a debate on half-timers. In 1899 he moved a resolution,[46] took a point of order, and spoke in two major debates – on half-timers and the eight-hour day. In 1900, again elected a teller, he spoke on the eight-hour issue and on a procedural matter; and moved the official vote of thanks to Co-operative Union representatives. In 1901, he intervened in a debate on half-timers, and was elected by Congress to its prestigious General Purposes Committee. By this time, he would almost certainly have had a seat on the TUC's executive, the Parliamentary Committee, had his way not been blocked by David Holmes, president of the Weavers' Amalgamation.[47]

Shackleton's inter-union associations took him away from Lancashire. According to his own recollection, he was travelling to London to take part in ministerial deputations and conferences with parliamentarians from about 1892.[48] In 1902 he was said to have been a member of every cotton union deputation that had 'waited upon the Home Secretary' in the preceding four years.[49] And London was not the end of it. In August 1897, he left England for the first time, crossing the Channel to attend the International Textile Congress in Roubaix, on behalf of the Weavers' Amalgamation. During April–June 1902, with the amalgamation's blessing, he accompanied six Lancashire cotton employers to the United States in order to investigate the textile industry there and, especially, the new Northrop loom.[50]

Labour in Politics

The issue of labour, or 'direct', representation on elected bodies was a matter of intense controversy among cotton trade unionists during the 1890s. Long-established Liberal and Conservative loyalties died hard. The strongest

44.   One supported local taxation on ground values, the other attacked employers' powers to deduct wages. TUC, *Report*, 1897, pp. 35, 54. As for his previous Congresses, he was mute at the first two, in 1890 and 1891; but at the third, in 1892, he moved the dismissal of a protectionist resolution, seconded a resolution on the eight-hour day, and intervened briefly in two other debates. Ibid., 1892, pp. 51, 53–6.

45.   It protested against strike-breaking by the wives of trade unionists, a particular problem for the weavers' unions. Ibid., 1898, p. 58.

46.   It concerned the fining powers of employers. Ibid., 1899, p. 68.

47.   Holmes – nominated by the amalgamation but subject to a vote of the whole Congress – had occupied a Parliamentary Committee seat since 1892, losing it temporarily in 1901 when he failed to win sufficient Congress votes. The politics of the TUC dictated that so long as Holmes was nominated by the weavers, Shackleton could not stand.

48.   *M.A.P.*, 26 January 1907, p. 111.

49.   *Colne & Nelson Times*, 11 July 1902.

50.   This trip came about after G. P. Holden of Darwen, a member of the party, approached the Darwen weavers' union with an offer to pay half of Shackleton's expenses. The union met the other half, and also paid its chairman £1 8s a week for acting as secretary during Shackleton's absence. DWA, *Minutes* (Ctee), 10 March 1902; 31 March 1902.

passions were stirred by proposals for direct representation at the national level, in parliament. The idea of direct representation at the level of local government tended to be more acceptable, subject to the proviso that union candidates were nominated without any reference to a political party. Thus, shortly before Shackleton left Ramsbottom, the local Trades Council decided to interest itself, 'as a non-political association', in local elections and 'when opportune ... bring forward Trade Union candidates'.[51] The Darwen Trades Council, quicker off the mark, had John Aspin, president of the weavers' union, elected to the Town Council there as early as 1891.[52]

Shackleton cut his formal connection with the Liberals when he moved to Darwen in 1894.[53] It has been claimed that he did this because 'as a paid union official he had felt it improper to be active in party politics'.[54] But on that reasoning, he should not have joined the Liberal Club in Ramsbottom either. It seems more likely that his decision had to do with the politics of the Darwen union itself. Either way, it was a critical decision because it made him eligible for nomination as a direct representative of labour. And so, in 1895, when Aspin stepped down from his North-east Ward seat, the Trades Council was able to nominate Shackleton. He won unopposed,[55] repeating the feat three years later. Then, in 1901, after the Trades Council's secretary, William Atkinson, won Central Ward at a by-election, Shackleton announced his retirement as a councillor on the ground of his union work.[56] But the replacement nominated by the Trades Council, a member of the spinners' union, apparently had Conservative associations, for when the Conservatives decided to oppose Atkinson in Central Ward, Shackleton was induced to re-contest his old seat as a non-party candidate. He was returned once again without opposition, after the spinner withdrew.[57]

51.   *Ramsbottom Observer*, 26 January 1894. Surprisingly, the Colne and Nelson weavers' unions, reputedly radical on the issue of direct representation, did not take similar action until 1898 and 1901 respectively. See Bealey, 'Northern Weavers', pp. 32–4.

52.   *Cotton Factory Times*, 27 September 1895.

53.   In 1900, however, he apparently spoke on Liberal platforms during the general election, and was thought to be 'ready to come forward as a Liberal candidate'. Clarke, *Lancashire and the New Liberalism*, p. 92. Not long after, it was said that he had refused a Liberal invitation in 1900 to contest the Darwen division, a solid Conservative seat. *Colne & Nelson Times*, 11 July 1902.

54.   Bealey and Pelling, *Labour and Politics*, p. 112.

55.   *Cotton Factory Times*, 1 November 1895.

56.   Ibid., 10 May 1901.

57.   Ibid., 13 September 1901; 8 November 1901. By 1902, Shackleton was on 15 council committees, and had been actively associated with other local enterprises – such as the Famine Funds of 1897 and 1900, concerned with India; the Lord Mayor's War (Relief) Fund, concerned with the dependants of Boer War servicemen; and the celebration of both Queen Victoria's Jubilee, in 1897, and Edward VII's Coronation in 1902. Moreover, his formal community involvement extended beyond Darwen. He was elected to the Board of Management of the Blackburn and East Lancashire Infirmary in 1900, and represented the Darwen weavers' union in the Blackburn Chamber of Commerce from 1896, later becoming a director of the chamber and a delegate to the annual conference of the Associated Chambers of Commerce. He remained on the Accrington magistrates' bench, although apparently not a regular attender of its Wednesday 'court days'. *Nelson Chronicle*, 11 July 1902.

The question of direct parliamentary representation, prompted by a Trades Council circular suggesting a conference about it, was on the agenda of the first general meeting of the Darwen union that Shackleton attended as secretary; but the outcome was inconclusive.[58] Three months afterwards, in a ballot conducted by the Textile Factory Workers' Association, his members rejected the principle by 1,900 votes to 1,421.[59] They rejected it a second time at a general meeting in 1895.[60] And four years later, they rejected it once again by deciding that the Darwen weavers would not be represented at a special London conference in February 1900.[61] This was the conference that gave birth to the Labour party, initially under the title of the Labour Representation Committee (LRC).

The LRC was a confederal body, its membership being confined to organizations, which meant that individuals could be formally part of it only by belonging to an affiliated organization. For financial reasons in particular, the affiliates most significant to its survival were trade unions. Initially, however, its union affiliations were limited. Then, just 17 months after its foundation, the Law Lords came to the rescue by handing down a decision in the Taff Vale case which not only, as intended, made trade unions liable for damages arising from their members' industrial actions, but also had the unintended consequence of assuring the LRC's future.[62]

Only legislation could remedy Taff Vale. There was no dispute in union circles about that. Whether or not remedial legislation depended on the direct representation of labour in parliament was a more open question. But, happily for the LRC, there were early illustrations of the unreliability of parliamentarians from the traditional parties.[63] The way in which the tide flowed at this time (and not only among the cotton unions) is shown by successive decisions of the Weavers' Amalgamation. In 1900, its General Council had

---

58. *Cotton Factory Times*, 10 August 1894.
59. Ibid., 9 November 1894. The Darwen spinners, on the other hand, endorsed it (by 95 to 45) – as did the cotton unions in general (by 40,805 to 37,752) and the weavers as a totality (by 27,804 to 25,271). Ibid., 28 February 1902. But these small majorities, coupled with an awkward compromise proposed by the association's leadership (involving James Mawdsley, of the Spinners, standing as a Conservative; and David Holmes, of the Weavers, standing as a Liberal), led to the matter being dropped following an 'unsatisfactory discussion' at a meeting of the association's constituent bodies. Ibid. See also Clegg et al., *History of British Trade Unions*, vol. 1, p. 299.
60. DWA, *Minutes* (GM), 29 July 1895. The resolution as adopted: 'That we do not support a representative of the [Weavers' Amalgamation] being put forward as a parliamentary candidate'.
61. Ibid., 22 January 1900. This followed a similar decision by the General Council of the Weavers' Amalgamation. *Minutes*, 13 January 1900. Beforehand, the Darwen executive committee had instructed its General Council delegates to vote *in favour* of the amalgamation being represented at the London conference. DWA, *Minutes* (Ctee), 8 January 1900.
62. See Martin, *TUC*, pp. 69–70.
63. For example: 'Great dissatisfaction has been given by certain Lancashire members in consequence of their action on the picketing question, which was discussed in the House of Commons on May 14th. These men went into the division lobby against the trades unionist workmen, although at the time of their election it was understood that they were favourable to a reversal of the Lords decision in the Taff Vale case.' *Cotton Factory Times*, 27 June 1902.

flatly rejected 'labour representation in Parliament' when responding to a letter from Ramsay MacDonald, secretary of the LRC, asking them to affiliate.[64] In January 1902, with the Taff Vale decision before it, the amalgamation somersaulted and instructed its leadership 'to take the necessary steps to secure direct representation in Parliament' by way of the Textile Factory Workers' Association.[65] This proposal did not commit the union to the LRC, and might have involved nothing more than reviving the 1895 scheme for cotton union candidates.[66] But no action followed. Then, six months later, the amalgamation had before it a motion explicitly proposing affiliation to the LRC. Its cautious response was to adjourn the matter pending the biannual meeting of the Textile Factory Workers' Association on 26 July.[67]

In the month that elapsed before that meeting, the situation was transformed by two events. The first was an announcement, on 26 June, that the Member of Parliament for the Clitheroe constituency in north-east Lancashire, Sir Ughtred Kay-Shuttleworth, had been elevated to the House of Lords in the Coronation honours list. The second was a meeting on 5 July at which it was decided that David Shackleton would be nominated as the independent Labour candidate in the consequential by-election.

64. Weavers' Amalgamation, *Minutes*, 22 September 1900.

65. *Nelson Chronicle*, 17 January 1902. Most union leaders, as Clegg et al. have argued, probably did not 'fully realise the dangers of their situation' following the Taff Vale judgement until January 1903, when it was announced that the union directly involved, the Amalgamated Society of Railway Servants, faced total costs of £42,000. On the other hand, these dangers had been brought home to the cotton union leaders all of a year earlier as the result of a picketing case, involving the Blackburn weavers, which the Weavers' Amalgamation had settled out of court at a cost of some £11,000. See *History of British Trade Unions*, vol. 1, p. 323; and Bealey and Pelling, *Labour and Politics*, p. 101.

66. See above, and Bealey and Pelling, *Labour and Politics*, p. 97.

67. *Cotton Factory Times*, 27 June 1902.

3

The Clitheroe By-election

The parliamentary constituency of Clitheroe was in 1902 a Liberal strong-hold, an oddity in east Lancashire. Following its creation in 1885, Sir Ughtred Kay-Shuttleworth had held it through five elections, either unop-posed or with majorities of 2,000 and more. It was based on a group of towns, 'all of them populous, flourishing ... full of intelligent life', and boasting 'twelve miles of continuous street lamps'.[1] Colne and the larger Nelson con-tained about half the division's voters, with most of the remainder in the towns of Clitheroe, Padiham, Brierfield and Barrowford.[2] Cotton weaving was the main source of employment.[3] Since weaving was a predominantly female occupation, and women did not have the franchise, there was little correspondence between the population and the voting strength of cotton workers. It is possible, however, that they accounted for as much as 40 per cent of all Clitheroe voters.[4]

There was a distinctively radical edge to working-class politics in Clitheroe, as compared with most Lancashire electorates. Both Nelson and Colne contained flourishing branches of the revolutionary Social Democra-tic Federation and the evolutionary Independent Labour Party (ILP).[5] The two biggest unions, the Nelson and Colne weavers, were part of the Weavers' Amalgamation, and had a record of taking up positions to the left of the amal-gamation's Liberal-oriented leadership.[6] They were the only cotton unions present at the London conference that set up the Labour Representation Committee (LRC) in February 1900. The Colne union was the first, and for some time the only, Lancashire weavers' union to affiliate to the LRC.

The Liberals of Clitheroe, in 1902, were displaying every sign of compla-cency. Their clubs in the smaller towns, according to a sympathetic observer, were 'on the decline', while the 'big clubs are social institutes for cards and

---

1. *Manchester Guardian*, 3 July 1902.
2. See Bealey, 'Northern Weavers', p. 29.
3. In Colne, at the previous census, 79 per cent of working women and 48 per cent of male workers were weavers: in Nelson, 62 per cent of employed males were 'at the loom'. *Manchester Guardian*, 9 July 1902.
4. See Clegg et al., *History of British Trade Unions*, vol. 1, p. 275.
5. See Howell, *British Workers and the Independent Labour Party*, pp. 52, 61.
6. See Bealey, 'Northern Weavers', pp. 32–4.

billiards'.[7] Many grumbled about the performance of their local member. Kay-Shuttleworth suffered, ostentatiously, from ill health. As he told a gathering of Liberal stalwarts at a tea in Gawthorpe Hall, his country home, 'his old foe – influenza – [had] attacked him, obliging him now to express regrets for his inefficiency in Parliament last Session, and his inability to hold meetings and address his constituents this autumn'.[8]

The announcement of his elevation to the House of Lords came out of the blue for almost everyone. It 'finds all political parties unprepared for the contest', a local paper reported.[9] Not quite all, as it happened.

Labour Prepares

In the autumn of 1901, eight months earlier, there were two items in the local press which might have suggested to the Liberals that Clitheroe was a pot about to boil over. One was an announcement that Philip Snowden of the ILP, well-known in the electorate as a brilliant speaker, was to give an address on 'Labour Representation' at an impending conference convened by the Textile Trades Federation of Nelson, Colne and District.[10] The other cited the lesson drawn, in the quarterly report of the Colne weaver's union, from the Taff Vale decision: 'ceasing to put our trust (for our own legislative work) in landowners and other members of the capitalist class, and sending instead a few able men of our own to take their places'.[11]

The pot began to bubble in January 1902. The Textile Trades Federation and the Colne Trades Council agreed to convene, 'under the auspices' of the national LRC, a conference of union officials in Nelson to discuss 'labour representation'.[12] A few days later, the local branches of the Social Democratic Federation (acting through the Clitheroe Division Socialist Council) tried to seize the initiative by announcing their firm intention to 'run a Socialist Trade Unionist candidate' at the next parliamentary election in Clitheroe, and by issuing a general invitation to an earlier conference on the matter.[13] In the event, the attendance at this conference was dismal, and it could only adjourn until after the LRC-sponsored conference which had been scheduled for 1 March.[14]

Trade unions, co-operative societies, and branches of both the ILP and the

---

7. *Nelson Chronicle*, 17 January 1902.
8. Ibid., 8 November 1901.
9. Ibid., 27 June 1902. The reference was to the Liberals and to the 'Conservative and Labour parties'.
10. *Colne & Nelson Times*, 4 October 1901. Snowden was a Yorkshire man, but had lived in Nelson for 10 years during his early manhood and thereafter maintained a close interest in Nelson and Colne.
11. Quoted in *Nelson Chronicle*, 11 October 1901.
12. *Colne & Nelson Times*, 10 January 1902.
13. *Nelson Chronicle*, 17 January 1902.
14. See *Colne & Nelson Times*, 7 February 1902.

Social Democratic Federation were represented among some 100 delegates at the 1 March conference.[15] The organizing committee circulated four resolutions beforehand. Three were adopted expeditiously, unanimously, and without amendment.[16] The fourth, though eventually carried in its entirety, was the subject of prolonged discussion and a number of attempted unsuccessful amendments. It read:

> That this conference is of opinion that in order to secure the best possible result from a body of Labour representatives in Parliament, the labour movement generally should unite in promoting Labour candidates in favourable constituencies, of which Clitheroe Division is one, and that these candidates should be run on the distinct understanding that they shall, if returned, loyally co-operate with a Labour party in Parliament in advancing the interests of labour, and that on all labour matters they should act together independently of all other parties.[17]

The discussion was dominated by an amendment proposing the addition of the words: 'That a Labour and Socialist candidate be brought out at the next election'.[18] The amendment's eventual rejection left the designation of a future candidate as simply 'Labour'; and this outcome was reportedly taken by those present to mean 'that the candidate should not be a Socialist primarily'.[19]

The conference formally adjourned for three months but, as fortune dictated, did not assemble again until Saturday 5 July.[20] In the meantime, the participating unions took the issue of financial support back to their members, whose reaction seems generally to have been overwhelmingly favourable.[21] That left the selection of a candidate. And when the conference reconvened, nine days after the announcement of Kay-Shuttleworth's peerage, delegates knew that the man they chose could be their Member of Parliament in a matter of weeks.

The Liberals

A few of them had the advantage of foreknowledge about the peerage. Early in June, Kay-Shuttleworth raised the question of his successor in a letter to

15. See ibid., 7 March 1902; and *Nelson Chronicle*, 7 March 1902.
16. Between them, they supported the principle of direct parliamentary representation; committed delegates to urge their unions to affiliate with the LRC; and asked all participating bodies to 'consider' how funds might be raised to meet both the campaign expenses and the maintenance of a successful Labour candidate.
17. *Colne & Nelson Times*, 7 March 1902.
18. *Nelson Chronicle*, 25 July 1902.
19. *Northern Daily Telegraph*, 11 July 1902.
20. The organizing committee later put the date back to 28 June, and then (because of the sudden postponement of Edward VII's Coronation, owing to his ill health) to 5 July.
21. Thus the Colne weavers' ballot registered a majority of 'nearly 20 to 1, in favour'. *Colne & Nelson Times*, 30 May 1902. The Nelson weavers' majority was 4,565 votes to 825. *Northern Daily Telegraph*, 10 July 1902. See also *Cotton Factory Times*, 30 May 1902.

the Liberals' parliamentary leader, Sir Henry Campbell-Bannerman. He suggested A. Acland, on the ground that Acland was not only 'admirable in every way', but 'likely to satisfy Labour party & avert a 3 cornered contest'.[22] He also asked that Herbert Gladstone, the Liberal Chief Whip, should let him know of anyone else 'available', and said he would shortly be seeing W. S. Catlow, the Clitheroe Liberals' chairman ('I can trust him, but shall bind him to great secrecy').

Acland was duly sounded out, but declined on health grounds.[23] Seven other names were mentioned in correspondence between Gladstone and Kay-Shuttleworth at this stage: Shaw Lefevre, Arnold Morley, Augustine Birrell, C. N. Lawrence, J. A. Bright, J. Stuart and Lane Woods.[24] After talking with Catlow, Kay-Shuttleworth told Gladstone (in a distinctly peevish tone) that the chairman 'feels inclined to run up to London & have conversations with you'.[25] He also said he inclined towards Morley and Lawrence, along with two new possibilities, J. Duckworth and P. Stanhope.

On 19 June, just a week before Kay-Shuttleworth's peerage was publicly revealed in the Coronation honours list, Gladstone met Catlow. The shortlist they agreed on is recorded in Gladstone's diary, following an unwary comment ('Labour trouble possible, but no L. candidate ready'): 'C. N. Lawson [Lawrence?] strongest available candidate. Duckworth & Stanhope possible.'[26] A week later, Stanhope had emerged as the front-runner. On the day Kay-Shuttleworth's peerage was made public, Gladstone telegrammed Catlow 'that S. meant to offer himself'.[27] But now, as he confided to a senior Liberal colleague, he saw shoals ahead: 'I am nervous about Clitheroe'.[28]

The Executive Committee of the Clitheroe Liberal Association met the next day, and set up a sub-committee 'to negotiate' with Stanhope, Birrell and (a new name) Franklin Thomasson.[29] The sub-committee decided to interview Stanhope after Birrell ruled himself out. Stanhope travelled to Colne on Wednesday 2 July, for an evening meeting with the sub-committee. That afternoon, on the Liberals' initiative,[30] Catlow and three colleagues met

22.   Kay-Shuttleworth to Campbell-Bannerman, 7 June 1902: Campbell-Bannerman Papers, vol. XVI, BM Add. MS 41221, fols. 57–60.

23.   Acland to Gladstone, 11 June 1902: Viscount Gladstone Papers, vol. LXXV, BM Add. MS 46059, fols. 219–20.

24.   The last two appear to have been trade unionists, but not from the textile industry – a distinct disadvantage, as Kay-Shuttleworth explained, because Clitheroe 'contains more weavers (cotton) than any other constituency in the Kingdom; & if a Labour man is put forward, I have little doubt that he would be one chosen from the Textile Trades'. Kay-Shuttleworth to Gladstone, 14 June 1902: ibid., fols. 227–8.

25.   Ibid., 16 June 1902: fols. 229–31.

26.   Diary entry, 19 June 1902: ibid., vol. CXLV, BM Add.. MS 46484, fol. 14 (p. 27).

27.   Gladstone to R. A. Hudson (secretary, National Liberal Federation), 27 June 1902: ibid., vol. XXXVI, BM Add.. MS 46020, fol. 150.

28.   Ibid.

29.   Nelson Chronicle, 4 July 1902.

30.   See Northern Daily Telegraph, 4 July 1902.

with four local trade union leaders. Catlow, according to his own account, opened with an appeal for unity behind the Liberal party. Some verbal sparring followed.[31] Then Catlow asked the critical question: 'supposing that a name [the trade unionists] might mention [were] considered by us, would they give power to their man to act ... upon all Labour questions directly on their behalf and otherwise ... be amenable to the Liberal Whip?' This question was put in the knowledge that, since the 1870s, trade union officials elected to parliament had customarily aligned themselves, on these terms, with the Liberals – being designated 'Liberal-Labour' men or, more familiarly, 'Lib-Labs'. The response unequivocally ruled out the Lib-Lab solution. 'To that question they said "No". They went as far as to say that if they put up a man he would not even ... be called a Liberal-Labour man, but would ... be a Labour man pure and simple – he would not have ... the word Liberal attached to him at all.'[32]

Stanhope was told of this exchange when he met the sub-committee. Nevertheless, by the time he returned to Manchester the same evening, he had agreed to 'place his services at the disposal of the party'.[33] It was understood that the sub-committee would recommend him to the Executive Committee the following evening, immediately before a meeting of the 600-member Liberal Council.

However, some time between leaving the Crown Hotel in Colne and reaching the Queen's Hotel in Manchester, Stanhope had second thoughts. And before he went to bed, he wrote a letter to Catlow in which he made three points. First, he would not stand if that meant 'a contest between Liberalism and organised and official forces of Labour represented in Trades Unions'; second, the afternoon meeting with the unionists 'does not give ... much present encouragement ... to the hope of a general agreement' on his candidature; and, third, in the event of a formal invitation from the Liberals, he would give 'a definite reply' only after 'consideration of ... its general reception' in the electorate.[34] In the light of this letter, the Liberal Executive Committee, on Thursday evening, decided against proposing his adoption to the Council. But the Council, after listening to both a reading of his letter and an

---

31. One trade unionist asked whether the Liberals were claiming 'the right to nominate'. The Liberals, while saying 'we could not exactly claim the right', nevertheless 'thought that we had a prior claim ... to have some say in the nomination'. They also claimed to be 'strongly influenced by the position of the Labour party' in their choice of candidate. *Nelson Chronicle*, 4 July 1902.

32. Ibid.

33. Ibid.

34. Ibid. As he explained in telegramese to Gladstone: 'While I have consented allow my name to be provisionally submitted to Liberal Council it is solely with object endeavour to promote an understanding between Liberal & Labour parties & implies no definite acceptance failing sufficient agreement between them.' Stanhope to Gladstone, 3 July 1902: Viscount Gladstone Papers, vol. LXXV, BM Add. MS 46059, fols. 247–8.

account of the meeting with the trade unionists, was reportedly more optimistic – the 'feeling' being that Stanhope might well be acceptable to 'the Labour party'.[35] A resolution asking him to accept nomination as the Liberal candidate was carried unanimously, 'amid applause'.[36]

Meanwhile, the Clitheroe Conservatives, slyly critical of 'the hurry the Liberals are making', played a waiting game.[37] Their leaders met in Burnley on the Wednesday afternoon when their Liberal counterparts were confronting the trade unionists. They narrowed the field of their possible candidates to two.[38] Then, like the Liberals, they awaited Saturday and the outcome of the adjourned Labour conference.

Labour Decides

Labour's preparations paid off handsomely in the assurance and despatch with which its spokesmen were able to act on 26 June when Kay-Shuttleworth's peerage was announced. In Colne, A. B. Newall, the local weavers' secretary and an initiating spirit in the preparations, immediately announced that 'a Labour candidate would be run'.[39] In London, Ramsay MacDonald, secretary of the LRC, was equally quick to confirm Labour's determination.[40]

Newall wrote to MacDonald the same day, to tell him that the sub-committee organising the 5 July conference was meeting that night to consider the 'names of likely men'.[41] The initial 'likely men', as set out in a sub-committee resolution made public some time later, were 'Councillor D. Shackleton, J.P., of Darwen, vice-president of the Northern Counties Weavers' Amalgamation; Mr W. H. Wilkinson, secretary of the Northern Counties; Mr J. Cross, secretary of the Blackburn Weavers' Association; Mr Philip

35. *Nelson Chronicle*, 4 July 1902.
36. *Northern Daily Telegraph*, 4 July 1902. Stanhope appears to have been emboldened by this. Beforehand, on Thursday, he was evidently resigned to Clitheroe slipping from his grasp, and told Gladstone that 'at present it looks as if it would be well to choose some Labour man, acceptable to both sides' – and he offered to contribute to the expenses of such a candidate. On Friday, in contrast, he was reassuring Gladstone by telegram: 'I have by no means abandoned possible candidature.' Stanhope to Gladstone, n.d., *c.* (BM notation) 3 July 1902: Viscount Gladstone Papers, vol. LXXV, BM Add. MS 46059, fol. 249; 4 July 1902: ibid., fol. 250.
37. *Burnley Express and Clitheroe Division Advertiser*, 5 July 1902. Not only was their organization 'in a very backward state', but it was obvious to all that their only chance of capturing the seat depended on both Liberal and Labour putting up candidates. *Weekly Standard and Express*, 5 July 1902.
38. *Burnley Express and Clitheroe Division Advertiser*, 5 July 1902.
39. *Nelson Chronicle*, 27 June 1902.
40. In a letter published in the *Daily Chronicle* on 27 June, he also pointed to the 'very large majorities' obtained in the ballots of rank-and-file trade unionists on the two issues of direct representation and the striking of a levy for a 'Parliamentary Fund'.
41. Newall to MacDonald, 26 June 1902: LP Archives, LRC 4/37.

Snowden, Mr John Hodge, of Manchester, and Mr W.C. Steadman, of London'.[42]

On the 28th Newall, acting for the Clitheroe 'Lab Rep'n Com'e', wrote to Shackleton (and, presumably, to the other five as well) inviting him to allow his name to be submitted, along with others, as one willing to be a candidate in 'the *direct* Labour interest'.[43] Shackleton promptly accepted. Of the others, at least Wilkinson and Cross, the two weavers' officials, just as promptly declined.[44] In any case, it is evident that Newall and his colleagues had plumped for Shackleton by the time four of them conferred with Catlow's Liberal delegation on the afternoon of Wednesday 2 July. For at this meeting the trade unionists, as reported, expressly 'urged the claims of Mr Shackleton'.[45]

The next day, when the Liberal Council opted for Stanhope, the executive of the national LRC held a special meeting in Colne. After discussions with 'a deputation of representative Trade Unionists', the executive decided to send two members to Saturday's selection conference.[46] The minutes of the meeting do not reveal whether the trade unionists expressed a preference for Shackleton – but it is clear that they did.[47]

The popular belief, on the eve of the Saturday conference, was that there would be two nominations, Philip Snowden, of the ILP, and Shackleton[48] – providing a straight choice between a fervent Socialist and a Liberal-leaning trade unionist. In that contest, from the start, the unionist had the edge because the power of the push for direct representation in Clitheroe depended, above all, on official union support.[49] And the unions' support was conditional on a candidate who was one of their own, as an anonymous weavers' official made clear at the time:

---

42. *Nelson Chronicle*, 4 July 1902. The comparatively careful elaboration of Shackleton's offices, and his placement first in the list, strongly suggests that he was favoured by its authors. Hodge, at the time, was secretary of the British Steel Smelters' Amalgamated Association and a member of the national LRC executive; Steadman was secretary of the Barge Builders' Union and chairman of the TUC's Parliamentary Committee.

43. Newall to Shackleton, 28 June 1902: SP. The letter, according to Shackleton, was preceded by a telephone message. *Colne & Nelson Times*, 11 July 1902.

44. See *Burnley Express and Clitheroe Division Advertiser*, 5 July 1902; *Weekly Standard and Express*, 5 July 1902.

45. *Nelson Chronicle*, 4 July 1902.

46. LRC, *Minutes*, 3 July 1902: `Infancy of the Labour Party', vol. 1, fol. 118.

47. This is evident from a decision made by the ILP's Parliamentary Committee, at its Friday meeting in Leeds, that 'Snowden should withdraw in Shackleton's favour provided the latter's position on the question of independence was satisfactory'. Quoted in Moore, *Emergence of the Labour Party*, p. 90.

48. See *Northern Daily Telegraph*, 4 July 1902; *Nelson Chronicle*, 4 July 1902.

49. As Stanhope put it to the Liberal Chief Whip: 'the real trouble is that the Labour [campaign for an independent candidate] springs from the Weavers' Unions and they have funds and a wonderful organization'. Stanhope to Gladstone, n.d., *circa* (BM notation) 3 July 1902: Viscount Gladstone Papers, vol. LXXV, BM Add. MS 46059, fol. 249.

It is not a Socialist we want – far from it; but a Labour man we intend to have ... The textile workers in Clitheroe are masters of the situation ... The textile workers of Lancashire have received loyal support from a number of county M.P.s, but in many cases we have had to go down almost on our knees to extract promises of support for proposals to benefit our class; and it is that which has made our members feel that they ought to have a representative of their own in Parliament.[50]

In the Church Street Co-operative Hall, Colne, on the afternoon of Saturday 5 July, Newall formally reopened the conference that had adjourned in March. There were 81 local delegates present. They represented five weavers' unions (Colne, Nelson, Clitheroe, Padiham and Todmorden), seven other unions, the Colne and Padiham Trades Councils, the Nelson Textile Trades Federation, the Barrowford Co-operative Society, some ILP branches and the Clitheroe Division Socialist Council (meaning the Social Democratic Federation) – whose delegates subsequently stormed out when the conference declined to add the word 'Socialist' to 'Labour'. There were also two representatives of the national LRC, Ramsay MacDonald and James Sexton, secretary of the Liverpool-based National Union of Dock Labourers and a member of the TUC's executive.

Before selecting a candidate, the conference decided on an annual levy of 6d per union member,[51] appointed a 'committee of management for the Clitheroe Division Labour party', and resolved to contest the Clitheroe by-election 'in the direct Labour interest'.[52] Newall then read from the chair a letter, dated that day, from Philip Snowden.

> Dear Mr Newall, – I understand that Mr Shackleton's name and my own are the only two now to be submitted to the conference that is to be held at Colne this afternoon. I have given the matter very careful consideration, and I have come to the conclusion to withdraw my name. Although I should appreciate very highly the position of Parliamentary representative for the Clitheroe Division ... I think that Mr Shackleton, as a trades union official and one so thoroughly acquainted with the staple trade and with the labour conditions of the district, has a far better claim, and would make a more useful representative.[53]

Newall then called for nominations. Only Shackleton's name was put forward. A motion inviting him to accept nomination as a parliamentary candidate was carried unanimously.

Why Shackleton? The answer is plain enough when it comes to the choice between Shackleton and Snowden, given the determination of the local union leadership to have a union man. But why Shackleton of all the non-Socialist cotton men? He was not a local. But, then, neither were Wilkinson and Cross, the other two cotton unionists in the initial list. All three, however, were prominent in the Weavers' Amalgamation, and that was almost

50. Quoted in *Westminster Gazette*, 4 July 1902.
51. This, assuming a base of 18,000 union members, was calculated to raise £450.
52. *Colne & Nelson Times*, 11 July 1902.
53. Ibid.

certainly the essential qualification. Shackleton (the younger of the three, which may or may not have mattered) was not only the amalgamation's vice-president but had played the leading role in its industrial negotiations since 1898. He was also a Darwen town councillor, a longstanding Accrington magistrate, and – as had been publicly suggested 'more than once in recent years' – a man with the makings of 'a worthy Labour representative in the House of Commons'.[54]

The Socialists Bite the Bullet

The choice of Shackleton inevitably disappointed the local Socialists, of all varieties. Clitheroe was widely regarded as a Socialist stronghold.[55] And in Snowden, the Socialists would have had a popular candidate, a man who had put a great deal of time and effort into proselytizing in Nelson and Colne. The local ILP leadership initially issued a palpably grudging statement,[56] which served to reinforce a public impression that both the ILP and the more extreme Social Democratic Federation were going to follow a policy of 'benevolent neutrality', rather than 'active alliance' with the LRC candidate, in the forthcoming election campaign.[57] The ILP's national leadership, however, was anxious to dispel this impression. 'We must not be seen', wrote Bruce Glasier, the party's chairman, 'to act as if we were either disappointed at Shackleton's selection, or were disposed to allow ourselves to be reckoned outsiders. It must be our campaign as well as that of the Trade Unionists.'[58] The national view prevailed, and shortly after Glasier's comment, the ILP's Clitheroe branches made amends with a 'manifesto' directly endorsing Shackleton.[59]

There was a broadly similar tussle within the Social Democratic Federation. Following Shackleton's selection, the federation's Nelson branch sent a list of four names to its London headquarters, asking that one be chosen to contest the by-election.[60] Headquarters responded by saying there was no reason either to support or oppose Shackleton.[61] The local branches, through the Clitheroe Division Socialist Council, took the cue and formally ruled

54. *Blackburn Times*, 12 July 1902.
55. 'Socialism is stronger in this division than in most'. Ibid., 5 July 1902.
56. 'Although Mr Shackleton does not ... acknowledge himself a Socialist, he is credited with being a very able and earnest trade union official, and it is believed that he will ... most scrupulously respect the terms of independence of Liberal and Tory politics upon which his candidature is being promoted.' *Colne & Nelson Times*, 18 July 1902.
57. *Northern Daily Telegraph*, 15 July 1902.
58. Glasier to Hardie, 13 July 1902: Glasier Papers, I.1.1902/35.
59. In doing so, the manifesto disingenuously claimed that there had been 'considerable misunderstanding ... with regard to the attitude of the Socialists'. *Nelson Chronicle*, 25 July 1902.
60. *Northern Daily Telegraph*, 8 July 1902. But the federation's branch in the town of Clitheroe publicly opposed this proposal. Ibid., 11 July 1902.
61. *Cotton Factory Times*, 18 July 1902.

out a Socialist candidate, saying they would wait to learn the campaign policies of the by-election candidates before 'instructing Socialists which ... to
support'.[62]

Liberal Stumbles

The local Liberals, on the other hand, provided a notably more substantial
source of resentment. Their anxiety to hold the seat was reflected in the speed
with which they moved to select Philip Stanhope. The scion of a noble
Liberal family and former MP for the nearby seat of Burnley, which he lost
in 1900 owing to his opposition to the Boer War, Stanhope had a reputation
as an 'advanced' Liberal and a 'friend of labour'. His selection, two days
before the 5 July conference, was plainly intended to spike Labour's guns.

When the stratagem failed, the Liberals were outraged. Forgetting the
warnings they had had from the time of the March conference in Nelson,[63]
they saw themselves as 'treated very shabbily' by union leaders who had
'sprung a surprise' on them, and demonstrated a 'high-handed and autocratic
spirit'.[64] Initially, too, they found it difficult to accept that Shackleton's nomination was Labour's last word. Many of them preferred to construe his selection as 'the hasty action of a few minor [union] officials', who had consulted
neither rank-and-file weavers nor 'the responsible leaders' of the Weavers'
Amalgamation.[65] They looked to the next meeting of the amalgamation's
General Council, on 12 July, for a correction. In the meantime, they pursued
a policy of deliberate deception.

On 8 July, three days after Shackleton's selection, Stanhope told the leadership of the Clitheroe Division Liberal Association that he had decided to
withdraw his name. The association did not make his decision public until
the evening of 14 July, having withheld it, as one report put it, 'for reasons
only known to the local leaders of the Liberal party'.[66] In the meantime, it was
put about that the association's selection committee had tried, but failed, to
see Stanhope in Manchester on the afternoon of 8 July. That evening, the
committee met in Nelson, where 'it was freely reported' that one of its members had talked about a telegram of withdrawal from Stanhope. At the end of
the meeting, Catlow blandly informed the press that 'he had not received a
telegram from Mr Stanhope to the effect stated'.[67]

---

62. Ibid., 25 July 1902.
63. As Ramsay MacDonald told the LRC executive, his 27 June letter in the London *Daily
Chronicle*, the leading Liberal paper, was (like Newall's parallel announcement in the local press)
directed precisely at 'making the Liberals hold their hands'. LRC, *Minutes of Special Meeting*,
Colne, 3 July 1902: 'Infancy of the Labour Party', vol. 1, fol. 118.
64. *Colne & Nelson Times*, 11 July 1902; *Blackburn Weekly Telegraph*, 12 July 1902; *Northern
Daily Telegraph*, 9 July 1902.
65. *Colne & Nelson Times*, 11 July 1902.
66. Ibid., 18 July 1902.
67. *Northern Daily Telegraph*, 9 July 1902.

Stanhope was party to the deception. The committee did in fact see him in Manchester on 8 July. But evidently, after telling the committee he had decided to withdraw, he was won around to the view that Shackleton's nomination lacked legitimacy and was likely to be overturned. This much is clear from a letter he wrote the next day, 9 July,[68] to Herbert Gladstone who had evidently been away. 'A sort of Conference', according to Stanhope, had selected Shackleton but it was 'very doubtful whether it was really representative of the Trades Unions'.[69] The conference's decision had led, he reported, to 'ructions amongst the Trades Unionists', and to a Weavers' Amalgamation meeting on the 12th which would 'protest against' Shackleton's nomination. In addition, the Socialists (accounting for 'from 1000 to 1500 votes') were 'determined at all hazards to run a candidate'. But closer to the bone: 'if Shackleton stands alone [i.e. without Liberal opposition], the Tories will fight him and will *win*'. As for the local Liberals, Stanhope told Gladstone, 'you will not get [them] to stand aside and accept Shackleton' in the existing circumstances. 'Catlow ... is in favour of dilatory tactics to see how matters shape themselves before the Liberals take any decided step. I think he is right.'[70]

The overriding intention of Stanhope's letter is clear enough. He was anxious that Gladstone should not foreclose the possibility of the Liberals putting up a candidate in the Clitheroe by-election. And since the letter made no mention of his own withdrawal (later announced as occurring on the day before he wrote to Gladstone), Stanhope gave Gladstone to understand that he remained the selected Liberal candidate.

On the day that Stanhope wrote to Gladstone, Catlow aimed higher, and sent a telegram to Campbell-Bannerman: 'Could you or Gladstone or both meet small Liberal deputation re political position Clitheroe Thursday evening [10th] wire time and place address.'[71] Later that morning, Catlow cockily remarked to a reporter that 'the nomination of a Liberal candidate was a certainty' – Clitheroe would not be 'surrendered to the Labour party'.[72] 'Some people', according to the same reporter, believed that Labour would 'withdraw Mr Shackleton' in the face of the Liberals' determination.[73]

Stanhope's letter created extreme uncertainty in Gladstone, as the latter's diary records: 'Cannot oppose Shackleton ... But if agreed on [Shackleton] a Tory might beat him owing to weavers' disunion. And a Lib. cand. might win

---

68. The letter, undated, has been archivally identified as *c*. 13 August, 1902. This is incorrect. From internal evidence, it was clearly written earlier, and in the week after Shackleton's selection on Saturday 5 July; and since it is headed (in Stanhope's hand) 'Wednesday', the correct date would be 9 July.

69. Stanhope to Gladstone, n.d., *c*. (BM notation) 13 August 1902: Viscount Gladstone Papers, vol. LXXVI, BM Add. MS 46060, fols. 15–16. See note 68.

70. Ibid.

71. Catlow to Campbell-Bannerman, 9 July 1902: ibid., vol. IV, BM Add. MS 45988, fol. 21.

72. *Northern Daily Telegraph*, 9 July 1902.

73. Ibid.

a 3 cornered fight.'[74] But his mind was cleared later the same day after hearing, along with Campbell-Bannerman, from Catlow's deputation. The two senior Liberals concluded that it was advisable, in the interests of their party, 'to unite on Shackleton'. And, with the help of Liberal MPs from Lancashire, they pressured Catlow into accepting Shackleton's nomination – provided he asked for a meeting with the local Liberals and expressed 'general agreement with Lib. policy'.[75]

The next day, Gladstone saw Sam Woods, secretary of the TUC, and John Burns, the leading Lib-Lab MP, and persuaded them to write, 'in my sense', urging Shackleton to meet with the Clitheroe Liberals.[76] Shackleton's supporters duly approached the Liberals, and a meeting was arranged for Monday 14 July, in Manchester.[77] Four Liberal and six Labour men (including Shackleton) attended. As Catlow later reported, the Liberals first proposed an arbitration to decide between Stanhope and Shackleton, the winner to campaign as either 'Liberal-Labour' or 'Labour-Liberal'.[78] Shackleton and his colleagues rejected this. In response to further Liberal questions, they declined either to accept Stanhope, or to allow Shackleton to stand, as a 'Liberal-Labour' or 'Labour-Liberal' candidate. The Liberals then asked if Shackleton would state in his formal election address that he was 'a Liberal in politics'. 'He said "No"', but added that he would explain 'his principles' in the address. In this case, the Liberals persisted, would he state 'what his previous convictions had been politically … and say he had seen no reason to modify them?' – 'He said "No".' The Liberals were offered just one crumb of comfort: if they refrained from putting a candidate forward in Clitheroe, the LRC would 'use its influence' to prevent Labour candidates opposing sitting Liberal MPs elsewhere in Lancashire.[79]

The Liberal delegation reported back to their selection committee the same evening. Immediately afterwards, it was officially announced that Stanhope had withdrawn his name six days earlier, on 8 July.[80] The Liberals' London leadership promptly expressed support for Shackleton's candidature.[81] What Gladstone had been hoping for at this point was an agreement with the cotton unions and the LRC which, 'in considn. of the … Lib. party in Clitheroe' accepting Shackleton, would remove the threat of any 'future [Labour] interference when a Lib. Member or candidate is in the field'.[82] But

74. Diary entry, 10 July 1902: Viscount Gladstone Papers, vol. CXLV, BM Add. MS 46484, fol. 17 (p. 32).
75. Ibid.
76. Diary entry, 11 July 1902: ibid., p. 33.
77. *Northern Daily Telegraph*, 14 July 1902.
78. *Nelson Chronicle*, 18 July 1902.
79. Ibid.
80. Though the letter (not telegram) in which he did so may have been dated 7 July. See ibid.
81. See *Daily Chronicle*, 16 July 1902.
82. Memorandum, 11 July 1902: Viscount Gladstone Papers, vol. CXXI, BM Add. MS 46105, fol. 322.

the Clitheroe Liberals, seeing it as a choice of 'surrender or ... fight',[83] had other ideas. They decided to ask Franklin Thomasson, of Bolton, to address the full Liberal Council as a potential candidate.

The 600 and more members of the Council gathered in Nelson on the evening of the 21st, only to be told that Thomasson had declined the invitation. Their immediate and unanimous reaction was to ask Catlow, their chairman, to accept the candidacy. He, too, declined. Then, in accordance with Gladstone's hope, he moved a resolution proposing that Shackleton, as 'an undoubted Liberal', should not be opposed.[84] But this was countered by an almost unanimously adopted amendment insisting 'that at all hazards the election be fought', and asking him to reconsider his refusal. Eventually, after a confusing discussion, Catlow agreed to think the matter over. He formally declined nomination by letter on 23 July.

That was where the action ended, but the bitter taste lingered. Catlow acknowledged to a journalist that local Liberal activists, almost to a man, remained hotly indignant at the policy forced on them by their London leadership.[85] Gladstone, understandably, chose to paint a completely different picture of their attitude, in a widely reported speech at Leeds later that week.

A Labour representative came into the field ... What had the Liberal party [in Clitheroe] done there? They had said, 'We will not oppose the representative of Labour. (Cheers.) He is a good Liberal ... [and] we are so anxious to have the great cotton industry of Lancashire worthily represented that we stand aside and sacrifice our own interest in ... the representation of Labour.' (Cheers.)[86]

The Clitheroe Conservatives had declared their hand a few days earlier. They would contest the seat only if the Liberals did. Just hours before the Liberal Council urged Catlow to stand, the Conservatives 'provisionally selected' a candidate but did not name him.[87] He never was named.

Labour's Bandwagon

Meanwhile, Labour had been organizing. Immediately after Shackleton accepted nomination, the 5 July conference had resolved to form district

83. *Nelson Chronicle*, 18 July 1902.
84. *Colne & Nelson Times*, 25 July 1902.
85. Ibid. Kay-Shuttleworth told Gladstone that he was 'much relieved' at the outcome, but the main point of his letter and its enclosures was to underline 'the extraordinary strength of the Liberal feeling in the constituency, and the resentment at the high handed action of the Labour people'. Kay-Shuttleworth to Gladstone, 23 July 1902: Viscount Gladstone papers, vol. LXXV, BM Add. MS 46059, fol. 259.
86. *Northern Daily Telegraph*, 26 July 1902.
87. *Colne & Nelson Times*, 27 July 1902.

election committees, linked to a central executive body.[88] The new executive met on 10 July, decided to call itself the Clitheroe Division of Lancashire Labour Representation Committee,[89] and elected Newall as its corresponding secretary.

Despite Liberal hopes and press predictions, there seems to have been no serious dissension among the trade unionists. On 9 July (the day Stanhope told Gladstone of union 'ructions'), a crowded general meeting of the Colne weavers' union roundly endorsed Shackleton's candidature.[90] On the 12th, the General Council of the Weavers' Amalgamation (which Stanhope had predicted would 'protest') did the same 'enthusiastically and unanimously'.[91] A general meeting of the Nelson weavers followed suit two days later.[92] And a well-known 'early opponent of labour representation',[93] David Holmes – president of the Weavers' Amalgamation and a Liberal stalwart – expressed warm support for the Labour candidate in his regular newspaper column.[94]

Labour opened its election campaign with a public meeting in Nelson on the evening the Liberal Council pressed Catlow to nominate. The supporting platform speakers were either locals or Weavers' Amalgamation officials (including Holmes and Wilkinson), or both.[95] The traditional resolution approving Shackleton's candidature was carried unanimously. Newall reported to Ramsay MacDonald, the following day, that Shackleton 'made a grand impression & was enthusiastically adopted' – adding gleefully: 'You will have seen from this morning's paper the pass that the Liberals are in.'[96] He also informed MacDonald of four further meetings to be held before nomination day, 1 August, each (unlike the first) involving a nationally prominent speaker.[97]

88.   The trade unions, a journalist commented, 'are being used to form the nucleus of the election committees. This employment of trade union machinery in electioneering is an interesting development ... [It] will give the Labour candidate a valuable advantage.' *Northern Daily Telegraph*, 8 July 1902.

89.   Ibid., 11 July 1902. Its letterhead soon after dropped 'of Lancashire', and replaced 'Committee' with 'Association'.

90.   See *Manchester Guardian*, 10 July 1902.

91.   *Cotton Factory Times*, 18 July 1902.

92.   *Nelson Chronicle*, 18 July 1902.

93.   Bealey and Pelling, *Labour and Politics*, p. 121.

94.   'In my opinion Mr Shackleton ... will make an ideal member of Parliament ... No one will certainly be better pleased than myself to see my personal friend and colleague take up the position of Parliamentary member.' *Blackburn Times*, 19 July 1902.

95.   While giving full support to Shackleton, however, the amalgamation's leadership was still undecided about affiliating to the LRC. The General Council meeting which applauded Shackleton's selection also postponed consideration of a proposal to affiliate, put by the Colne weavers. *Minutes*, 12 July 1902.

96.   Newall to MacDonald, 22 July 1902: LP Archives, LRC 4/40.

97.   These were Fred Brocklehurst, of the ILP, at Colne on the 23rd; MacDonald himself at the town of Clitheroe on the 24th; Lady Dilke, of the Women's Trade Union League, at Brierfield on the 30th; and Philip Snowden at Padiham on the 31st.

On nomination day, accompanied by Holmes, Cross of the Blackburn weavers, and a number of union officials from the constituency, Shackleton presented himself at the Clitheroe Town Hall. At noon, eleven nomination papers were submitted on his behalf, 'all of them … signed by working men and officials of trades unions'.[98] The Acting Under-Sheriff, sitting for the High Sheriff, waited until 12.30 p. m. before declaring that there were no other nominations. He waited another hour to hear any objections to the nomination. He then declared Shackleton duly elected. The new MP moved a vote of thanks to the Acting Under-Sheriff, and was 'warmly congratulated by his friends and a few gentlemen who had assembled in the vicinity of the Town Hall'.[99] It was done.

The Issue of Independence

Shackleton's formal 'election address', announcing his candidature and outlining his policy concerns, dealt first and most lengthily with matters that, in his words, 'directly interest and affect trade unionists'.[100] These, in the order he dealt with them, were the Taff Vale and anti-picketing judgements, workers' compensation legislation, old-age pensions, housing, cheap train tickets for workers, eight-hour legislation, electoral reform, payment of MPs, and women's suffrage. Beyond matters of direct union interest, he declared himself in favour of free trade, 'nationalization of land, mines, minerals, and railways', shorter parliaments, the abolition of the House of Lords, arbitration in international disputes, stricter liquor-licensing laws, free and secular education, and Irish home rule. Later, in response to questions from the floor during his campaign, he added two items to this list: support for the disestablishment of the Church of England and opposition to compulsory vaccination.

The issues of education and liquor-licensing reform attracted especially intense public attention, each generating an association created for the express purpose of questioning Shackleton and any other candidates.[101] More unusual, for the times, was the prominence achieved by a third issue, women's suffrage. This came to the fore because the levy funding Shackleton's campaign and parliamentary salary had been imposed on female and male unionists alike,[102] which meant that the bulk of his financial support came from voteless women and girls. Emmeline Pankhurst, down from

---

98. *Cotton Factory Times*, 8 August 1902.
99. *Nelson Chronicle*, 8 August 1902.
100. *Cotton Factory Times*, 25 July 1902.
101. These were the Clitheroe Division Temperance Electoral Association and, on education, the Central Protestant Electoral Council for the Clitheroe Division. *Northern Daily Telegraph*, 31 July 1902.
102. An initial proposal to limit the levy to adult males was dropped, presumably because it would not have raised enough money without being set at a prohibitive level.

Manchester shortly before his campaign began, bluntly told a Clitheroe audience that Shackleton 'ought to do something for [women] in return' for their monetary contribution.[103] Shortly afterwards, he publicly conceded 'it was unfair that they should be called upon to pay ... and not have a voice in his [election]', and spoke as well of 'broader principles' justifying the claim that 'women should have a say in the government of this great nation'.[104] Pankhurst was evidently mollified. She not only spoke for him at his Brierfield meeting, but later complained that his performance on the suffrage issue 'has not received the attention in the Labour papers which it deserves'.[105]

But the truly central issue of the Clitheroe by-election was altogether different. It was embodied in Shackleton's claim that he stood apart from the three major political movements of his day – Liberalism, Conservatism and Socialism. The problematic aspect of this claim concerned Liberalism, for there was never any question of his wish to stay clear of Conservatism and Socialism. On the other hand, he was known to have been a formal Liberal up to 1894, and was widely associated with the Liberal cause thereafter. Up to this time, too, as we have seen, the standard practice of such a trade union official, when elected to parliament, was to identify himself as a 'Lib-Lab' who would act independently on 'labour' matters, but otherwise submit to the Liberal party's whip.[106]

In these circumstances, it is understandable that Bruce Glasier of the ILP, hearing of Shackleton's Manchester meeting with the Clitheroe Liberals on 14 July, should have been worried about the possibility of some 'Liberal compact business' being done.[107] Newall, who was at the meeting, saw the need to reassure ('set your mind at rest', was the way he put it) Ramsay MacDonald on the point. 'Dear Mac. Dont [sic] be alarmed ... there was no compromise.'[108] What 'no compromise' meant was spelled out more precisely in a letter Shackleton wrote about the same time to John Burns.

> I met the leaders of the Liberal Party yesterday, and explained to them my views on public matters, and as one who has been an advanced Radical all his live [sic], I

103.   Colne & Nelson Times, 25 July 1902.
104.   Ibid.
105.   Labour Leader, 2 August 1902.
106.   The Lib-Lab MPs, however, were few in number (there were only eight in parliament at the time of the Clitheroe by-election), and that seems to be part of the explanation of the LRC's growing support among Liberal trade unionists. The 'main Liberal offence so far as organised workers were concerned' had nothing to do with policy, Kenneth Brown argues, but was rather 'the constant [Liberal] rejection of their wish to be represented in Parliament by men of their own social class'. First Labour Party, p. 11.
107.   Glasier to Hardie, 15 July 1902: Glasier Papers, I.1. 1902/36. Despite a reassurance from Snowden, Glasier was convinced that the meeting had been a mistake, and went ahead with a fabricated press 'interview', initially published in the Manchester Guardian, which threatened a Snowden candidacy if Shackleton compromised with the Liberals. See Poirier, Advent of the Labour Party, p. 149; and Manchester Guardian, 18 July 1902.
108.   Newall to MacDonald, 17 July 1902: LP Archives, LRC 4/39.

think they were satisfied on that point. The only question on which we could not agree was, their request, that I should allow myself to be nominated as a Liberal-Labour or Labour-Liberal Candidate ... The only thing that stands between the Liberal Party and myself now is the name.[109]

Shackleton's position on the name was thoroughly pragmatic. 'From many years experience of the Textile people', he confided to Burns, 'I have come to the conclusion, that to openly ally myself with any Party, other than Labour, would be disastrous to the cause of Labour Representation in this County.'[110] In his public statements at this time, he made effectively the same point. But he tended to do so in terms implying that 'Labour' was above party, or at least non-party, which left open the possibility of supporting Labour without altogether abandoning an original party allegiance. Thus, a day or two after writing to Burns: 'I cannot definitely ally myself with any political party. The trade unions, whose candidate I am, are composed of men of all parties, and if I were to declare myself a Liberal candidate it would ... be to ruin this election and all future attempts to get direct Labour representation.'[111] And, again, as he put it at his inaugural campaign meeting in Nelson the following week, 'no official of a trades organisation has the right to expect the members to ... contribute towards his support as a member of Parliament, and at the same time be ... tied to any political party'.[112]

At this time, too, Shackleton distilled the message of his political independence into one oft-repeated sentence: 'I am a Labour candidate pure and simple.'[113] Sometimes he was pressed. As by one journalist: 'You are a Labour man first and a Liberal after?' 'No,' he replied, 'I am not a Liberal at all. I am a Labour man purely and simply, and as far as anything but Labour is concerned, my ideas are progressive.' Being progressive included support for 'some of the Socialists' ideas which are practicable, such as the municipalisation of as many monopolies as we could get hold of'. The journalist pressed again: 'You are not a Socialist?' – 'No; I simply call myself a Labour man'.[114]

But, as a Labour man, whom precisely did he represent? In its second annual report a few months earlier, the LRC's national executive had emphasised the aim of '*Labour* Representation ... not merely ... *Trade* Representation', and argued (with a particular eye to the contemporary practice of the Miners' Federation) that there was 'danger ... in action which makes the Labour member the representative of one trade rather than of the general

109. Shackleton to Burns, 15 July 1902: Burns Coll., BM Add MS 46298/81.
110. Ibid.
111. *Northern Daily Telegraph*, 19 July 1902.
112. *Colne & Nelson Times*, 25 July 1902. Later in the same meeting, both his view and his terminology were corroborated by A. Smith, president of the Nelson Overlookers' Association, who moved the resolution formally adopting the candidate. ' If Mr Shackleton had for one instant lent an ear to the advisability of tacking himself to any party, whether a Liberal, or a Tory, or a Socialist, or any party distinction, [this] meeting would not have been held to support his candidature.'
113. *Cotton Factory Times*, 11 July 1902.
114. *Colne & Nelson Times*, 11 July 1902.

interests of wage-earners'.[115] Shackleton, it seems, saw no such danger. At this time, to judge from his public pronouncements, he thought of himself as primarily a trade representative. Interviewed shortly after his selection, he described himself as 'a man elected to represent the textile workers' and talked of a general feeling that 'the textile workers ought to have direct representation', before briefly acknowledging that, as well, 'it will be my duty to watch closely over the interests of all classes of Labour'.[116] The newspaper reports of his campaign speeches suggest a similar emphasis on the role of trade representative. The pattern, in one sense, was set for him at the outset of the inaugural meeting in Nelson, when the chairman referred to the 'splendid example' of the miners' MPs.[117] Shackleton himself referred approvingly to the miners' example at the Colne meeting.[118] It was left to others at his campaign meetings to press the notion of a broader representational role.[119]

There is little doubt that in stressing the narrower role, Shackleton was echoing the popular perception. Thus, celebrating his election, the *Cotton Factory Times* described him as 'the first Lancashire textile labour representative in the House of Commons'.[120] And over two years later, a less friendly editorialist not only wrote of the 'special and peculiar nature' of Shackleton's parliamentary position as 'a Trade Representative', but affirmed that 'this constituency [Clitheroe] is content to be represented in the House by a Cotton Trade Representative'.[121]

Shackleton himself, as it happened, had by then come round to (or decided it was safe to embrace publicly) the broader conception of his role. Less than six months after his election, he told a journalist from the *Westminster Gazette*, 'I did not stand as a textile man pure and simple, but as a Labour man'.[122]

115.   *Labour Party Foundation Conference*, p. 59.
116.   *Northern Daily Telegraph*, 7 July 1902.
117.   *Colne & Nelson Times*, 25 July 1902.
118.   See ibid.
119.   At Nelson it was D. Ormerod, an ILP member, who directly condemned the miners' MPs as 'sectional'; and at Colne, it was Newall. Ibid. At Padiham, it was Snowden, with a barbed remark to the effect that 'they did not want representatives of just one industry'. *Nelson Chronicle*, 8 August 1902.
120.   8 August 1902.
121.   *Colne & Nelson Times*, 27 January 1905.
122.   Quoted in *Nelson Chronicle*, 30 January 1903. A little earlier, too, he had elaborated on the point at some length in a speech at Ashton-under-Lyne. 'He had no sympathy with sectional representation. – (Hear, hear.) … In no single constituency that he was aware of could a cotton operative rule the roost himself. – (Hear, hear.) They ought to look at it in a broader sense than that of mere textile representation. – (Hear, hear, and applause.) He … was not returned as a textile representative. He was returned as a Labour representative.' *Cotton Factory Times*, 16 January 1903.

The Consequences of Clitheroe

The LRC executive formally hailed Shackleton's election as 'one of the greatest triumphs ... Labour has ever had'.[123] The feelings of Socialists were predictably mixed. Keir Hardie put the best face on it by linking it to 'the activity and energy of the I.L.P.', and suggesting it would 'stimulate Labour elsewhere to put candidates into the field'.[124] In a characteristically florid editorial, Blatchford's *Clarion* said it proved 'the workers had but to signify their determination at the polls, and no power dare stand against them' – adding, for good measure, that '"Labour Representation" is the "Open Sesame" to the cave where the political robbers have hitherto concealed their plunder.'[125] Further left, the Social Democratic Federation's paper conceded that Clitheroe marked 'another stage in the growth of the movement for Labour Representation', but warned darkly against the dangers of relying on men like Shackleton whom 'the wirepullers of the capitalist parties will welcome'.[126]

Comment in the general press was limited.[127] Local observers on the Liberal side were inclined to interpret the by-election as the outcome of 'one of the most remarkable pieces of political self-abnegation ever recorded in the history of party politics'.[128] A different tack and a larger perspective came easier in London, where a Liberal editorialist could hope that Clitheroe was 'the first fruit of a better understanding' – despite the admitted 'feeling of soreness' among the Liberals there.[129] That 'soreness', in fact, points to the most significant feature of the by-election.

Shackleton's walkover, in the face of the local Liberals' hot resistance, was the most convincing electoral victory that the LRC had ever had. Before then, its only successes were Richard Bell's at Derby, and Keir Hardie's at Merthyr Tydfil, in the general election of 1900 – both of them depending on tacit local Liberal support and the easier circumstances of a two-member constituency.[130] This aspect of the Clitheroe by-election was well understood

---

123. *Labour Party Foundation Conference*, p. 91.

124. *Labour Leader*, 9 August 1902.

125. *Clarion*, 8 August 1902.

126. *Justice*, 9 August 1902.

127. The press and the public, it has been argued, were preoccupied with the illness of King Edward and with his Coronation, which occurred a week after the by-election; and besides, Clitheroe was a long way from London. Halévy was the first to make these points: see his *Imperialism and the Rise of Labour*, pp. 278–9.

128. *Nelson Chronicle*, 1 August 1902.

129. *Daily News*, 2 August 1902. The soreness is evident in the splutter of rage evoked by a Conservative paper's claim that Shackleton owed his win to the Conservative's threat of a three-way contest, which allegedly persuaded the Liberals to withdraw rather than risk a Conservative victory. This 'fanciful theory', a local Liberal editorialist sneered, 'would be amusing if it were not too absurd to notice' – and then embarked on a painfully laboured rebuttal. *Nelson Chronicle*, 1 August 1902.

130. See Bealey and Pelling, *Labour and Politics*, pp. 44–50.

by the Liberal party's national leadership. For it was following Clitheroe – and before the more famous, but less controversial LRC victory at Woolwich[131] – that serious negotiations about electoral sharing began between the LRC and the Liberals.[132] These dealings, confined mainly to Ramsay MacDonald and Jesse Herbert (Gladstone's secretary), eventually produced the secret agreement which underwrote the LRC's triumph in the general election of 1906.[133]

Also underwriting that triumph, partly because it strengthened MacDonald's negotiating hand in relation to the Liberals, was the way Shackleton's election persuaded the cotton unions to throw in their lot with the LRC, sooner rather than later. Before then, along with the miners, they had represented by far the most significant source of union opposition to the LRC. A week before the by-election (but with its outcome a foregone conclusion), the biannual meeting of the Textile Factory Workers' Association gave Shackleton a 'hearty' reception that left the *Cotton Factory Times* reporter in no doubt that the cotton unions were about to change their position on the issue of direct representation.[134] He was right. And the change was radical enough to be reflected before long in their joining the LRC. Once that happened, there were few who still doubted that the nascent Labour party had a future.

131.   A London electorate, which in itself ensured better exposure in the metropolitan press, Woolwich was won for the LRC by Will Crooks in March 1903, from the Conservatives, with the public support of the local Liberal organizations. See ibid., p. 144. Later, in July the same year at Barnard Castle, Arthur Henderson scored the LRC's only other by-election win before the 1906 general election. Both Woolwich and Barnard Castle have been fairly judged – and for much the same reasons – as 'less remarkable' than Shackleton's success at Clitheroe. Clegg et al., *History of British Trade Unions*, vol. 1, pp. 381–2.
132.   See Bealey and Pelling, *Labour and Politics*, p. 125.
133.   See ibid., pp. 140–6, 156–9.
134.   1 August 1902. And not only the unions. His own paper also changed tack after Shackleton's win and, as Peter Clarke has pointed out, 'made constant propaganda for the L.R.C., which only two years previously it had deprecated'. *Lancashire and the New Liberalism*, p. 92.

4

The Member for Clitheroe, 1902–1906

On 25 April 1903, nine months to the week after Shackleton won Clitheroe, his wife, Sarah, at the age of 38, bore him a son. The boy, unlike either of his two dead brothers, was given Shackleton's first name, David. This suggests a certain sense of self-importance on the part of a man who had lately acquired what Will Crooks, his new parliamentary colleague, described as 'the privilege of being able to attach the magic letters "M.P."' to his name.[1]

The 'magic' lay in the effect of those letters on the public standing of their possessor. True, as a raw MP from the north of England, Shackleton might not initially carry great weight in London.[2] But in north-east Lancashire, it was an entirely different matter.

The Local Scene

Before the by-election, Shackleton's positions as Accrington magistrate and Darwen town councillor were key determinants of his local standing. As the member for Clitheroe, he had no need of them in this sense, as well as less time to give to them. He resigned from both before long.

He also loosened his ties with the primary source of his local standing, the Darwen Weavers' Association. Early on, he made it known that he would like to keep the secretaryship 'if arrangements satisfactory to the Association can be come to'.[3] He had his way. The union appointed an assistant secretary, John Parkington, who took up his duties early in October. Both Shackleton and the union paid a price for this arrangement. His salary at the time of the by-election was £2 5s a week. The executive, when it proposed an assistant secretaryship, decided ('if asked for our opinion') to recommend £1 10s for the post, and a new salary of £1 5s for Shackleton.[4] This was accepted by the general meeting, which meant that the union paid an additional 10s a week for the privilege of having an MP as its part-time secretary.

---

1. Quoted in Haw, *From Workhouse to Westminster*, p. 205.
2. Except, of course, in Labour circles. Thus, a month after his election, he was given a place of honour on the platform at the TUC's annual Congress in Holborn, which he would otherwise have attended with the rights of an ordinary delegate.
3. *Blackburn Weekly Telegraph*, 2 August 1902.
4. DWA, *Minutes* (Ctee), 11 September 1902.

Despite its willingness to accommodate Shackleton, the Darwen union had still not committed itself to his political sponsor, the Labour Representation Committee (LRC). And while it was moving in that direction, there was plainly serious opposition that took time to overcome. Three months after the by-election, the union's membership voted overwhelmingly (4,998 votes to 978) in favour of the principle of direct representation.[5] Two months later, its executive came out in support of the Textile Factory Workers' Association affiliating to the LRC.[6] But it was almost a year before the union itself finally took the plunge, and affiliated on its own account, sending two delegates to the LRC's 1904 conference.[7]

Other cotton union bodies moved faster. The results of the ballot initiated by the Textile Factory Workers' Association (see Chapter 3) were announced six months after the by-election. Direct representation was endorsed by a majority of four to one (84,154 votes to 19,856).[8] When the association's biannual meeting subsequently considered the question of LRC affiliation, some delegates spoke of being 'used by the Socialists', but Shackleton made a speech which was said to have 'soon killed that bogey'.[9] The meeting voted overwhelmingly in favour of affiliation. Days later, the association's delegates attended the annual conference at which Shackleton was first elected to the LRC's executive.[10]

He remained vice-president of the Weavers' Amalgamation. By the beginning of 1905, the general buoyancy of the cotton industry encouraged the amalgamation to claim a 7½ per cent increase in wage rates, involving full restoration to the levels applying before the great strike of 1878. He was the amalgamation's spokesman in press interviews about the claim, and his name (followed by those of Wilkinson, the secretary, and Holmes, the president) headed the published list of the negotiating team that won a 5 per cent

5. *Cotton Factory Times*, 21 November 1902.

6. DWA, *Minutes* (Ctee), 26 January 1903.

7. Ibid., 7 December 1903. The strength of the opposition within the union is reflected in the fact that more than two years after the Clitheroe by-election, the executive twice adjourned consideration of a circular proposing the formation of a Darwen LRC. When it did finally bite the bullet and send delegates to a meeting on the matter, nothing eventuated. Ibid., October–November 1904.

8. See *Cotton Factory Times*, 6 February 1903. In the case of the weavers, the majority was closer to five to one (54,637 votes to 11,352).

9. *Labour Leader*, 7 February 1903.

10. The total membership of the Textile Factory Workers' Association was 103,000, and it affiliated on this basis. But this did not, as has been claimed by Bealey and Pelling (*Labour and Politics*, p. 120), swell the LRC's affiliated union membership by 103,000 (or its coffers by the precise amount of its affiliation fee – amounting to £51 10s), because some of its constituent unions had affiliated earlier on an individual basis. Among them were eight local weavers' unions (including those at Colne, Nelson and Clitheroe), mustering a total of 18,139 members; and six of these (the exceptions were the Ramsbottom and Bacup unions) are recorded as being affiliated at least a year earlier. LRC, *Executive's Report and Agenda*, 1903, 1902: LSE, Coll Misc 196, vol. I, fols. 161–2, 78–81.

increase, and the promise that the remaining 2½ per cent would be considered in the New Year.[11]

In July 1905, Wilkinson fell ill. Shackleton took over his functions.[12] Holmes's health was also a concern, even before he had 'a rather serious relapse' in January 1906.[13] Again, Shackleton filled the gap.

Meanwhile, within the Clitheroe constituency, the Clitheroe Division Labour Representation Association had held its first annual conference in November 1902.[14] The conference, as well as electing a standing executive,[15] decided that Shackleton should be paid £300 a year from the levy on affiliated trade union members.[16] A high value was evidently placed on this financial relationship. For when the Textile Factory Workers' Association offered to take over the 'burden' of Shackleton's financial support a year later, the Clitheroe LRC's leaders firmly rejected the offer on the ground that their 'personal connection' with him 'would be weakened were he to be the nominee of the general body of textile workers'.[17]

11. See *Cotton Factory Times*, 20 January 1905; 31 March 1905.

12. As he wrote in August: 'I have been doing this [Wilkinson's] work for [the] past five weeks. I am likely to have to continue to do so for many weeks to come. This has made me very busy of late.' Shackleton to Middleton, 20 August 1905: LP Archives, LRC 25/284. He was too optimistic. His 'many weeks' extended into many months.

13. See *Cotton Factory Times*, 22 December 1905; 19 January 1906.

14. See *ibid.*, 17 October 1902. The use of 'association', instead of 'committee', appears to have signified that membership was open to individuals as well as organizations. Most of the national LRC's local branches followed the centre's example by not allowing direct individual membership. See McKenzie, *British Political Parties*, p. 469. The Clitheroe branch, its formal title notwithstanding, is hereinafter referred to as the Clitheroe LRC.

15. One of those elected was the ebullient Newall, whose career in the labour movement came to a sad end a few months later: 'Mr A. B. Newall, J.P., secretary of the Colne Weavers' Association, has disappeared. It is reported that there are some defalcations in his accounts.' *Labour Leader*, 11 July 1903.

16. Clitheroe LRC, *Minutes*, First Ann. Conf., 22 November 1902: LP Archives, LRC 6/108/2. This meant, with his salary from the Darwen weavers, a total salary from these two sources of £365 per annum, or about £7 a week. It is not known whether he was entitled to any allowances (in relation, for example, to travel) or had any other sources of income while he was an MP, although it is likely that he received some payment from the Weavers' Amalgamation after mid-1905. State payment of MPs was still 11 years off. Those supported by trade unions received a variety of payments. According to a contemporary survey formal annual salaries paid ranged from a low of £250 (which John Burns received from the Engineers) to a high of £450 (which Richard Bell received from the Railway Servants), £200 of the latter being Bell's salary as the union's secretary. But, with the addition of 'house, coal and gas, and travelling expenses' to his formal salary of £400 (from the Northumberland Miners), T. Burt's real income was certainly greater. And: 'Rumour has it that Ben Pickard [Yorkshire Miners] makes about £700 a year, but', commented the writer, 'I have my doubts.' At he same time, the Miners' Federation was reported to 'have finally decided' on a uniform amount of £350 per annum for their MPs, plus first-class railway fares and any salary they might draw from a union office held at the same time. *Nelson Chronicle*, 9 May 1902. See Clegg et al., *History of British Trade Unions*, vol. 1, pp. 281–3, for payments in earlier times.

17. *Nelson Chronicle*, 8 January 1904; *Colne & Nelson Times*, 8 January 1904. The Clitheroe LRC leaders would also have known that their 'burden' was soon to be considerably lightened.

The local Liberals, on the other hand, riven with 'unrest and resentment' after Shackleton's win,[18] were in dire straits. A member gloomily reported in mid-1903 that 'our organization is falling to pieces like a rope of sand, our subscriptions have fallen down twenty-five per cent, we cannot get a meeting together ... and most of our active supporters ... are openly declaring that they will vote Tory if there is a Tory candidate in the field'.[19] Lord Shuttleworth, whose peerage had been the start of it all, was anxious for a reconciliation with Labour, while recognizing that 'the difficulties are pretty considerable'.[20] Eventually, his patience exhausted, he tried to strongarm the local Liberals by attaching a condition to his party subscription (£50) for 1904: he would consider withholding further subscriptions if they refused to give 'active support' to Shackleton at the next election.[21] He was officially and firmly rebuffed. Then, as 1905 opened, the Clitheroe Liberals collapsed, and 'decided finally to disband their organisation'.[22] But the resentment remained. And so it was a matter for comment, a month later, when an obscure Liberal town councillor 'had the courage to range himself on the side of Mr Shackleton'.[23] Seven months later, it was still a matter for comment when a more significant defection occurred: 'We congratulate Mr D. Parker on being the first prominent Liberal to publicly identify himself' with Shackleton.[24]

The congratulations came from a Liberal editorial writer who, like some others outside the Labour camp, had been favourably impressed by the performance of the local member. In particular, Shackleton won frequent applause for his practice of touring the electorate, addressing public meetings, when parliament was in recess.[25] He developed a reputation for accessibility. 'He is always approachable, and his constituents' ... communications

A year earlier, the third national LRC conference had set up a Parliamentary Fund designed to pay LRC MPs a maximum of £200 a year and, in the case of each LRC-endorsed parliamentary candidate, a quarter of the returning officer's fee. It also directed that, unless a general election intervened, the fund should not be drawn on before it reached £2,500. It exceeded that figure by mid-1904, and the LRC's national executive resolved to pay maintenance at the rate of £200 per annum from 1 July: LRC, *Executive Annual Report for 1904-5*, LP Archives, LRC 19/75. A week later Shackleton received his first quarterly payment of £50. Letter to Shackleton, 8 July 1904: ibid., LRC 16/393. But the money went to the Clitheroe LRC. *Cotton Factory Times*, 26 January 1906.

18. *Nelson Chronicle*, 15 August 1902.
19. Quoted in Poirier, *Advent of the Labour Party*, p. 202.
20. Shuttleworth to Campbell-Bannerman, 18 July 1903: Campbell-Bannerman Papers, vol. XVI, BM Add. MS 41221, fols. 66–7.
21. *Nelson Chronicle*, 1 April 1904.
22. *Nelson Leader*, 27 January 1905.
23. Ibid., 24 February 1905.
24. Ibid., 29 September 1905
25. In the year he initiated this routine, he was reported as visiting 'every town and hamlet in his constituency'. *Nelson Chronicle*, 25 September 1903.

are not shelved by a private secretary.'[26] He also cultivated the local press to good effect.[27] Nor did it hurt his local standing when he could be mentioned in honourable connection with both a noble patron and stern parliamentary responsibility: 'Mr Shackleton has been placed ... on the National Patriotic Fund Committee ... on the motion of H.R.H. the Duke of Connaught. He has also been placed on the [parliamentary] Standing Committee for the consideration of all bills relating to trade, shipping, and manufactures. Labour is undoubtedly moving.'[28] As the 1906 general election loomed, a Liberal editorialist remarked that Shackleton had 'strengthened his [electoral] position so much' since 1902 because he had been so 'attentive to his duties ... both inside and outside the House of Commons'.[29]

Independence and the Labour Representation Committee

For the LRC's leadership, at the moment the Clitheroe by-election was settled, the key question was whether, in Bruce Glasier's words, 'Shackleton would run true'.[30] Would he maintain an independent position in relation to the Liberal party? His Liberal sympathies were longstanding and well known. Compounding their unease was the fact that neither of the union bodies in which he held an official position was yet affiliated to the LRC.

Before the by-election, the House of Commons contained 10 members who were thought of as specifically working-class representatives. Eight were Lib-Labs, openly associated with both the Liberal party and particular trade unions (the Miners' Federation accounting for five of them), with John Burns and the ageing Henry Broadhurst the most prominent. The other two of the ten had been elected in 1900 as LRC candidates. One was Keir Hardie, a leading member of the Independent Labour Party (ILP). The other, Richard Bell, was a railways union official who had wanted to stand as a Lib-Lab, but was prevented from doing so by his union. From the time of his election, Bell maintained a 'persistent liaison' with the Liberals, even during 1902, when he was chairman of the LRC executive.[31] His behaviour prompted the 'Newcastle Resolution', adopted by the LRC's annual conference in February 1903, which formally prohibited LRC parliamentarians and candidates from promoting or identifying with either the Liberal party or the Conservative party.

26. *Nelson Chronicle*, 25 September 1903. Perhaps a dig at his predecessor, Kay-Shuttleworth?
27. As a mention in a Conservative newspaper demonstrates: 'Mr Shackleton loses no opportunity of watching the interests of his constituents. It is to this vigilance of the Member for the Clitheroe Division that we are indebted for a copy of the Report of the Committee of the House of Commons on the Colne Corporation Bill, Mr Shackleton sending it to us with a kindly written note that "it may interest" us.' *Colne & Nelson Times*, 14 April 1905.
28. *Cotton Factory Times*, 4 March 1904.
29. *Nelson Leader*, 8 December 1905.
30. Quoted in Morgan, *Keir Hardie*, p. 130.
31. Bealey and Pelling, *Labour and Politics*, p. 134.

Glasier's worst fears seemed confirmed when Shackleton chose Bell and John Burns for his formal introduction to the House of Commons.[32] But Snowden intervened, and Shackleton agreed to Hardie in the place of Burns.[33] Glasier's fears, nevertheless, were almost certainly re-kindled when Shackleton, following his introduction, attended a private dinner given by Sir Charles Dilke, a Liberal with close links to the TUC leadership.[34]

First impressions apart, Shackleton quickly emerged as a public advocate of independent Labour representation. He urged the principle at numerous meetings of trade unionists during 1902 and 1903. Newall was pleased: 'Shackleton is taking a splendid stand on independence, and compares well with Bell.'[35] Shortly after this comment, Shackleton was elected to the LRC's national executive. In October 1903, while Will Crooks and Arthur Henderson still hesitated,[36] he formally accepted the parliamentarians' pledge of solidarity by signing the LRC's constitution.[37] By this time, however, he was already embroiled in the first of two early disputes in which his loyalty was called into question.

Franklin Thomasson, who had declined to stand against Shackleton at Clitheroe, was the Liberal candidate in a by-election in the Accrington division. His opponent was Thomas Greenall, the endorsed LRC candidate. The Accrington Trades Council secretary, W. Wareing, seeking prominent speakers for Greenall's inaugural meeting, suggested a number of possibilities to Ramsay MacDonald, the national LRC secretary, but emphasised that Shackleton 'would be especially welcome'.[38] Shackleton, however, declined to speak in support of Greenall. When MacDonald pressed him, he replied that it would be 'an act of folly', because of the Clitheroe episode, if he were to speak against Thomasson.[39] And he would not budge ('I see no reason to change my attitude'),[40] despite a direct request from Wareing, and a further plea from MacDonald after Wareing, out for blood, pressed the LRC

32. Newall to MacDonald, 2 August 1902: LP Archives, LRC 4/41.
33. See Bealey and Pelling, *Labour and Politics*, p. 192.
34. See *Cotton Factory Times*, 8 August 1902.
35. Newall to MacDonald, 2 February 1903: LP Archives, LRC 6/109.
36. Crooks won Woolwich for the LRC in March 1903; and Henderson, who did not sign the constitution until July 1904, won Barnard Castle in July 1903.
37. He wrote: 'I enclose you[r] "constitution" duly signed, with my objection marked thereon'. Shackleton to MacDonald, 22 October 1903: LP Archives, LRC 10/415. The nature of his objection is not specified, but it probably had to do with the words 'or resign' in the clause requiring LRC candidates to pledge they would abide by decisions of the LRC's parliamentary group. For three months later at the 1904 conference, seconded by Hardie, he successfully moved the deletion of those two words. See *Labour Party Foundation Conference*, pp. 176–7.
38. Wareing to MacDonald, 23 August 1903: LP Archives, LRC 10/441.
39. Shackleton to MacDonald, 1 September 1903: ibid., LRC 10/442.
40. Shackleton to MacDonald, 8 October 1903: LP Archives, LRC 11/418.

executive for disciplinary action.[41] The executive declined to move against him because, as MacDonald explained to Wareing, the LRC's MPs had 'a perfect right to refuse to support' an LRC candidate – 'so long as they did not oppose one of our candidates or did not appear on the platform of candidates for whom we were not responsible'.[42] Wareing and the Accrington LRC were not mollified. But the greater storm, on a similar issue, lay ahead.

In June 1904 the Liberals won two by-elections. In neither case did the LRC put up a candidate. At Market Harborough, the Liberal candidate was Philip Stanhope, of Clitheroe fame; at Devonport, it was J. W. Benn. At the time, Shackleton was chairman of the LRC executive and had been involved in well-publicized negotiations with Richard Bell about Bell's refusal to sign the LRC constitution ('the pledge') and his action, in January, when he publicly congratulated the Liberal winner of a by-election in Norwich that had been contested by the LRC.[43] The Devonport incident, as it came to be called, involved Shackleton, Henderson and, to a lesser extent, Crooks.[44] And it was serious enough to 'nearly split the party'.[45]

It began on 10 June with a meeting organized in Market Harborough by the Leicestershire Temperance Union, at which Shackleton and Henderson spoke against the government's Licensing Bill. Subsequently, the meeting appears to have expressed support for Stanhope's candidature in the by-election. The two of them, this time accompanied by Crooks, then spoke again on 14 June in Devonport (on the prompting of the local LRC) at a meeting held under the auspices of the Free Trade League. The furore that ensued focused almost exclusively on this meeting.[46] The spark that lit the fire was struck by the Liberal-oriented *Westminster Gazette* in an article quickly taken up by the provincial press. The anonymous writer, commenting on the Market Harborough meeting, said that Shackleton and Henderson had

41. The *Manchester Guardian* (8 October 1903) picked up the story, and reported 'a rumour' of an agreement between Shackleton and the Clitheroe Liberals, but also suggested that a letter from MacDonald effectively 'dispelled' that allegation.

42. MacDonald to Wareing, 2 November 1903: 'Infancy of the Labour Party', LRC LB 3/52–3.

43. See Bealey and Pelling, *Labour and Politics*, pp. 194–7. At Norwich, both Shackleton and Henderson (Crooks had declined) appeared on the platform with the LRC candidate, an ILP man, and spoke against the Liberal. See Poirier, *Advent of the Labour Party*, p. 210.

44. The three of them, moreover, had stirred Socialists' suspicions of their independence a few weeks earlier when they had spoken from the same platform as Bell, John Burns and a number of Liberal MPs at a 'monster' (70,000) Hyde Park demonstration against the use of indentured Chinese labour in South Africa. *Nelson Leader*, 1 April 1904.

45. Bealey and Pelling, *Labour and Politics*, p. 208.

46. Probably, it seems, because it was the only one which press comment repeatedly implied was a specifically 'Liberal meeting, and that the three M.P.'s were on the Liberal platform'. *Labour Leader*, 5 August 1904. The furore also focused on Shackleton and Henderson, presumably because, unlike Crooks, they were both executive members – Shackleton having been chairman since February.

spoken in support of Stanhope as a 'Temperance Reformer', not as a Liberal.[47] On the forthcoming Devonport meeting, he predicted that the Liberal, Benn, would be given 'the strenuous support of organised labour' by Shackleton, Henderson and Crooks 'armed with the full authority of the Labour Representation Committee'.[48] Following press reports of the Devonport meeting, there was a torrent of protest from local LRCs, ILP branches, and trades councils under Socialist leadership.[49] The privately expressed fury of Pete Curran, an ILP union official and an LRC executive member, is symptomatic: 'these people [Shackleton, Henderson, Crooks] will have to be dealt with … the movement will have to be purged of the undesirables'.[50] Bruce Glasier, as the new editor of the ILP's *Labour Leader*, perforce trod more moderately in public. While convinced that 'Devonport has put us back two or three years … [and] tied a millstone round the neck of the L.R.C', he assured his readers that the culprits were guilty, not of treachery, but simply 'a grave error of judgement'.[51] H. M. Hyndman of the Social Democratic Federation (writing under the pseudonym, 'R. B. Suthers') was predictably less charitable: the 'Labour Party must purge its ranks of wobblers'.[52]

But there was no purge. The LRC executive, after hearing Shackleton's and Henderson's explanations, accepted that they 'did not appear under Liberal auspices nor attend any Liberal meeting'.[53] Hyndman, of course, sneered about 'a white-washing'.[54] But three weeks later, his editor, Robert Blatchford, was the first to acknowledge that the information on which so many denunciations had depended was tainted. Hyndman, said Blatchford, had been 'a little too hasty in denouncing [Shackleton, Henderson, and Crooks] on no better evidence than … statements in Liberal papers' which were, 'it appears, untrue'.[55] Glasier and the *Labour Leader* followed suit a week later.

> Echoes of the 'Devonport incident' continue to be heard. It still provides material for questions at the close of nearly every I.L.P. meeting. The form in which these questions [is] almost invariably put indicates that the real facts of the incident are still not clearly understood, even by our own people. The old saying about giving

47. *Westminster Gazette*, 13 June 1904.
48. Ibid.
49. It did not help matters when Bell, as the uproar mounted, leaked to the press a letter in which Shackleton had asked him to throw his weight behind Stanhope's candidacy. See *Norwich Daylight*, 18 June 1904.
50. Curran to Hardie, 24 June 1904: Francis Johnson Corr., 1904/19.
51. *Labour Leader*, 24 June 1904.
52. *Clarion*, 24 June 1904.
53. LRC, *Minutes*, 30 June 1904: LSE, Coll Misc 196, vol. 1, fols. 254–5. At the same time as it exonerated them, the executive also appointed Shackleton and Henderson, along with MacDonald, to represent the LRC at the Amsterdam Congress of the Second International in August. For a brilliantly biting account of this Congress, see Tuchman, *Proud Tower*, pp. 435–7.
54. *Clarion*, 8 July 1904.
55. Ibid., 29 July 1904.

a lie a start and it cannot be overtaken is very well illustrated by the still prevailing belief in the statements first published in the Liberal press.[56]

In its next annual report, the LRC executive announced that the principle of independence did not preclude its MPs from co-operating with 'Free Trade organisations'.[57] Shackleton had already acted on this assumption, speaking against Joseph Chamberlain's protectionism from a Rossendale platform alongside the Duke of Devonshire and other Liberal and Conservative notables. A Nelson paper rejoiced at finding 'our Member in such good company', but wondered whether he had 'secured the consent of the L.R.C.'.[58]

Ironically, the Devonport incident, raising as it did the spectre of cosy deals with the Liberals, came some months after MacDonald and Hardie had concluded a secret electorate-sharing arrangement with the Liberal party's leaders. Between January and September 1903, without the knowledge of their colleagues on the LRC executive, they had determined the constituencies in which the Liberals would give LRC candidates a clear run in return for corresponding LRC co-operation in others.[59] The agreement, hurriedly concluded in the expectation of an autumn election in 1903, operated at the general election of January 1906.

'Providing Sport for the Philistines'

Shackleton formally took his place in the House of Commons in August 1902, a few days before the summer recess. On 3 November he asked his first question (about legislation governing conditions in cotton-weaving sheds), and four days later devoted his maiden speech to the Conservative government's Education Bill. Five months and four more speeches later, he had

---

56. *Labour Leader*, 5 August 1904. Glasier then set out 'the bare and actual facts of the matter' in the form of eight points – two of which do not quite square with the one really detailed account by an eyewitness of what was done and said at the Devonport meeting. The *Western Daily Mercury*, 15 June 1904, devoted a full broadsheet page, with seven columns of tiny type, to accounts of a number of meetings held the previous day (14 August) in relation to the Devonport election. The 'Free Trade and Labour Union', sometimes abbreviated to the 'Free Trade Union', figured prominently in these activities, and was identified with the meeting addressed by Shackleton and his colleagues. The local LRC leadership was almost certainly involved in the Union; but, despite the *Labour Leader's* claim (point 1) that the meeting was 'organised by the Plymouth, Stonehouse, and Devonport L.R.C.', the LRC was plainly not the formal sponsor. In the second place, and more important, the *Labour Leader* claimed (point 7): 'No direct reference was made to the election by the three principal speakers'. But the *Mercury* report suggests otherwise. Henderson: 'said Devonport had a splendid opportunity of striking a blow at this retrograde Government'. Shackleton: 'and Devonport must show their deprecation of [the government's] action on Monday next'. Crooks: 'So was he (the speaker) and his friend Benn – (loud cheers) ... Mr Crooks ... urged his hearers ... to do the right thing on Monday next – (cheers).'

57. *Labour Party Foundation Conference*, p. 209.

58. *Nelson Leader*, 18 November 1904.

59. See Bealey and Pelling, *Labour and Politics*, ch. VI.

charge of the private member's bill that represented the TUC's first, and most modest, attempt to counter the Taff Vale judgement.

His introduction of the bill focused considerable public attention on the new member for Clitheroe. Both the trade unions and the Employers' Parliamentary Council mobilized to lobby MPs. The *Cotton Factory Times*, with 'Mr Shackleton's Bill' the subject of its main editorial, predicted 'a battle royal between the forces of capital and labour ... in the House of Commons'.[60] The *Manchester Guardian*'s correspondent praised his second reading speech as 'a model of clear and telling exposition, delivered with an unaffected ease which many older hands might have envied'.[61]

There was, however, a darker side to Shackleton's early parliamentary career. The LRC group, of which he became the third member, after Hardie and Bell, initially had little substance. Bell's recalcitrance saw to that. In the immediate aftermath of the 'Newcastle Resolution', and in direct defiance of its terms, he was busily arranging a meeting with Liberal MPs in order to discuss co-operative action. He repeatedly denied any agreement to hold weekly meetings of the three-man 'Labour Group' while parliament was sitting.[62] And he not only continued to champion Liberal causes throughout 1903, but in October refused point-blank to sign the LRC constitution ('the pledge'). Bell, however, was not the only problem.By mid-1903 the group had acquired Crooks (in March) and Henderson (in July). Quite apart from Bell, according to Hardie, it still failed to act as a group. 'A little more cohesion and organisation', he wrote, 'would be welcome.'[63] But Hardie himself may well have been part of the problem, to judge from a complaint Shackleton made to MacDonald.

> You will remember [Shackleton wrote] that at the Joint Conference ... [about] the Royal Commission on the Trade Disputes Bill, I suggested ... that a question should be put across the floor of the House. This ... was defeated by the casting vote of the Chairman. I regretted this decision but have loyally adhered to it. I see from Friday's order sheet that Mr Keir Hardie has put a question down much on the lines I suggested. As [you are] Secretary to the L.R.C., I call your attention to this.[64]

At the start of the 1904 parliamentary session, the group was put on a more formal footing at a meeting of four of the five LRC MPs, Bell refusing to attend.[65] No chairman was appointed, but Shackleton was made secretary,

60. *Cotton Factory Times*, 8 May 1903.
61. *Manchester Guardian*, 9 May 1903. The Speaker, dwelling on a technical flaw, effectively gutted the bill. But, despite the Prime Minister's intervention against it, it was defeated by only 30 votes. *Parl. Debs.*, 8 May 1903, vol. 122, cols. 204–11.
62. Bell and Hardie exchange, 9–16 March 1903: Francis Johnson Corr., 1903/31ff.
63. *Labour Leader*, 22 August 1903.
64. Shackleton to MacDonald, 28 June 1903: LP Archives, LRC 9/383/1.
65. 'Bell was in the House but did not attend although duly warned & even reminded by Henderson who went for him at the hour of meeting.' Hardie to Glasier, 'Sunday', n.d.: Glasier Papers, I.1. 1904/42.

and it was agreed to hold regular weekly meetings.[66] 'This is very important', Hardie remarked in one of his *Labour Leader* columns.[67] But his enthusiasm soon waned. 'The group', he wrote a few weeks on, 'doesn't appear to be making much of a show.'[68] Bruce Glasier thought so, too: 'as a fighting factor [it] has practically ceased to exist'.[69] That was one view. But just a month later, reporting on an all-night sitting to deal with a government bill involving a tax on coal, the *Labour Leader*'s parliamentary correspondent, 'J. H. H.' (J. H. Harley), conveyed a somewhat different impression – certainly so far as Shackleton, at least, was concerned:

> Mr Will Crooks ... went home between twelve and one [a.m.] ... But Mr Shackleton sat with the miners' representatives till half-past four the next afternoon, sleepless, unwearied ... About seven in the morning ... Mr Shackleton saw his opportunity. Mr Henderson was away in the North addressing meetings, and Keir Hardie is not able yet to endure extra fatigue, so our comrade Shackleton was the sole representative of the L.R.C. on the field of battle. He flatly told the Premier that ... the effect of this coal tax had been to reduce wages, shorten hours, and seriously to affect the conditions of working class families ... I have had many testimonies as to the effectiveness of this speech ... The House was crowded all the time the Labour man was orating, and the Premier's face was literally as white as a sheet. But the silence was even more impressive as Mr Shackleton proceeded to point out that Mr Balfour [the Prime Minister] had simply insulted organised Labour all over the country ... Of course the Liberal stalwarts cheered to the echo.[70]

J. H. H.'s plaudits registered, for Shackleton, a pleasant interval between the earlier Devonport incident and another storm, this time centred on the Lib-Lab, John Burns.

At the start of the 1904 session, there had been a second meeting involving the LRC MPs. This time Bell attended. It was a joint meeting with the nine Lib-Lab MPs, at which (after Burns, as the *Labour Leader* carefully put it, had 'generously [offered] to stand aside in favour of Mr Keir Hardie') John Burns was elected the chairman, and Bell and Crooks 'the Whips of the Labour

---

66.   Shackleton kept minutes of these meetings. This is clear from a letter in the Labour Party Archives, written by Shackleton's son, addressed to Morgan Phillips and dated 20 February 1956. In it, David Shackleton, junior, describes 'a book' he was sending Phillips as 'the original minutes of the Labour Representation Group in the House'. The whereabouts of this book is unknown. I am indebted to Stephen Bird for this information.

67.   *Labour Leader*, 9 April 1904.

68.   Hardie to Glasier, (June) 1904, Glasier Papers, I.1.1904/37.

69.   Glasier to Hardie, 17 June 1904: ibid., 1904/36.

70.   *Labour Leader*, 20 July 1904. And before this parliamentary session ended, Shackleton, together with Crooks, again won the admiration of J. H. H. 'I cannot resist paying a tribute to the little body of men who fought Mr Balfour all this week, from twelve often till four o'clock in the morning. Mr Lloyd George, Mr McKenna, Mr Will Crooks, Mr Shackleton ... morning after morning as I watched their gallant fights I realised what a small body of men may do in Parliament if they work with one heart and mind!' Ibid., 19 August 1904.

Party'.[71] Late one evening a few weeks later, for some reason Burns chose to destroy this promising alliance between the Lib-Labs and the LRC MPs. At the time, a resolution on wage rates in state factories and shipyards, moved by Shackleton, was before the House of Commons. Burns proposed an amendment. Shackleton promptly accepted the amendment, remarking that 'it more clearly expressed the object he had in view',[72] and shortly afterwards moved the closure of the debate in an attempt to secure a vote before the House rose. But as Burns – an MP since 1892 – surely anticipated, the Speaker ruled against a closure on the ground that the amendment had been introduced too late to allow adequate consideration.[73] The resolution, accordingly, lapsed. This strange episode excited little comment at the time, but almost six months later was the source of a blazing public row between Burns and Shackleton.

The trigger was a question put to Shackleton at the TUC's annual Congress about the issue at stake in his aborted resolution. In his reply, Shackleton claimed that Burns knew the terms of the resolution beforehand, and said that the amendment would have been incorporated without question if he, as mover, had known of it before the debate. He ended his reply by charging Burns with the responsibility for preventing the House 'from coming to a definite decision on the matter'.[74] A second questioner asked whether Burns 'was present when the resolution was prepared'. Shackleton replied: 'No. He is not a member of the [LRC] group, and we could not recognize him.'[75] Stung by reports of these remarks, Burns shot off a long and widely publicized letter to the press. In it, he vehemently denied setting out to sabotage Shackleton's resolution, and took particular umbrage at his exclusion from the LRC group.[76] Shackleton responded with an interview in which he explained why he believed that Burns had intended, as the interviewing journalist put it, to 'wreck the resolution'.

71. *Labour Leader*, 6 February 1904.

72. *Parl. Debs.*, 23 March 1904, vol. 132, col. 574. The amendment, in effect, involved substituting the words 'Trade Union rate' for 'standard rate'.

73. Beforehand, the procedural point had been quickly taken by Balfour, the Prime Minister, who expressed surprise at Burns's action, 'because it was quite impossible for the [relevant] departments ... to examine [the amendment], and it would obviously be most improper for the House ... to come to a decision upon it after three-quarters of an hour's debate'. But then, as Balfour shrewdly concluded, he 'did not suppose that [Burns] desired that the House should be asked to vote on this matter'. Ibid., cols. 576–7.

74. TUC, *Report*, 1904, p. 83.

75. Ibid., p. 84.

76. Burns mistakenly believed that Shackleton had said 'we do not [as against 'could not'] recognize Mr Burns', which he described as an 'inspired taunt' and a 'petulant ebullition of pique'. He poured scorn on the LRC group ('a clique of political tyros and economic fledglings') and its 'travesty of political independence and impotent isolation', charging it with 'a policy of intolerant exclusion of myself and many other politicians from helping in the settlement of Labour matters'. Quoted in *Colne & Nelson Times*, 16 September 1904.

Just let me tell you what happened the previous night [before the resolution was introduced]. Mr Crooks, Mr Henderson, and I were talking over the matter in the tea room of the House of Commons, when Mr Burns came up and said, with an air of great significance, 'I have a surprise in store for you to-morrow'. We pressed him to say what he meant, but he only replied mysteriously, and walked away. It is that action that we complain of. The debate had been on for two hours before I knew what Mr Burns was going to do ...

You see the point? We had a possible three hours, quite enough, for the discussion of a straightforward issue. But just as the time is nearly exhausted, Mr Burns comes forward with a new point, disclosing an apparent difference in the Labour party itself. Why did he not tell us of his intention the night before, instead of propounding his delphic utterance, and then walking off with his tongue in his cheek?[77]

It was all grist to the enemy's mill. 'This pretty little quarrel', the Conservative *Pall Mall Gazette* sneered, showed what happened when 'men of immature judgement' were entrusted with legislative responsibilities that rightly belonged only to 'men of education'.[78] And the *Globe*'s editorialist, chuckling about these 'so-called Labour leaders ... as jealous of each other as peacocks', saw their 'squabbling' as a preview of the consequences 'if more of their class' entered parliament.[79] Friends, discomfited by this demonstration of the tension between the LRC group and the Lib-Labs, naturally drew a different conclusion. 'Providing sport for the Philistines', as the *Cotton Factory Times* put it, 'ought to be strictly tabooed.'[80]

A Choice is Made

The 1904 Congress, at which Shackleton aired his grievance with Burns, also saw his accession to the TUC's executive body, the Parliamentary Committee. In effect, he succeeded to the seat which had been held for most of the previous 20 years by a Lancashire weavers' official. The Weavers' Amalgamation had annually nominated its president, David Holmes, from 1892; but in 1904 it nominated Shackleton. He had to fight for the nomination. In a first-past-the-post ballot involving four candidates, he won by a plurality of 40 votes to Holmes's 35, with 14 votes going to the other candidates.[81] His win

77. *Labour Leader*, 16 September 1904. Shackleton's insinuation of calculated duplicity was backed up by Crooks, in a letter to the press. He said he had approached Burns beforehand, asking him 'to support Mr Shackleton's motion'; and added that, since 'the motion was upon the table from March 17th to March 23rd, it ought to have been possible to arrange the [Burns] amendment earlier'. *Cotton Factory Times*, 16 September 1904.
78. Quoted in *Nelson Leader*, 16 September 1904.
79. Quoted in *Colne & Nelson Times*, 16 September 1904.
80. *Cotton Factory Times*, 16 September 1904.
81. Weavers' Amalgamation, *Minutes*, 9 April 1904. As printed, the minutes of the April meeting record only the names of the four candidates, who were nominated at this meeting. The ballot was held a month later, on 14 May. But the only record of the precise distribution of votes is in the April minutes, where the voting figures have been entered by hand, against the names of the candidates, in the copy of the printed minutes that survives in the Public Record Office, Preston.

in the TUC election was less questionable. He obtained more votes than any other successful candidate for the 12 executive vacancies, a feat he was to repeat the following year.

For the better part of five months thereafter, Shackleton was thus the only person simultaneously a member of the labour movement's two major executive bodies, the Parliamentary Committee and the LRC Executive Committee. This, predictably, placed him in a 'sometimes uncomfortable position'.[82] In January 1905, he let it be known that he was not seeking re-election to the LRC's executive. It is probable that he intended to make this choice from the time he won the Weavers' Amalgamation ballot for the TUC position.

His last formal duty as an LRC office-holder was to preside over its fifth annual conference, at which there were moves from the right, first, to weaken the principle of independence from the Liberal party and, second, to restrict conference representation to trade unionists. Shackleton spoke strongly against each proposition in his presidential address.[83] Both were defeated.

Shortly after the conference, on the LRC's initiative, a meeting of the full executives of the LRC, the TUC and the General Federation of Trade Unions[84] was held at Caxton Hall to work out 'a common plan of action at the approaching general election'.[85] Under the resulting Caxton Hall agreement, as it was called, the TUC undertook to endorse all of the LRC's candidates, while the LRC accepted the TUC's right to endorse Lib-Lab candidates. It was also agreed to form a joint consultative body. Shackleton, although new to the Parliamentary Committee, was one of a three-man TUC delegation which subsequently negotiated the constitution of a tripartite 'Joint Board'. He was there again, as a member, when the Joint Board met for the first time in November 1905.

The Caxton Hall agreement followed a second attempt, the day before, to establish a working partnership between the Lib-Lab and LRC parliamentarians. Once again, Burns was elected chairman, and Bell one of two whips.

---

82. Bealey and Pelling, *Labour and Politics*, p. 206. For example, in his last weeks as LRC chairman, in January 1905, he was involved in an exchange of correspondence in which he and MacDonald, on behalf of the LRC, took an extremely tough line about an alleged lack of consultation by the TUC. See LP Archives, LRC 19/207–21.

83. *Labour Party Foundation Conference*, p. 219. Union representatives, in any case, formed a majority in both the conference and the executive at the time. On the executive, nine seats were reserved for union representatives, one for the local trades councils, three for the ILP, one for the Fabian Society and one for the secretary (which gave the ILP another seat owing to MacDonald's election).

84. The GFTU had been set up (like the LRC) under the TUC's auspices, but earlier in 1899, primarily to run a central strike fund.

85. *Labour Leader*, 24 February 1905. The LRC's initiative was prompted by a decision of the TUC's 1904 Congress. This Congress, while the first formally to concede that resolutions about the LRC constitution were beyond its jurisdiction, also authorized the Parliamentary Committee to endorse parliamentary candidates regardless of their acceptability to the LRC. See Martin, *TUC*, p. 90.

Despite ILP reservations,[86] the arrangement this time worked well enough, by all accounts – and, in particular, ensured a second reading for the unions' Trade Disputes Bill in March.[87] It seems to have survived even Burns's deep disagreement with his colleagues over the government's Unemployed Workmen Bill.[88] According to Clegg, Fox and Thompson, Shackleton's role during this whole episode was central. It was he, they say, who 'engineered' the election of Burns and Bell, and thereafter 'stage-managed the [LRC and Lib-Lab] group's activities during the session on behalf of the Parliamentary Committee'.[89] Their larger conclusion is that Shackleton, along with Henderson, effectively laid the foundations of the parliamentary Labour party at this time. 'In 1905 ... the careful argument, the crucial lobbying, and the beginnings of genuine organization were provided by Shackleton, assisted by Henderson. Behind the temporary facade of Burns, their efforts at last gave the group something of the force and cohesion it had so far lacked.'[90]

The Burdens of Office

The newness and the smallness of the LRC group combined to exacerbate problems arising from the inevitable shortfall between its members' performance and their supporters' expectations. J. H. Harley, who should have known better, fuelled suspicions on the left with an invidious comparison, when he remarked that the Irish Nationalist MPs 'don't spend the best of their time outside the House, like ... the Labour men'.[91] The allegations of absenteeism, based on published parliamentary division lists, eventually reached such proportions that MacDonald, as LRC secretary, was obliged to publish a spirited defence. He emphasized, among other things, the 'constant demand for the handful of [LRC] members for Sunday and week-end meet-

---

86. See *Labour Leader*, 24 February 1905.

87. Burns's leadership in relation to this bill is described as 'little short of heroic' by his biographer; and Bealey and Pelling, too, have him 'marshalling his men with all the adroitness of an experienced and skilful parliamentary tactician'. Brown, *John Burns*, p. 102; *Labour and Politics*, p. 210. But J. H. Harley, the *Labour Leader*'s parliamentary correspondent, devoted just one implicitly dismissive sentence to him: 'John Burns could be seen everywhere; now he was in the House, now talking in the Lobby, and anon you could see him rapidly hurrying along the corridor.' Otherwise, Harley focused on Shackleton and Henderson: 'nothing could have been better than the tactful way ... they watched every step of the progress of the Bill. They smoothed over the difficulties, they got to know the moves of their opponents.' *Labour Leader*, 17 March 1905.

88. See Brown, *John Burns*, pp. 103–4.

89. *History of British Trade Unions*, vol. 1, p. 373n.

90. Ibid., p. 372.

91. *Labour Leader*, 3 March 1905. Subsequently, after talking with an unnamed Labour MP who spoke about the weight of correspondence and of meetings, Harley made amends. 'The more I look into the matter, the more I feel that we don't always allow for the terrific strain on the few men who chance to get elected in the early days of a great Parliamentary party.' Ibid., 17 March 1905.

ings', and the fact that 'Trade Unions [expected] their [MPs] to do regular delegate work'.[92]

Shackleton's commitments during 1905 were certainly more various, and probably more demanding, than MacDonald's defence suggests. As already noted, and apart from more local obligations,[93] he was the Weavers' Amalgamation's chief negotiator on its 7½ per cent wage claim from early in the year, its acting secretary from mid-year, and its *de facto* president as well, by the year's end. In June, he attended the International Textile Workers' Conference in Milan, becoming one of two British representatives on the International Committee it spawned.[94] Most significantly, he was a member of the TUC's Parliamentary Committee throughout the year – and an acknowledged leader of it.[95]

There were other demands on his time, too. One came from the Association to Promote the Higher Education of Working Men (later famous as the Workers' Educational Association), founded in 1903 under the inspiration of Albert and Frances Mansbridge. When Albert Mansbridge belatedly moved to enlist the TUC's support, it was Shackleton whom the Parliamentary Committee 'provisionally appointed' to the association's executive committee;[96] and five months later, to its advisory council.[97] Again, he was (and had been since 1903) the treasurer, and only male executive member, of the Women's Trade Union League, an organisation founded by middle-class women in 1874, initially as the Women's Protective and Provident

92.   Ibid., 18 August 1905.

93.   He was still formally required to put in some time at the office of Darwen Weavers' Association; and, although he had resigned from the Darwen Town Council on entering parliament, his expressed wish for a continued association with the council's Technical Instruction Committee meant he was still a member of its Weaving Sub-committee.

94.   *Cotton Factory Times*, 22 September 1905.

95.   His inclusion in the TUC's three-man negotiating team following the Caxton Hall meeting was an early indication of this. In addition, the Parliamentary Committee's minutes show a clear reliance on Shackleton, above other MP-members, for information and action to do with parliamentary arrangements, and for comments on bills of interest to the TUC. He was also exceptionally punctilious in his attendance at its meetings. TUC Parliamentary Committee, *Minutes*, 1905, *passim*.

96.   TUC, PC, *Minutes*, 19 January 1905.

97.   Ibid., 20 May 1905. As an executive committee member he had initially recommended that 'the Association should be encouraged in every possible way' by the Parliamentary Committee. Ibid., 9 March 1905. But later, presumably on his recommendation, the TUC executive decided against continuing his appointment, on the ground that 'they could not find the time, owing to the pressure of other matters, to have one of their members represent them' in this way. Ibid., 18 May 1905. Two days afterwards, however, the committee agreed to appoint both Shackleton and Bell to an 'Advisory Council' of the association.

League, with the aim of promoting trade unionism among working-class women.[98]

Early in December 1905, he formally replaced his ailing colleague, Wilkinson, on the council of the British Cotton Growing Association. The association, a public company set up by Lancashire employers and unions in 1902, sought to increase the production of raw cotton and diversify its sources in the hope of avoiding 'cotton famines' and market manipulation by American interests.[99] Shackleton's appointment was almost immediately followed by a doubling (from £500 to £1,000) of the Weavers' Amalgamation's shareholding.[100] Even before his appointment, he often spoke on its behalf.

Finally, there were two older and deeply felt, but probably less time-consuming commitments. One was to the Co-operative movement.[101] He attended its major conferences and, from the beginning of 1905, was member of a joint committee of the TUC and the Co-operative Union.[102] The other commitment was to the Independent Order of Rechabites,[103] a substantial friendly society associated with the temperance movement.[104] He often spoke on its platforms after becoming an MP.[105]

98.   See Clegg et al., *History of British Trade Unions*, vol. 1, p. 470; Lewenhak, *Women and Trade Unions*, ch. 5. Shackleton's union, the Darwen Weavers' Association, had affiliated to the league three years before he became its treasurer. He regularly chaired the league's Annual Private Conference held in conjunction with the TUC's Congress, and its reports recounted his activities in connection with parliamentary questions and ministerial deputations on women's issues. See Tuckwell Papers.

99.   The association's finances depended not only on donations from cotton unions and mill-owners, but also on collections taken up among cotton workers. By 1908 it had obtained 'only a little more than half' of the £500,000 which was its target; but the value of the cotton produced under its auspices had increased from £29,000 in 1903 to 'the vast sum' of £400,000 in 1907. *Cotton Factory Times*, 10 April 1908.

100.   Ibid., 22 December 1905.

101.   'Co-operation', he told an interviewer, was 'the twin sister of trade unionism'. *Co-operative News*, 31 January 1903.

102.   TUC, PC, *Minutes*, 21 December 1904.

103.   The order (its local branches were called 'tents') was named after Jonadab, son of Rechab, who instructed his household and descendants neither to drink wine nor to live in houses. *Jer.* 35; Graetz, *History of the Jews*, vol. I, p. 200.

104.   Its membership, far outstripped by those of the Manchester Unity of Oddfellows and the Ancient Order of Foresters (over 700,000 each), and the Hearts of Oak (400,000), matched the Druids, the Free Gardeners, and the Shepherds. See Gilbert, *Evolution of National Insurance in Great Britain*, pp. 165–8.

105.   Following the Clitheroe by-election, he was congratulated in its journal as 'a present member and past officer' of the order, the Accrington Good Samaritan Tent No. 234 held 'a congratulatory tea and meeting' in his honour, and the Blackburn and District Rechabites' Union organized a public meeting at which he gave 'a lengthy address on the drink question and Rechabitism'. *Rechabite and Temperance Magazine*, vol. 33, October 1902, p. 237; December 1902, p. 282.

The General Election of 1906

On the day the Balfour government resigned, in December 1905, Shackleton was scheduled to speak at a meeting in Nelson. As a result, he opened his campaign for the impending election that night. A day or two later, his electoral position was strengthened by well-founded rumours that Campbell-Bannerman wanted him in the new Liberal government.[106] Informed opinion was confident that he would be returned unopposed for a second time.[107] Even some of his firm supporters, it was said, regretted the expected 'walkover' in a constituency where parliamentary elections had been uncontested for 14 years. Once again, Clitheroe electors would be reduced to 'passive onlookers in the great political fight', unable to share in 'the attendant excitements and activities'.[108]

However, a few days before nominations were due on Wednesday 17 January, there were rumours of a nameless 'Tariff Reform [Conservative] candidate', though most discounted them.[109] But on the Tuesday, Bernard Joseph Belton arrived in the town of Clitheroe and 'announced his intention of contesting the constituency on Independent lines'.[110] On the Wednesday, Shackleton went to Burnley for the funeral of David Holmes, quite unaware of Belton. The agent who went to Clitheroe to lodge his nomination, too, had no thought of 'a contest'.[111] Almost everyone, indeed, was taken by surprise: the news 'fell like a bombshell', and the general reaction was 'utter amazement and disbelief'.[112]

Belton, a brewer from Weybridge, Surrey, was a tariff reformer and a Roman Catholic. He had been educated at Stonyhurst College in Clitheroe, and had two sons there at the time of his nomination. He said he had been invited to become a candidate by 'those who feel themselves oppressed in the

106. 'When Sir Henry Campbell-Bannerman was forming his Government it is not much of a secret that he would have liked to include Mr D. Shackleton.' Quoted from 'a contemporary' in *Colne & Nelson Times*, 17 April 1908. C. P. Scott, editor of the *Manchester Guardian* and an influential Liberal, was the go-between. He was to remind Shackleton of the episode 20 years afterwards. 'Do you remember the half offer (it would have come off all right) of the Cabinet which I brought to you when you were at the head of the then little Labour party? You – quite rightly – wouldn't take it then because your party was not strong enough.' Scott to Shackleton, 19 December 1925: SP.
107. Thus the ILP's *Labour Leader* (5 January 1906), with apparent satisfaction, announced that he 'will probably occupy the unique position of being the only Labour candidate to have a walk over' – that is, be unopposed. Lord Shuttleworth agreed. Seeking to play some part in the Liberals' election campaign, he told Campbell-Bannerman: 'I am not wanted in the Clitheroe Divn. – where Shackleton walks over.' Shuttleworth to Campbell-Bannerman, 29 December 1905: Campbell-Bannerman Papers, vol. XVI, BM Add. MS 41221, fols. 85–6.
108. *Nelson Leader*, 5 January 1906.
109. *Cotton Factory Times*, 19 January 1906.
110. *Labour Leader*, 19 January 1906.
111. *Cotton Factory Times*, 19 January 1906.
112. *Nelson Leader*, 19 January 1906.

matter of religious education'.[113] Catholic hostility to Shackleton on the education issue seems to have dated from late 1903 when he became a vice-president of the Northern Education League, a body committed to secular education and the repeal of the Conservatives' Education Act of 1902. His acceptance of the vice-presidency had raised an immediate storm of protest from local Catholics, and he had in fact been threatened then with opposition at the next election.[114]

Shackleton did not take Belton's challenge lightly. 'Our organisation is ... ready for the fray,' he told a reporter on Wednesday evening, 'and ... we intend to take no risks.'[115] Starting at Padiham the following evening, he addressed crowded meetings throughout the electorate in the week that elapsed before polling day.

Belton, in contrast, ran a distinctly lightweight campaign. He addressed only one public meeting. He seems to have relied instead on 'literature', mainly 'of a pictorial character', in which he called on Catholics 'not to hand their schools over to the Socialists'.[116] His formal, published address to electors advocated 'religious instruction for the poor', the amendment or repeal of the liquor-licensing laws, together with 'one vote one value, and ... giving women their rights as voters'.[117] His open public support was limited. It was said that he had 'no recommendation except those given by the Catholics and publicans'.[118] And even then, there were Catholics who came out for Shackleton.[119] To the local Conservatives, he was an embarrassment. They publicly branded his candidature 'ill-advised', and 'not serious'.[120]

On polling day, both candidates toured the constituency. Belton started off in a stagecoach 'driven in fine style' to Nelson, then went to Barrowford and Padiham by car, and returned to Burnley again by stagecoach – scattering, en

113.   Ibid. The principal source of the invitation was probably the Catholic Rector of Nelson, the Reverend Father Smith, who (as later recalled) gave Belton 'active assistance' during his campaign. *Colne & Nelson Times*, 18 September 1908.

114.   See *Nelson Chronicle*, 2 October 1903.

115.   *Nelson Leader*, 19 January 1906. And they did not – if Shackleton's election expenses of 'a little over £600' are any guide. *Cotton Factory Times*, 2 March 1906.

116.   *Burnley Express and Clitheroe Division Advertiser*, 27 January 1906.

117.   *Nelson Leader*, 19 January 1906.

118.   Ibid., 26 January 1906.

119.   Thus, the Nelson branch of the United Irish League issued a manifesto 'placing on record the services Mr Shackleton had rendered the Irish cause, and appealing for votes on behalf of the Labour candidate'. *Burnley Express and Clitheroe Division Advertiser*, 27 January 1906.

120.   *Colne & Nelson Times*, 19 January 1906. The Conservatives of Burnley, on the other hand, could afford to be a little more charitable. They reportedly admired Belton's 'British pluck', and were grateful for 'the amusement he ... afforded' and the way he added to 'the gaiety of the people' with his candidature. *Burnley Express and Clitheroe Division Advertiser*, 24 January 1906. A Liberal journalist put a totally different construction on the 'amusement' afforded by Belton's campaign, describing his election address as 'funny and foolish' and detailing contradictions that, the writer claimed, had made Belton 'the laughing-stock of the whole constituency'. *Nelson Leader*, 26 January 1906.

route, 'thousands of hand-bills ... amongst the interested spectators'.[121] Shackleton toured by car. And he always regretted that.

The result was what everyone predicted. But the size of the majority (as always, there were a few who said they had suspected it all along) was a surprise. In a letter to the editor, 'A Lancashire Lad' had beforehand appealed for 'at least 4,000 of a majority'.[122] Shackleton doubled that to 8,207 – well in advance of the majorities recorded by other successful LRC candidates in the 1906 general election. The *Cotton Factory Times* had the grace not to be wise after the event. Its editorialist wrote of an 'astounding ... simply amazing' majority.[123]

The voter turnout was remarkable, given that the contest was universally perceived as one-sided. The official figures (announced by the Returning Officer, Mr Fullalove, of the legal firm Southern and Fullalove) were: Shackleton 12,035; Belton 3,828; spoiled papers 40. That, given 20,613 registered voters, meant a turn-out of 77 per cent.[124]

In this moment of triumph, however, Shackleton struck a suddenly sombre note at the celebration his supporters had arranged in the Clitheroe Weavers' Institute. After reading out Mr Fullalove's figures, and expressing his thanks, he asked the audience to 'pardon him making anything in the nature of a speech', in view of the 'regrettable accident ... at Burnley'.[125] On polling day, the car in which he had been touring the constituency struck and killed a young father of two. This tragedy was to stay with him.

121. Ibid.
122. Ibid., 19 January 1906.
123. *Cotton Factory Times*, 26 January 1906.
124. The average for the general election was not much higher at 82.6 per cent. Butler and Freeman, *British Political Facts 1900–1965*, p. 141.
125. *Nelson Leader*, 26 January 1906.

5

The Labour Leader as Parliamentarian, 1906–1907

The general election produced a Liberal government with a massive majority in the House of Commons. It also produced an independent Labour party of some parliamentary substance. Over the five following years, Shackleton was a towering presence in the labour movement. Initially, he owed this ascendancy largely to his parliamentary role. Two events in 1906 saw him emerge as a clearly major figure in this respect. One was the election of officers by the LRC-endorsed parliamentarians. The other was the passage of the Trade Disputes Act.

The Party Chairmanship

Before the general election, Shackleton had been one of a four-man 'Labour group' – as they called themselves – in the House of Commons. After it, he was part of an initially self-styled 'Labour party in Parliament', an official party of 29 members which quickly became 30.[1] They constituted, in Joseph Chamberlain's phrase, 'the labour earthquake.'[2] In their social origins, they were a remarkably homogeneous lot by the standards of Continental left-wing parties. All of them were born of working-class parents, and all but two had first entered employment as manual workers.[3] Nevertheless, they were ideologically split between those who said they believed in Socialism and those who said they did not. One of them later described them as being 'pretty evenly divided between the Trade Union view of things represented by David Shackleton ... and the more extreme [Socialist] element voiced by Keir Hardie.'[4] But nominal Socialists, although their precise number is uncertain, seem actually to have formed 'a clear majority.'[5] Despite that, it was by no means a foregone conclusion that the leader of the new party (unusually, for the House of Commons, to be entitled 'chairman') would be a

1. J. W. Taylor, an ILP member whose candidature was backed by a union outside the LRC, joined the LRC grouping shortly after parliament met.
2. Quoted in Martin and Rubinstein, *Ideology and the Labour Movement*, p. 143n.
3. Ramsay MacDonald started as a clerk; Philip Snowden as a junior civil servant.
4. Barnes, *From Workshop to War Cabinet*, p. 83.
5. Bealey and Pelling, *Labour and Politics*, p. 276.

Socialist. At least one of the Socialists, Philip Snowden, thought that 'Shackleton would easily be elected.'[6] The Labour Party in Parliament formally met for the first time on 12 February. The meeting was attended also by the non-MP members of the LRC's executive committee, and it was chaired by Arthur Henderson, the committee's current chairman. Its first, and most momentous decision, was that the party would sit on 'the Opposition side of the House', and would not form 'a separate section with the other [Lib-Lab] Labour Members.'[7] Then it proceeded to elect a chairman.

Shackleton wanted the chairmanship. That much is clear from the fact that he allowed his name to go forward. So, too, did Keir Hardie – at least when it came to the crunch. But before the meeting (according to an unsigned letter written in his hand, a month earlier), he had been reluctant, foreseeing a personal incompatibility: 'It is no affectation on my part to say that Nature has not equipped me for a position as Leader of a Party; a Pioneer I may be, but a scheming Leader never.'[8] Moreover, there is evidence of a strong feeling among his senior ILP colleagues that he should not stand. Thus, when Ramsay MacDonald raised the question of the parliamentary leadership with some local LRC members, and they insisted that 'Hardie was the man', he predicted 'a serious split in the party' if Hardie became chairman.[9] Bruce Glasier was of the same mind. The day before the leadership election, he wrote a letter that – while strenuously stroking Hardie's ego – stressed the importance of keeping the unions onside, and pleaded for his withdrawal: 'It will do a power of good if it is known that you voluntarily declined.'[10]

> My idea is that you should not accept nomination ... unless it unexpectedly happens that the feeling in favour of your doing so is *unanimous* and *enthusiastic* – and hardly even were it so. It is much more important ... that you should be free to lead the Socialist policy, than that you should be stuck in the official chairmanship where you would be bound for unity and decorum's sake to adopt a personal attitude acceptable to the moderates ... If Henderson, Shackleton or even Barnes [an ILP member] accepts the position, you nevertheless will be the fighting front. Besides ... if a Trade Unionist takes the post it will tend to keep the Trade Unions ... loyal to the movement.[11]

He also urged him to 'speak magnanimously of the Trade Unions' claim' to the chairmanship in his withdrawal speech.

6.   Snowden, *Autobiography*, p. 125. This judgement, it should be said, was based on Snowden's belief at the time that the Socialists were outnumbered.
7.   Labour party, *Minutes of Parliamentary Meetings*, 12 February 1906.
8.   (Hardie) to R. B. Cunningham Graham, 5 December 1905: LP Archives, Francis Johnson Corr. 1905/188(i).
9.   George Dallas to Mrs [Mary] Macarthur, 7 February 1906; ibid., 1906/59(i).
10.   Glasier to Hardie, 11 February 1906: Glasier Papers, I.1.1906/23.
11.   Ibid.

But Glasier's advice fell on deaf ears. The next day, when Henderson called for nominations, and Will Crooks moved 'That D. J. Shackleton be the Chairman', Hardie said nothing.[12] Nor did he say anything when George Barnes proposed 'That J. Keir Hardie be the Chairman'. There was then a show of hands. It was a tie: 13 each. After recording this result, the minutes of the meeting report: 'A ballot was then taken when there voted 14 for D.J. Shackleton and 15 for J. Keir Hardie.'[13] The three additional votes in the ballot came from the two candidates and MacDonald, all of whom had abstained in the show of hands. MacDonald certainly voted for Hardie, despite the latter's doubts[14] – though, as MacDonald confessed to Glasier, he had done so 'with much reluctance.'[15]

12.   Labour party, *Minutes of Parliamentary Meetings*, 12 February 1906.

13.   Ibid. This account, drawn from the handwritten minutes of the meeting, conflicts with the conventional account of the election, which has it that there were *three* votes all told (one show of hands and two secret ballots) and that both the show of hands and the first ballot were drawn. See Bealey and Pelling, *Labour and Politics*, pp. 278–9; Elton, *Life of James Ramsay Mac-Donald*, p. 132; McLean, *Keir Hardie*, p. 117; Marquand, *Ramsay MacDonald*, p. 96; Morgan, *J. Ramsay MacDonald*, p. 40; Morgan, *Keir Hardie*, p. 155; Moore, *Emergence of the Labour Party*, p. 103; Pelling, *Short History of the Labour Party*, p. 20. Only Morgan, in *Keir Hardie*, gives actual voting figures (14 each in the first ballot, and 14 to 15 in the second); and only Elton and Bealey and Pelling indicate their source. Elton, whose book was published earliest (1939), relied on verbal information ('I am told, by one who was present …'), and so did Bealey and Pelling whose informant, interviewed as late as 43 years after the event, was Edward Pease, who attended the meeting as a non-MP member of the LRC Executive Committee. Among those at the meeting as new MPs, Philip Snowden discussed the election in his memoirs (*Autobiography*, p. 125) without specifying either the number of ballots or the voting figures, while J. R. Clynes (*Memoirs*, vol. I, p. iii) mentioned Hardie's election but also without detail. John Hodge (*Workman's Cottage to Windsor Castle*) and George Barnes (*From Workshop to War Cabinet*) both ignored the matter. The newspaper reports of the time either had nothing to say about the details of the election or were totally at odds. Perhaps significantly, because it is a paper particularly prominent in the bibliographies of labour historians, only the *Cotton Factory Times* (16 February 1906), a strong supporter of Shackleton, seems to have suggested that there were two tied votes, and a third deciding vote: 'Twice it was even voting, and the final was a majority of one for Hardie.' The London *Daily Chronicle* (13 February 1906), without mentioning the number of times votes were taken, was unusually precise in recording that Hardie was elected by 15 votes to Shackleton's 14. The *Northern Daily Telegraph* (13 February 1906) specified only two votes, but one of them was a formality: 'The first vote gave Mr Hardie a majority of one over Mr Shackleton. When the vote was put a second time Mr Hardie was declared to have been unanimously elected.' The *Nelson Leader* (16 February 1906), evidently unaware that Henderson chaired the meeting, gave a version altogether its own: 'The voting at first resulted in a tie, but [MacDonald] … gave his casting vote in favour of Mr Hardie.' The *Colne & Nelson Times* (16 February 1906), like the greater part of the interested press, reported simply that Keir Hardie had been elected chairman, and Shackleton vice-chairman; and that was the end of the detail.

14.   See Elton, *Life of James Ramsay MacDonald*, p. 132.

15.   Quoted in Morgan, *Keir Hardie*, p. 155. John Hodge later claimed to have switched his own vote from Shackleton to Hardie. Bealey and Pelling, *Labour and Politics*, p. 279. If that was so, there had to be a second shift in allegiance, from Hardie to Shackleton, registered in the ballot as well.

1   David Shackleton is seated on the extreme left of this photograph of the General
Purposes Committee of the 1901 Trades Union Congress. The others, from left to
right, are Allen Gee (Textile Workers), J. Jenkins (Shipwrights), Pete Curran
(Gasworkers) and J. Haslam (Miners).
Trades Union Congress.

THE POSITION AT CLITHEROE.

First HOOLIGAN—"You have a go at him."
Second HOOLIGAN—"No; you knock him down and I'll jump on him."

2 *Daily Dispatch*, 14 July 1902: SP.

In August 1902 Shackleton was elected Member of Parliament for Clitheroe as an independent Labour candidate. Although he won unopposed, neither the local Liberal party nor the local Conservative party gave him even tacit support. 'The Position at Clitheroe' depicts their active hostility, at a time when each was planning to put up a candidate. Their later refusal to support him, after he proved unassailable, is depicted in 'Come and Be Killed'.

"COME AND BE KILLED."

[The Clitheroe ducks have so far proved themselves to be remarkably shy.]

3 *Manchester Evening Chronicle*, 24 July 1902: SP.

4   This photograph was taken in February 1906, and includes all 29 of the successful LRC-endorse
candidates, but not J. W. Taylor, who joined the party shortly afterwards. Those seated are, left to right
T. Wilson, A. Wilkie, Ramsay MacDonald, Arthur Henderson, Keir Hardie, Shackleton and Will Croc
Among those standing, John Hodge is third from the left and Philip Snowden is eighth from the righ
Unknown newspaper: SP.

5   The parliamentary Labour party's leaders, from left to right: Arthur Henderson,
G. N. Barnes, Ramsay MacDonald, Philip Snowden, Will Crooks, Keir Hardie, John
Hodge, J. O'Grady and Shackleton.
Unknown newspaper: SP.

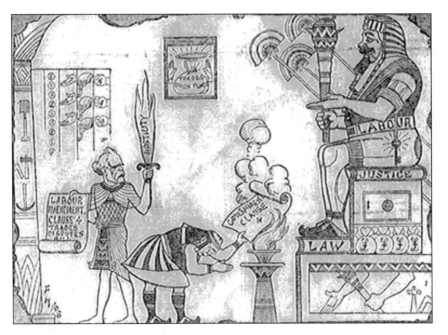

'Fragment of an old Egyptian fresco recently brought to light at Westminster'.

6 'The Burnt Offering'. With Shackleton as Pharaoh and Keir Hardie as sword-bearer, this cartoon depicts the Liberal government's concession on the critical clause in the Trade Disputes Bill of 1906.
Unknown newspaper: SP.

"THE MONEY OR —!"

[A big fight would take place next session on old-age pensions unless the Government brought in a practical proposal. He put the sum required at £15,000,000.—Mr. Shackleton, M.P.]

The sign of our age is
Unrest about wages,
Unrest about politics, morals and crime ;
And all this confusion
Impels this conclusion :
We live in a very remarkable time.

Excitement, sensation,
And fierce agitation
Disturb ancient Parties asleep in their beds.
They cry " Lord preserve us ! "
And, terribly nervous,
Doubt whether they stand on their heels or their heads.

And here's a poor couple
Not young, and not supple,
Who, plodding their slow and deliberate course,
Are set all a-quiver
By " Stand and deliver ! "
A knight of the road on a very strong horse !

" Look here, you old duffers,
Humanity suffers," [kind,
Cries he ; " I'm a knight of the chivalrous
And mean to help quickly
The old and the sickly.
I want fifteen millions—which you'll have to find."

They stagger, they stutter,
They gasp in a flutter
" But where shall we find it ? " He thunders
" Beware !
My plan's clear as crystal :
The cash or—the pistol ! [affair."
But where you will find it—well, that's your

Not young, and not supple,
That worried old couple
Regard the strong horseman with agonised fear,
And totter off, racking
Their brains in attacking [year.
That problem : to find fifteen millions next
DEMOCRITUS.

7   The cartoon depicts Shackleton in the saddle, his pistol trained on the Liberal Prime Minister, Sir Henry Campbell-Bannerman, and the Chancellor of the Exchequer, H. H. Asquith. Legislation introducing non-contributory old-age pensions was subsequently enacted by the Asquith government in 1908, with the Labour party's support.
Unknown newspaper (? February 1907): SP.

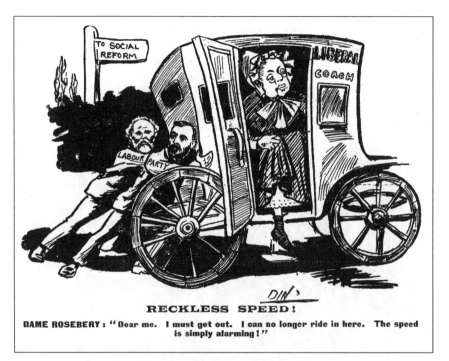

RECKLESS SPEED!

DAME ROSEBERY : *"Dear me. I must get out. I can no longer ride in here. The speed is simply alarming ! "*

8 The abandonment of the Liberal party by Lord Rosebery, a former Prime Minister, is here attributed to the impact of the Labour party – represented by the black-bearded Shackleton and the white-bearded Keir Hardie – on the Liberal government's social policies.
Unknown newspaper (? 1907): SP.

THE "KNOTS" CONGRESS.

The Trades Union Congress now sitting at Nottingham, under the presidency of Mr. D. J. Shackleton, is confronted with many knotty problems to untangle.

9   Unknown newspaper, September 1908: SP.

THE MAIN PROP OF PEACE.

MR. SHACKLETON, M.P., at Nottingham: If the other buttresses were as strong as this, the wall would never come down.

10   *Manchester Evening News*, 9 September 1908.

9 and 10   The TUC's Nottingham Congress in 1908 was the first of two presided over by Shackleton. The two cartoons draw a sharp distinction between the domestic and the foreign 'problems' confronting the Congress and its president.

LEADERS OF THE LABOUR MOVEMENT IN CONFERENCE

LEADERS OF THE LABOUR MOVEMENT IN CONFERENCE

'A special meeting of the officials of the Labour Party, the [General] Federation of Trades Union and the Trades Union Congress met yesterday at the offices of the Federation of Trade Unions un the presidency of Mr. D. J. Shackleton, M.P., to discuss the case of Osborne v. A.S.R.S.'

11   Shackleton stands in the centre of the group, with the white-bearded Keir Hardie to his imme left, and Ramsay MacDonald seven faces to his right.
Unknown newspaper, 1909: SP.

12   Trades Union Congress Parliamentary Committee, 1910. Front row, left to right: W. J. Davis (Brassworkers); M. Arrandale (Machine Workers); C. W. Bowerman (Compositors); J. Haslam (Miners), *Chairman*; D. J. Shackleton (Weavers), *Vice-Chairman*; W. Thorne (Gasworkers); J. Sexton (Dock Labourers); J. Jenkins (Shipwrights). Back row, left to right: W. J. Bolton (Clerk to Committee); J. A. Seddon (Shop Assistants); H. Emery (Bakers); W. Mosses (Patternmakers); J. Hill (Boilermakers); J. H. Williams (Musicians); W. Mullin (Card Room Operatives); H. Gosling (Watermen).
Trades Union Congress: SP.

13   The general election of January 1910. Shackleton (left) and his wife
acknowledge the crowd on polling day in the Clitheroe electorate. A street scene
(right) on the same day. Inset portrait: T. Smith, Shackleton's Tariff
Reform opponent.
Daily Sketch, 22 January 1910: SP.

14 Shackleton, in July 1910, on the point of entering the House of Commons to move the second reading of his Parliamentary Franchise (Women) Bill.
Daily Sketch, 12 July 1910: SP.

15 Inside the House of Commons, Shackleton moved the second reading of his women's suffrage bill before an audience that, as the sketch-artist saw it, was either indifferent or hostile.
Daily Graphic, 12 July 1910: SP.

"THE UNPARDONABLE SIN."
Execration of Annan Bryce for laying Shackleton a stymie.

16   Bryce had apparently intended to demonstrate his contempt for Shackleton's
bill by breaching an ancient House of Commons convention that proscribed passing
between the Speaker and the Member addressing the House. He set off along the
floor of the House while Shackleton was speaking, but 'turned about and slunk
back' when 'there went up from both sides of [the] crowded House a shout of
expostulation and execration'.
Punch, 20 July 1910: SP.

17   '"Shack" and Jill went up the hill,
to fetch a pail of water.
(This is as far as the verse goes at present.)'
The task ahead, as seen by one cartoonist the day after Shackleton moved the
second reading of his women's suffrage bill.
Unknown newspaper, 12 July 1910: SP.

COTTON OPERATIVES' GIFT TO FORMER OFFICIAL.

18 A presentation on behalf of the Textile Factory Workers' Association to mark Shackleton's departure from the trade union movement. From left to right: W. C. Robinson, Sarah Shackleton, W. Mullin, Shackleton, J. Cross, and Mrs and Mr A. H. Gill.
Daily Dispatch, 1911: SP.

19 John Hodge, the first Minister of Labour, with Shackleton.
SP.

20 Shackleton (centre), with Lloyd George, the Prime Minister, on his right and Bonar Law, Chancellor of the Exchequer, on his left.
Daily News (1917?): SP.

Shackleton was declared 'Vice-Chairman', without a further vote.[16] His supporters' disappointment was tempered by the widespread belief that Hardie would be chairman for one year only. As a *Cotton Factory Times* editorialist put it: 'We should have preferred to see [Shackleton] appointed ... [but there] is a feeling that Mr Hardie has done a good deal of the "spade work" during the past twenty years, and that for one session his services should be recognised.'[17]

Hardie, in fact, was chairman for two years – but, for the greater part of that time, in name only. His bad health was one problem. His temperament was another. For he was not an organization man. He found the humdrum details of parliamentary business distasteful, and tended to neglect them. He was also remiss when it came to attending meetings or consulting his colleagues before taking action, and was apt to depart without warning to address audiences in Scotland, the North of England, or the Continent. Early evidence of 'his waywardness, his inaccessibility, his frequent absences from the ... House' meant that by mid-1906 his parliamentary colleagues (according to MacDonald) were 'coming to decisions without consulting him.'[18] Snowden was more blunt: 'Hardie's leadership of the party [is] a hopeless failure.'[19]

Almost from the start, then, Shackleton was for much of the time the effective party chairman. Moreover, in that first year, his leadership position was stunningly underscored by his role in relation to the Trade Disputes Act. This measure, designed to remedy the Taff Vale judgement, is indisputably the Labour party's most signal legislative achievement before the First World War.

Three years earlier, as a raw MP, Shackleton had been put in charge of the labour movement's first Trade Disputes Bill, as we have seen. This, in its original form, would have given unions only limited protection against legal action for damages arising from strikes. But subsequently, the TUC's Congress boldly opted for complete immunity from legal action; and this was the principal feature of the Trade Disputes Bill which was introduced (in each case by a friendly Liberal, owing to the fortunes of the ballot for private members' bills) in 1904 and again in 1905.[20] Shortly before the 1906 general election, Shackleton and two other members of the TUC's Parliamentary Committee were sent to talk to the new Liberal Prime Minister, Campbell-Bannerman. They reported that he had 'admitted the urgency of the matter,

16.   Labour party, *Minutes of Parliamentary Meetings*, 12 February 1906.
17.   *Cotton Factory Times*, 23 February 1906. Similarly, Hardie was elsewhere described as the 'sessional chairman', and as one of the 'sessional officers'. *Daily Chronicle*, 13 February 1906; *Colne & Nelson Times*, 16 February 1906.
18.   Morgan, *Keir Hardie*, pp. 160–1.
19.   Quoted in ibid. The passage of time, however, had worked its magic when Snowden came to write his memoirs. Then he mildly remarked that 'Hardie was not a success as a chairman.' *Autobiography*, p. 125.
20.   See Clegg et al., *History of British Trade Unions*, vol. 1, pp. 322, 369.

and [had] promised that a Bill on the general lines of the Parliamentary Committee's [bill] should be introduced at an early date and without any unnecessary delay', following the election.[21]

Soon after the election, however, it became known that Campbell-Bannerman's cabinet was deeply divided on the issue. The TUC leadership moved swiftly and publicly to have its bill of 1904 and 1905 reintroduced by a private member, this time a Labour member who had won a place in the private members' ballot. The government responded, eventually, by countering with a Trade Disputes Bill of its own, which proposed a much more limited protection for union funds. A hastily convened meeting of all Labour and Lib-Lab MPs, together with the TUC's Parliamentary Committee, decided that Shackleton on his own should be sent to talk again with Campbell-Bannerman. He reported back, later the same evening, to the Parliamentary Committee. His news was startling. The Prime Minister, with a radically different government bill before the House, had nevertheless 'promised to support our [private member's] Bill when [it was] brought forward for discussion.'[22]

The TUC's bill came up for its second reading the next day. Campbell-Bannerman was true to his word. During the debate, he intervened and effectively sabotaged the current version of his government's bill. Not only did he throw his weight directly behind the TUC's measure ('My advice to the House is to pass the Second Reading of this Bill'), but he insisted that the differences between the two bills turned on 'a point of detail' and would be 'possible ... to adjust.'[23] His speech, without a doubt, turned the tide in favour of the principle of complete trade union immunity.[24]

The outcome was a radically amended government bill which moved through the various, slow stages of the legislative process over the following nine months. During this time, it was Shackleton who chiefly handled continual consultations with Liberal backbench allies, led by Sir Charles Dilke, and frequent negotiations with the government, both on and off the floor of the House.[25] During the critical committee stage, in July and August, he was the only Labour party member to speak to the bill – in accordance with the caucus decision 'that we put up one official speaker, and that he be Mr Shackleton.'[26]

On the evening before the Trade Disputes Act received the royal assent, a celebratory dinner was held under the joint auspices of the TUC, the Labour party, and the General Federation of Trade Unions. Shackleton was the guest of honour. Keir Hardie proposed the toast to 'Our Guest', and others made

21. TUC, PC, *Minutes*, 21 December 1905.
22. Ibid., 29 March 1906.
23. *Parl. Debs.*, 30 March 1906, vol. 155, col. 54.
24. Possible reasons for Campbell-Bannerman's action are canvassed by K. D. Brown in Wrigley (ed.), *History of British Industrial Relations 1875–1914*, pp. 128–9.
25. See Clegg et al., *History of British Trade Unions*, p. 395.
26. Labour party, *Minutes of Parliamentary Meetings*, 24 April 1906.

complimentary speeches. It was Shackleton himself, however, who struck perhaps the truest note when he spoke of the Act as 'a success passing all [our] dreams.'[27]

Shackleton's parliamentary leadership was demonstrated on other occasions during 1906.[28] But it was, above all, his handling of the Trade Disputes Bill which ensured that he would be seen as Hardie's logical successor – at least by those outside the party. As early as August, the provincial press took up a story emanating from 'one of the [London] society papers' which had named him as the parliamentary party's next chairman. The *Nelson Leader* saw 'nothing very novel' in this report: 'Most people [already] think Mr Hardie will not be re-elected, and that Mr Shackleton … will replace him.'[29] And five months later, at the close of the Labour party's annual conference in Belfast, Hardie himself seemed to put this conclusion beyond doubt.

A longstanding and passionate advocate of votes for women, he had spoken strongly in support of a conference resolution endorsing a private member's bill that proposed a limited form of women's suffrage. The conference opted instead for total and immediate enfranchisement. Shortly after this decision, Hardie was required to move a ceremonial vote of thanks to the Belfast Trades Council and the press. He seized the opportunity to threaten his stunned audience with his resignation: 'if the [successful women's suffrage] motion … was intended to limit the action of the party in the House of Commons, I shall have to seriously consider whether I shall remain a member of the Parliamentary Party.'[30]

Hardie's outburst, made within days of the parliamentary party's first meeting for 1907, inevitably put his re-election as chairman in doubt. It was interpreted in the Liberal and Conservative press as giving 'early succession to the leadership' to Shackleton, who in any case was seen as having 'overshadowed Mr Hardie during the last session of Parliament.'[31] For its part, the ILP's *Labour Leader* was uncertain about Hardie's future. But it sought to defuse his threat by reassuring its readers that he and the ILP would stick to the Labour party, regardless of whether he was re-elected chairman or became 'an ordinary member of the group.'[32]

Shackleton, in the meantime, was acting – and acting, it seems, in Hardie's

27. TUC, *Report*, 1907, p. 63.
28. Two which attracted particular comment involved the membership of a committee of inquiry (when he secured, in effect, a prime ministerial backdown on the floor of the House) and Horatio Bottomley's attempt to introduce a bill permitting street betting (which Shackleton purportedly 'killed' with a single speech). See Chapters 9 and 10 below.
29. *Nelson Leader*, 24 August 1906.
30. *Labour Leader*, 1 February 1907.
31. *Colne & Nelson Times*, 1 February 1907; *Nelson Leader*, 1 February 1907. More bluntly, Hardie's leadership was described as 'never more than a titular leadership'. Ibid., 8 February 1907.
32. *Labour Leader*, 8 February 1907.

favour.[33] Some time before the Belfast incident, he and Henderson had told Hardie that they intended to back his re-election, which would have made it a foregone conclusion. After Belfast, both of them wrote to him. Henderson's letter simply threw the ball into Hardie's court: 'you have placed Shackleton and myself in a very difficult position. As you know we desired your unanimous re-election ... This ... will be impossible unless something can be said to minimise the effect of your statement ... Can you ... suggest ... the best course to follow?'[34] Shackleton, on the other hand, took a more positive line. He suggested, as a possible way of clearing the air, that the issue raised by Hardie's statement should be the first item considered at the parliamentary party's meeting. 'I am hoping we shall be able to arrange matters, and no one will be more pleased than myself if this can be done.'[35] It could be done, as it turned out. But it took time and, on Shackleton's part, some ingenuity in formulating motions.[36]

Hardie was in the chair when the parliamentary party met on the evening of 11 February. Again, the non-MP members of the Labour party's Executive Committee attended.[37] Most of the meeting was taken up with a convoluted debate about procedure. The issue was whether the election of officers should be replaced by 'the programme' (meaning, more specifically, the bill on women's suffrage which Hardie had championed at Belfast) as the first item of business.

After initial discussion, John Hodge moved that the programme be dealt with first. Henderson moved an amendment proposing an immediate election of officers, the programme to be dealt with the following day. This amendment was adopted by 15 votes to 6 in the only vote recorded at the meeting. After further discussion,[38] Henderson asked Hardie 'to make a statement with regard to his position before proceeding with the election of officers'. Following Hardie's statement and more discussion (both unrecorded in the minutes), Henderson moved 'That we thank the Chairman for his services during the past Session, and express regret that we cannot allow him a free hand on the Women's Suffrage Bill'. MacDonald riposted with an amendment proposing that the election of officers be held immediately, the

33 .   Bruce Glasier suspected that Shackleton was 'secretly pleased' because the outburst had put Hardie's re-election in jeopardy. Thompson, *Enthusiasts*, p. 149. But that does not square with Shackleton's behaviour.

34.   Henderson to Hardie, 4 February 1907: LP Archives, Francis Johnson Corr., 1907/32.

35.   Shackleton to Hardie, 3 February 1907: ibid., 1907/31.

36.   It was certainly not the straightforward process that Morgan implies: 'Soon Hardie was having second thoughts about the wisdom of his action. He was duly re-elected party chairman for the 1907 session.' *Keir Hardie*, p. 169.

37.   They were present, as the minutes put it, 'to co-operate in drawing up the programme for the coming Session'. Labour party, *Minutes of Parliamentary Meetings*, 11 February 1907.

38.   In the course of which it was agreed that if the election 'did not take up too much time', the programme should be dealt with that evening.

issue of the bill to be postponed 'until we see the result of the [election] ballot'. It was at this point that Shackleton appears to have intervened.

'Subsequently', the minutes laconically note, both Henderson's motion and MacDonald's amendment were withdrawn in order to allow three motions to be put consecutively. All of them were moved by Shackleton. The first ('That the party do not introduce or back the Women's Suffrage Bill') was carried with just one dissentient – Hardie, almost certainly. The second, affirming the party's authority in relation to the ballots for private members' bills, was carried unanimously. The third went, circuitously, to the heart of the matter. In the event of a 'Women's Suffrage Bill' coming before parliament, each Labour member was to be 'allowed freedom of action upon it' – but only in the case of 'questions which the party in meeting assembled [the caucus] has not decided either to support or oppose.'[39] There was just one dissenting vote; and, again, that was certainly Hardie's. The election of officers followed immediately. There were no contests, and each nomination was unanimously accepted. Shackleton, seconded by Henderson, nominated Hardie as chairman. Shackleton himself was re-elected vice-chairman. Hardie, plainly, had undertaken to abide by the majority decision on the two motions he opposed. In other words, in the face of the clear implication of his Belfast statement, he agreed to accept party discipline on the women's suffrage issue. And that, as Shackleton obviously intended and Hardie obviously wanted, cleared the way for a second term as chairman.[40]

The *Labour Leader*, welcoming Hardie's re-election, explained it in terms that not only ignored Shackleton's crucial role but implicitly depicted him as a thwarted, if worthy, opponent. 'Mr Shackleton commands the highest respect and trust of the whole movement. But to trade unionists as well as Socialists a change in the chairmanship … especially at this juncture, would have given rise to a feeling that dissension had arisen in the party.'[41] The point was broadly confirmed, but with a significant variation in emphasis, a little while later by T. F. Richards, a Labour MP and ILP member, speaking at Nelson. There was 'not the least doubt', Richards explained, that Shackleton would have been elected chairman if only 'the newspapers had left the Labour Party alone', and not tried to 'dictate' to the party by advocating his election – because this forced the party to conclude that it would be 'unwise to accept [such] dictation'.[42]

In the event, Hardie was effectively chairman for only a few more weeks. He fell seriously ill in April. In May, Shackleton travelled to Wemyss Bay, on

---

39.   Ibid.
40.   Hardie's humbling backdown clearly contradicts Robert McKenzie's claim of his 'considerable reluctance' to stand for re-election. *British Political Parties*, p. 337.
41.   *Labour Leader*, 15 February 1907. But a year later – suggesting now that a failure to re-elect Hardie 'would have been regarded as a concession to the Liberal attack upon him as a Socialist' – the *Labour Leader* charitably recalled that 'Mr Shackleton himself fully agreed with this point of view'. Ibid., 10 January 1908.
42.   *Colne & Nelson Times*, 22 February 1907.

the Clyde coast, where Hardie was convalescing. He laid down, gently it seems, conditions under which Hardie might return to the chairmanship; and on behalf of the party offered financial support for the sea voyage Hardie's doctors had advised.[43] Hardie was grateful, and eager to make amends. 'I have thought over what you said,' he wrote to Shackleton, 'and can promise whole heartedly that I will obey the wishes of the party in the matter of meetings and the like ... I cannot tell how deeply the offer of the party, and the way in which you conveyed it, moved me.'[44] He chaired one further meeting of the parliamentary party, 'for the purpose of bidding farewell' before embarking on an eight-month voyage round the world,[45] but formally remained chairman until January 1908. Shackleton was officially the party's acting chairman during this time.

Another Choice is Made

In January 1907, before his outburst at the Belfast conference, Hardie had made it known that, if given a second year as parliamentary chairman, he would not stand again for the position. From that time, as the *Labour Leader* put it, Shackleton was 'by common consent [within the party] regarded as the chairman-elect'.[46] Hardie's illness and Shackleton's acting chairmanship publicly underlined the point, and inspired repeated press comments assuming his succession. Things, it seemed to most observers, were falling into place for Shackleton. The chairmanship would be his for the taking in January 1908.

In the meantime, however, he accepted an appointment as one of two union representatives on a Home Office committee of inquiry into the use of artificial humidity in cotton-weaving factories.[47] The Humidity Committee, as it came to be known, met for the first time in Manchester on 13 December, not long after Shackleton returned from the American Federation of Labor's convention, which he attended on behalf of the TUC.

Three weeks later, shortly before Ramsay MacDonald sent out the notices for the meeting at which the parliamentary party was to select Keir Hardie's successor, Shackleton sent each of the Labour MPs a copy of a formal letter he had written to MacDonald. In it he said: 'I cannot accept any office for the coming session.'[48] The reason he gave his colleagues, he explained to a

43. See Hughes, *Keir Hardie*, p. 147. However, for the more ambitious round-the-world voyage on which he eventually embarked, Hardie relied on the financial support of the Salvation Army and a wealthy American industrialist. See Morgan, *Keir Hardie*, pp. 172–3; McLean, *Keir Hardie*, p. 127.

44. Hardie to Shackleton, n.d. (post-8 May, 1907): LP Archives, LP/PA/07/1/99.

45. Labour party, *Minutes of Parliamentary Meetings*, 4 July 1907.

46. *Labour Leader*, 10 January 1908.

47. The committee, chaired by a retired civil servant, also included two employers' representatives as well as the Professor of Pathology at Victoria University, Manchester. The other union member was Joseph Cross, Shackleton's predecessor at Darwen and by now secretary of both the Weavers' Amalgamation and the Textile Factory Workers' Association.

48. Shackleton to MacDonald, 3 January 1908: MacDonald Papers, PRO 30/69/5 69951.

journalist, was that 'the work of the Humidity [Committee] … was of the greatest importance to the cotton workers, who claim his first interests; and his work on this subject would prevent his giving to Parliamentary work the time that he felt was due from the chairman of the party'.[49]

Shackleton's decision startled everyone, his colleagues as well as the press. Snowden admitted this at the time: 'I may say that [it] came as a great surprise to the members of the Labour party', who had thought his chairmanship 'a foregone conclusion'.[50] But the public reason he gave for it, his membership of the Humidity Committee, evoked varying responses. Some professed to take it at face value. And so he was seen as putting 'the interests of the cotton operatives before personal honour', and paying 'a compliment to the Clitheroe Division' by seeking 'to render more effective service to his constituency'.[51] Others were more sceptical. And their responses ranged from the scornful ('only a trumpery [reason]') to the doubtful ('a committee of this kind does not involve very continuous or exhausting labour').[52]

Historians of the labour movement have sided with the sceptics, and accepted an interpretation of Shackleton's motives which first surfaced in an early biography of Ramsay MacDonald.[53] Shackleton's decision, on this view, was motivated by anger. The evidence is a letter written by MacDonald late in 1907.

> A storm seems to be brewing. I was told the other day that Shackleton is so angry with criticisms passed upon him in the *Labour Leader* that he is to decline to stand for the Chairmanship of the Party in Parliament. I understand that he is to write a letter to the members. In this he is to give as one reason that he has been appointed to the [Humidity] Commission [*sic*] which will take him away three days a week, but his friends are being acquainted with the I.L.P. cause for his decision … When in London the other day he did not hint anything of this kind to me, but he spent an afternoon and evening with Henderson talking things over with him. That alone looks as though the cause of division was T.U. v. Socialism.[54]

---

49. *Manchester Guardian*, 7 January 1908. This is the full extent of the reason as given in his formal letter to MacDonald. But in a more personal (not circulated) covering letter, he mentioned two other commitments as well. 'The work of the [TUC] Parliamentary Committee, my duties as the Weavers President, and this "Humidity" Committee make it quite impossible for me to add the responsibility of Chairmanship of the Party.' Shackleton to MacDonald, 3 January 1908: MacDonald Papers, PRO 30/69/5 69951.

50. *Nelson Leader*, 17 January 1908.

51. *Colne & Nelson Times*, 10 January 1908.

52. *Nelson Leader*, 17 January 1908; *Colne & Nelson Times*, 10 January 1908. Shackleton himself was reported as claiming that the Humidity Committee would occupy him 'for two days every week during the greater part of the forthcoming session'. *Pioneer*, 11 January 1908. In the event, this was probably not far off the mark (see below).

53. Elton, *Life of James Ramsay MacDonald*.

54. Quoted in ibid., pp. 159–60.

On the same evidence, Clegg, Fox and Thompson suggested that the specific source of his anger was 'probably' to be found in an article published in the *Labour Leader* of 6 September 1907.[55]

The sceptics were right in one thing. A man of Shackleton's temperament and working style (see Chapters 9 and 10) would not have seen the Humidity Committee as a bar had he really wanted the chairmanship. On the other hand, the assertion that such a man made a decision of this nature simply out of anger at some mildly critical comments, published four months earlier, stretches credulity too far. An accumulated anger is more believable, and he had long been a target of attacks from Socialist quarters.[56] But to fasten on anger alone, as an explanation of his decision, is to ignore two other factors which could not have failed to have played some part in his thinking. One is his election to the chairmanship of the TUC's Parliamentary Committee late in 1907. The other is his experience as the parliamentary party's vice-chairman and acting chairman during 1906 and 1907.

It is likely that the die was cast as early as September 1907, when he accepted the TUC chairmanship. He would have known long since that the succession to Hardie was his for the taking. But accepting the party chairmanship in January 1908 would certainly have meant withdrawing from that of the the TUC. Wearing both hats was ruled out – even if the attitudes of colleagues and the weight of dual responsibilities had allowed it. For the Liberals' emerging programme of social reform had already created competition between the TUC and the Labour party for the role of chief working-class mouthpiece in dealings with the government.[57] No great foresight was required to envisage the excruciating conflicts of interest that the two

55.   Clegg et al., *History of British Trade Unions*, vol. 1, p. 389 and n. 4. Written by 'J. H. H.' (Harley), this article in the *Labour Leader*, 6 September 1907, referred to Keir Hardie's illness and discussed his presence in the House – if not altogether without qualification – in decidedly lyrical terms. It then moved on to an assessment of Shackleton (reproduced in full below, with emphasis added) which, while mixed, was far from uncomplimentary: 'Shackleton ... made a careful and conscientious leader. He paid more attention to the details of leadership than Hardie did ... He is sincere, courageous, and unaffected, and if *during the latter part of the session he failed to show the highest qualities of leadership, it is because no man who is not a Socialist can be an ideal leader for a party which in the main consists of Socialists*. During the last session ... he was least successful in questions such as that of the House of Lords, which ... raise general constitutional issues. His speech on the Government resolution anent the Upper House was a very disappointing performance, and was quite eclipsed the next evening by the speech which Henderson delivered on the same subject.' The italicized passage in this quotation is the one that Clegg, Fox and Thompson designated as critical in provoking Shackleton's anger.

56.   MacDonald, worried by increasing friction between the party's trade unionist MPs and their ILP colleagues, in May 1907 appealed to Glasier, as editor of the *Labour Leader*, to try to ensure that ILP comment on the doings of the parliamentary party came from 'our old wise folk ... who have known the difficulties of public administration and who do not put their trust in fireworks & windbags'. MacDonald to Glasier, 31 May 1907: Glasier Papers, I.1. 1907/81.

57.   See Martin, *TUC*, pp. 112–13.

chairmanships, in tandem, would have entailed. A choice had to be made. Shackleton almost certainly made that choice when he accepted the TUC chairmanship.

By September 1907, as well, there were at least two good reasons why the chairmanship of the parliamentary party should have held less attraction for Shackleton than it had in February 1906. One had to do with the standing of the chairman. The intervening months would have brought home to him the fact that most of his parliamentary colleagues were determined that the position should amount to little more than a 'figurehead.'[58] Outsiders, at the time, thought of the chairman as possessing the 'privileged position of ascendancy ... which the Liberals and Conservatives accorded to their Leaders.'[59] But the reality was quite different, as Philip Snowden made abundantly clear in a newspaper article he wrote shortly after Shackleton publicly withdrew his claim:

> The chairman of the Labour Party is in no sense a leader of the party ... He is just the chairman of the party meetings, and when appointed by the party voices its decisions in the House. But it is just as likely that some other member may be selected for a special occasion ... The qualities required in the chairman ... are not so much those of a leader, as the possession of a business ability and a knowledge of the rules of the House.[60]

The accuracy of Snowden's depiction is confirmed by the early assumption that the chairmanship was a rotating position. And as MacDonald wryly commented, before Shackleton rejected it: 'to take the job on for a period of two years, at the maximum, is a bit discouraging for a start.'[61]

In the second place, the intervening months would also have brought home to Shackleton the discomforts of working in harness with Socialists.

---

58. This term, applied to the chairmanship, was used by MacDonald in 1910. Quoted in Elton, *Life of James Ramsay MacDonald*, p. 190.

59. McKenzie, *British Political Parties*, p. 302. Thus, from a columnist purporting to address Shackleton on his decision not to stand: 'And it is not a little thing that you are pushing aside; it is a thing that many clever and ambitious men would envy you. To be the leader of the Labour Party just when it is on the threshold of a larger world ... really that is something. It is better, perhaps, than being the chairman of the Parliamentary Committee of the Trades Union Congress.' *Ideas*, 11 January 1908: SP.

60. *Nelson Leader*, 17 January 1908. The indiscipline underlying this depiction is reflected in MacDonald's comment that both the Liberals and the Conservatives 'are beginning to see that we are all leaders and that they cannot accept anything which any officer [of the parliamentary Labour party] may say'. MacDonald to Glasier, n.d. [1909]: Glasier Papers, I.1.1909/100. George Barnes, much later, confirmed MacDonald's perception: 'We ... were rather loose in our discipline in those days. We could not be otherwise. Most of our men had had many a stiff fight with authority before getting [to parliament] ... and they were difficult to manage.' *From Workshop to War Cabinet*, pp. 82–3.

61. Quoted in Elton, *Life of James Ramsay MacDonald*, p. 161. Shackleton later echoed this sentiment: 'I have long felt that the position of Chairman should be of a more permanent character than it is at present.' Shackleton to MacDonald, 8 February 1910: MacDonald Papers, PRO 30/69/1154 69951.

Up to 1906, Hardie had been the only Socialist in the LRC's four-man parliamentary group. And of the others, not only were the political inclinations of Henderson and Crooks identical to Shackleton's, but (as he told more than one journalist) he regarded them as 'friends', his 'pals.'[62] The ideological balance was reversed following the 1906 general election. Of the new Labour party's 30 MPs, only 7 were officially sponsored by the ILP, the rest being sponsored by trade unions or a divisional LRC. But probably 18, all told, were members of the ILP, and one other belonged to the Social Democratic Federation.[63]

A group with such a pronounced Socialist majority was bound to be less comfortable for Shackleton. Tension, in any case, was inevitable between Socialists and Liberal-leaning trade unionists. Shackleton himself displayed at this time a keener awareness of the disparate character of the Labour party. He started to talk about it in terms an 'alliance', a 'federation', or 'a combination of a Trades Union element (composed of Tories, Liberals, and Socialists) with the Independent Labour Party.'[64] In his public statements, he repeatedly affirmed that the alliance was working well, and he stressed the common denominator underpinning it: 'While [the trade unionists] may not endorse all the aims of our more idealist [Socialist] friends, at least we are cordially agreed on all essential economic and social measures that promise to redress the hardships of the workers today.'[65] But he was constantly confronted with the different vision of the Socialists – as when Snowden, for example, told a Sunday audience that the party's objective was 'the emancipation of the workers ... from landlordism ... capitalism, and ... the forces of slavery', and declared that he (Snowden) would not be a member if it had 'no higher ideal ... than to get a Trade Disputes Bill, a Workmen's Compensation Bill, and old age pensions' enacted.[66] The next day, in direct response, Shackleton insisted before another audience that these three measures, in themselves, fully justified 'the existence of the Labour Party, as it is at present constituted.'[67]

These differences in outlook gave rise to deep antagonisms, which were compounded by personality clashes. As early as the summer of 1906, according to Hardie's major biographer, 'tensions within the party were becoming almost intolerable.'[68] By the autumn, Shackleton was publicly pleading for unity. 'He hoped that nothing would be said, either in the House of Commons or out of it, which would prevent that solidarity of the Labour Party in

---

62. Unknown newspaper, 4 March 1905; 15 February 1908: SP.
63. See Bealey and Pelling, *Labour and Politics*, p. 276.
64. *Labour Leader*, 28 September 1906.
65. Ibid., 1 February 1907.
66. *Colne & Nelson Times*, 28 September 1906.
67. Ibid.
68. Morgan, *Keir Hardie*, p. 159.

the House ... which now existed.'[69] But, as he showed a few weeks later when addressing a more congenial audience, even he was not above a public sneer at his Socialist colleagues.[70]

The climactic demonstration of the gulf between Shackleton and the Socialists in the party came in July 1907 during a by-election in the Yorkshire seat of Colne Valley. The seat was unexpectedly won by Victor Grayson, an independent Socialist who had been nominated by local Labour interests despite a directive from the Labour party's national executive that the Liberal candidate should not be opposed. Shackleton was one of an executive sub-committee which recommended that no support be given to Grayson's campaign.[71] He would scarcely have been pleased when the ILP's national executive defied the recommendation by passing a motion of support for Grayson, and sending Snowden to Colne Valley to speak for him. But worse was to come. In an extraordinary breach of party discipline, Hardie himself, still the parliamentary party's chairman, weighed in with 'a warm message of support' that was extensively used in Grayson's campaign.[72] And apart from this, Grayson's victory produced not merely some unsavoury scenes in the House of Commons but, as Shackleton might well have predicted, a lengthy period of strife within the party outside parliament.[73] If there was, in fact, a defining moment in 1907 when anger at the Socialists tipped Shackleton's decision against the party chairmanship, then the occasion is much more likely to have been provided by the Colne Valley by-election in July than by the *Labour Leader*'s article in September.

The article was published in the issue dated 6 September, during the week the TUC's annual Congress met in Bath. Shackleton had probably read it by the morning of the 7th when the TUC's executive, meeting a few minutes before the last session of the Congress, resolved 'that Mr Shackleton be elected Chairman for the ensuing year'.[74] It is not impossible that the article was a factor in his decision, maybe even the last straw which tipped the balance so that he accepted the TUC's chairmanship, instead of declining it in expectation of the party's. Or perhaps he simply tucked the article away in

69. *Labour Leader*, 28 September 1906.

70. 'To say that [under minimum wage legislation] everybody should at once receive ... 30s a week was nonsense. He did not suppose that even a Socialist member would get up in Parliament and make such a proposal. – (Laughter.)' *Cotton Factory Times*, 2 November 1906.

71. Shackleton, in fact, moved the recommendation, which went further than MacDonald had wanted to go. See Thompson, *Enthusiasts*, p. 152.

72. Morgan, *Keir Hardie*, p. 174.

73. Grayson's win, against a Conservative as well as a Liberal, hugely excited the more militant elements in the party's Socialist wing. One result, 'during the next two years [was] a succession of disastrous by-elections with candidates promoted locally against the advice of the [national] leaders'. Clegg et al., *History of British Trade Unions*, vol. 1, p. 411.

74. TUC, PC, *Minutes*, 7 September 1907. The content of the Shackleton papers suggests that he did not subscribe to Socialist journals. But it seems unlikely that he did not, at least, have his attention drawn to the article by someone at the Congress.

his mind as a conveniently specific reason to give some confidants when the time came, as he knew it would four months later, to announce that he had no intention of succeeding Hardie. However that may be, one thing is certain, and that is the inadequacy of an anger-with-the-Socialists explanation which focuses exclusively on negative aspects of the party and its chairmanship. For this approach overlooks the positive attractions of the TUC chairmanship.

The TUC Option

There is a revealing conclusion to the letter in which MacDonald told Glasier of Shackleton's intention to decline the party chairmanship.[75] After saying he was 'very sorry that Shackleton should be so offended' by the *Labour Leader*'s criticisms, MacDonald ended by remarking: 'He probably has a reason, but to throw down his crown! What more can one say than that it is an unkingly act?'[76] MacDonald, in other words, could not imagine that there might be another crown, within reach, which Shackleton valued more highly. And yet that was a clear implication of Shackleton's decision. He placed more value on the crown he already wore as chairman of the TUC's Parliamentary Committee.

One does not have to search far for reasons why he should have preferred the kingdom of the TUC. In the first place, by mid-1907, he could have had no doubt whatever that the Parliamentary Committee offered a far more comfortable environment. It was more compact.[77] Above all, it was ideologically both more congenial and more homogeneous. The nominal Socialists on it were a tiny minority and, in any case, much less assertive than their parliamentary counterparts. Of nine MPs on the Parliamentary Committee in 1907 (three Lib-Labs and six, including two Socialists, in the Labour party), there was 'little difference of outlook' in matters involving the unions, and 'all were Lib-Labs in spirit'.[78] There was thus none of the ideological friction that bedevilled the parliamentary Labour party.

Secondly, in the Parliamentary Committee, unlike the parliamentary party, Shackleton's personal ascendancy was assured. There was no Hardie or MacDonald, not even a Henderson, to challenge his leadership. One sign of his ascendancy is the fact that he became chairman of the Parliamentary

75. This is the letter which appears to be the only evidence for the conventional explanation that Shackleton's sole motivation was anger at criticisms in the *Labour Leader*.

76. Quoted in Elton, *Life of James Ramsay MacDonald*, p. 161.

77. Its membership, including the secretary, was increased from 13 to 17 at the time Shackleton became its chairman.

78. Clegg et al., *History of British Trade Unions*, vol. 1, p. 392. One of the Socialists, Will Thorne, although a member of the extreme Social Democratic Federation, 'was no doctrinal purist and found little difficulty in working with his colleagues on the Parliamentary Committee'. Another, George Barnes, a senior member of the ILP, similarly 'was able to agree with the others on most issues'. Ibid.

Committee just three years after joining it. This was highly exceptional. The committee was relatively stable in its composition from year to year, and its chairman (elected by and from itself) had traditionally been a long-serving member. His ascendancy was evident also at the annual Congress. At the Liverpool Congress of 1906, he again (see Chapter 4) headed the list of successful Parliamentary Committee candidates, and was elected to one of the two coveted positions on a delegation to the American Federation of Labor's convention.[79] At the 1907 Congress in Bath (when he became chairman), he was unopposed under a new system for electing an enlarged Parliamentary Committee, but won a hotly contested place on the delegation to the American Federation of Labor's convention by 1,285,000 votes to the runner-up's 715,000.[80]

The extent of his ascendancy is indicated by the Parliamentary Committee's extraordinary decision, as the Nottingham Congress of 1908 drew to a close, that he continue as chairman 'for a further period of twelve months, said election however not to be a precedent'.[81] Nobody, since the 1870s, had held the TUC chairmanship for more than one year; nor has anyone done so since Shackleton's time. A further indication is the role he played at the Sheffield Congress of 1910, when he was technically vice-chairman to the elderly James Haslam, a miners' union official who suffered from a weak voice and an uncertain grasp of procedure. The TUC secretary, W. C. Steadman, would normally have helped Haslam with points of procedure but was absent through illness. In the result, as the *Labour Leader*'s correspondent put it, the TUC's 'sturdy giant' took over, becoming a 'second unofficial chairman', and providing 'the spectacle of Mr Shackleton putting questions to the vote and making announcements, while at the same time [giving] the replies from the platform when the Parliamentary Committee is attacked.'[82]

The TUC's 'crown' thus promised Shackleton far more comfort than the party's.[83] But it promised more than just comfort. It also promised influence. For by latter months of 1907, he would have been well aware that the TUC, in the circumstances of the time, rivalled the party as a source of political weight.

Labour's success in the 1906 general election had persuaded many on the left that the TUC was played out. The party had emerged conclusively as the movement's specialized political organ, so the argument ran, and that meant

---

79. In the event, he did not go to America that year because of his parliamentary responsibilities in relation to the Trade Disputes Bill.

80. TUC, *Report*, 1907, p. 196.

81. TUC, PC, *Minutes*, 12 September 1908. Given that Hardie's example had established the convention of a two-year tenure of the parliamentary party's chairmanship, it is possible that Shackleton may have negotiated the second term as a quid pro quo for renouncing the party chairmanship.

82. *Labour Leader*, 16 September 1910.

83. He would have found ample confirmation of this in Arthur Henderson's wretched experience as party chairman during 1908 and 1909. See, e.g., Leventhal, *Arthur Henderson*, pp. 32–3.

the TUC had lost its once-distinctive role as the movement's principal mouthpiece in dealings with MPs and government ministers.[84] In other words, the TUC was redundant.

> The Parliamentary Committee of the Congress continues to meet, and passes bombastic resolutions ... It has outlived its usefulness ... It is as dead as old Marley, but it perversely refuses to lie down and get buried. The unreasoning persistence of the thing ... costs us a good round sum of money every year, besides involving some foolish waste of effort. And the money and effort might profitably be placed at the disposal of the Labour Party.[85]

This refusal to 'lie down and get buried' had a threatening consequence for the Labour party in parliament. The party's aspirations, at this time, were essentially the limited aspirations of a pressure group, rather than the governmental ambitions of a true party. And that fact thrust it into direct competition with the TUC's leadership. Thus, throughout 1906, the Trade Disputes Bill was the focus of the party's parliamentary concerns; and the bill's progress depended on frequent negotiations with government, with Liberal backbenchers, and on the organizing of other parliamentary initiatives. But it was the Parliamentary Committee, not the party, which primarily and formally handled these matters.[86] The party's leaders – other than Shackleton with his two hats as both a Parliamentary Committee member and the party's principal spokesman on the bill – were completely overshadowed. One outcome of this, the following year, was a lively dispute in Labour circles about apportioning credit for the legislation between the party and the TUC.[87]

The competition between them was brought into the open in January 1907. The Parliamentary Committee decided to publish a circular about old-age pensions and also to convene a meeting of Labour and Lib-Lab MPs on the issue.[88] But contrary to recent practice, in what seems to have been a deliberately provocative initiative, it did not invite the parliamentary party's

---

84.   It was also seen as having disowned all claim to an industrial role with the formation of the General Federation of Trade Unions (in 1899); and it had, as well, handed over to the federation the main responsibility for the international representation of the trade union movement. See Martin, *TUC*, pp. 84–5.

85.   *Clarion*, 16 March 1906. This view was reflected in the Amalgamated Society of Engineers' decision to disaffiliate from the TUC in 1907 because 'the old-time functions of the Congress have become obsolete'. Quoted in Clegg et al., *History of British Trade Unions*, vol. 1, p. 408n. It was also reflected in unsuccessful Congress resolutions, in 1908 and 1910, which effectively proposed that the TUC should amalgamate with the Labour party and the General Federation of Trade Unions.

86.   See Martin, *TUC*, p. 115.

87.   For example, at the 1907 Congress a delegate complained that the annual report gave the impression that the TUC, rather than the Labour party, was chiefly responsible for the Trade Disputes Act and the Workmen's Compensation Act. The Congress chairman blandly retorted that the issue of credit 'was quite a matter of opinion'. TUC, *Report*, 1907, p. 137.

88.   TUC, PC, *Minutes*, 16 January 1907.

whip to sign the notice of meeting. The party's executive swiftly protested against the breach of protocol. But MacDonald, after reading the TUC's circular, perceived a far more substantial threat behind the procedural issue:

> I think that we will have to come to some arrangement by which the P.C. is to keep within its own bounds ... There is not the least doubt but that an attempt is being made by the P.C. to cover the whole of our ground and to elbow us out ... I can see that before long the tables will be turned upon us and instead of our Conference being regarded as the only one of importance, the T.U.C. will do everything that is necessary and we shall have nothing but a few contentious remnants ... I think we have been too friendly for some time with the P.C., and it is imposing upon us in consequence ...
>
> I am not at all sure that Old Age Pensions is after all the most important work that the Labour Party has got to do next Session. Perhaps the most important work is to let the P.C. know that we are going to stand no nonsense.[89]

The party's executive took MacDonald's point. It proposed to the TUC (and, purely as a matter of form, to the General Federation of Trade Unions as well) that an attempt should be made to 'systematize' the agendas of their separate annual conferences, in order to avoid 'overlapping and possible confusion of decisions'.[90] The TUC leadership did not oppose this proposal. But then, after seeing the agenda for the TUC's forthcoming Congress, the party executive produced a lengthy list of items which it wanted either amended or deleted – some because they proposed parliamentary action by the Parliamentary Committee, but most, it seems, because they concerned issues of a political rather than an industrial character. The Parliamentary Committee's response to the party's list was blunt and unequivocal. None of the items, it declared, was 'outside the scope of [the TUC's] normal work'.[91]

The Parliamentary Committee's minutes show that Shackleton was present both at the first meeting in January, when the provocative initiative on old-age pensions was approved, and at the second meeting in May when the party's agenda changes were rebuffed. The minutes do not record movers or seconders, or whether the respective motions were adopted unanimously or by majority vote. There can be no question, however, that Shackleton was in favour of both. It is inconceivable that two such uncompromising decisions could have been carried without the support of a man who was not only offered an extraordinarily early elevation to the TUC's chairmanship a few months later, but was the parliamentary party's vice-chairman at the time of the first decision, and its acting chairman at the time of the second. In any case, his subsequent behaviour leaves no room for doubt that he favoured the TUC against the party on the 'overlapping' issue.

The public opportunity for affirming his personal position on the issue came at the annual Congress whose agenda the TUC leadership had refused

---

89. MacDonald to Hardie, 30 January 1907: LP Archives, Francis Johnson Corr., 1907/29A.
90. TUC, PC, *Minutes*, 5 March 1907.
91. Ibid., 16 May 1907.

to amend. At the time, moreover, he was still acting chairman of the parliamentary party. A delegate implied that Congress should not concern itself with the question of the reform of the House of Lords, but instead should leave the matter to the Labour party. Shackleton responded with a resounding affirmation of the breadth of the TUC's concerns. 'If Mr Knee thinks that the Trades Union Congress exists only for Workmen's Compensation Acts and things like that he has got a very poor idea of our mission. I take it that this movement of ours embraces reforms applying to the whole of the community.'[92] And he made the point again, just days before formally renouncing the party chairmanship, at a joint meeting of the Parliamentary Committee and the Labour party executive which had been convened because of the party's concern about 'overlapping'. MacDonald, on the party's behalf, had urged that 'the work of the two bodies should be strictly defined'. Shackleton, for the Parliamentary Committee, replied that he and his colleagues 'were against any proposition limiting their power to put on the Congress Agenda any resolution sent [to them] by affiliated societies.'.[93]

It is certain, too, that by the time of this joint meeting Shackleton was convinced that the TUC carried more weight than the party in the immediate task of shaping the Liberal government's policies. He made this clear in the course of responding to MacDonald's initial statement. 'The Labour Party', he said, 'is naturally antagonistic to every Government: the Parliamentary Committee are in a somewhat different position, and are of the opinion that it would weaken the power of Labour generally to give up their right to approach Ministers.'[94] The Parliamentary Committee's later report to Congress was more specific, explaining the 'somewhat different position' of the TUC leaders in terms of an ability to approach ministers 'with greater freedom, and, from some points of view, greater influence' than the party.[95]

There was, however, no question of abandoning the party. On the eve of its Hull conference in January 1908, Shackleton was reported as expressing his 'loyal appreciation ... of the Socialist wing'; and at the conference itself he affirmed 'the hope that nothing would occur [there] to rupture the basis of the alliance between the Socialists and the Trade Unionists.'[96] His hope was soon put to the test.

On the second day of the conference, the delegates overwhelmingly rejected one proposal to include a Socialist objective in the party's constitution and another to adopt a 'national programme' of policies. Shackleton did not speak in either debate. The next day, however, he led the opposition to a third proposal which, unlike the earlier two, made no attempt to tamper with the party's constitution but simply, and cleverly, expressed 'the opinion' that

92. TUC, *Report*, 1907, p. 160.
93. TUC, PC, *Minutes*, 19 December 1907.
94. *Ibid.*
95. TUC, *Report*, 1908, p. 85.
96. *Labour Leader*, 24 January 1908.

the party 'should have a definite object, the socialisation of the means of production, distribution, and exchange'.[97] This proposal, he warned, endangered 'the federal understanding' on which the party's unity depended. The resolution was carried, against him, by 514,000 card votes to 469,000.

> The Socialists were frantic with joy. They danced and shouted, and waved hats and red handkerchiefs, and took no notice of the pathetic protests of the president's tea-gong. Amidst the clamour the war song of the Socialists was raised, and the menacing chorus of 'The Red Flag' was nearly finished before the chant was drowned by indignant shouts of 'Order.'[98]

Surveying this scene, Shackleton might well have reflected with relief on his decision to decline the parliamentary party's chairmanship.

At Westminster, a few days later, he nominated Arthur Henderson for the position. After unanimously approving Henderson's appointment, caucus resolved 'that Mr Shackleton be thanked for the manner in which he discharged the duties of Chairman in the absence of Mr Hardie during last session.'[99]

97. *Cotton Factory Times*, 24 January 1908.
98. Ibid. James Holmes, of the Amalgamated Society of Railway Servants, later claimed that his union's 70,000 votes were mistakenly cast in favour of the resolution, instead of against it, owing to a 'blunder' by one of its delegates. *Daily Chronicle*, 23 January 1908.
99. Labour party, *Minutes of Parliamentary Meetings*, 28 January 1908.

6

The Labour Leader as Trade Unionist, 1908–1910

When Keir Hardie snatched the parliamentary party's chairmanship from him, in February 1906, Shackleton was acting as both president and secretary of the Weavers' Amalgamation, and had just negotiated an agreement with cotton employers securing the second part of the 7½ per cent wage increase won the previous year (see Chapter 4). His load lightened a month later, when Joseph Cross was appointed secretary after the ailing Wilkinson finally resigned. Then, in May, the amalgamation's annual meeting formally elected him president in place of the late David Holmes.

He remained secretary of the Darwen Weavers' Association for another year, before resigning. Some months afterwards, in October 1907, he was bid farewell at a 'social evening' in Darwen.[1] By that time, he was chairman of the TUC's Parliamentary Committee, and within a few weeks of announcing his decision to decline the chairmanship of the parliamentary Labour party.

In 1908, consistent with this decision, there was a clear shift in his priorities. He withdrew, in February, as the Labour party's representative on the Standing Orders Committee of the House of Commons, explaining that 'he would not be able to put in a regular attendance at its meetings'.[2] His involvement in parliament itself fell away sharply. The conventional, quantifiable yardstick of parliamentary diligence, at the time, was participation in voting divisions; and, in the session ending in the summer of 1908, he was well behind most of his Labour colleagues in this respect.[3] But a more convincing measure of the extent to which he abandoned parliament as a sphere of action is provided by his speeches, and other interventions, as recorded in *Hansard*. In 1903, his first full year as an MP, he gave nine speeches and made ten other interventions (including four formal questions); and in each of the next four years, exceeded this tally in both respects.[4] In 1908, with just four speeches

---

1. *Cotton Factory Times*, 25 October 1907.
2. Labour Party, *Minutes of Parliamentary Meetings*, 25 June 1908.
3. In a list of 32 Labour MPs, he ranked 26th with an attendance rate of 123 (the highest in the list was 228) out of a total of 239 divisions. *Labour Leader*, 7 August 1908.
4. 1906, of course, was exceptional because of his responsibilities in relation to the Trade Disputes Bill. In that year, he gave 29 speeches and made 24 other interventions (including 14 questions). In 1907, when he was acting chairman for much of the session, his tally was 12 speeches and 16 other interventions (including 10 questions).

and three interventions, he was well under the 1903 standard; and he remained under that standard in 1909 and 1910 as well. This change of emphasis was the subject of public comment during 1908, a local journalist echoing a common explanation that 'trade matters' were the reason for Shackleton's 'absence from his Parliamentary duties'.[5] In fact, a good deal of time plainly went into his involvement with the Humidity Committee, the public reason he had given for refusing the party chairmanship.[6] Up to late September, too, he was embroiled in 'very lengthy negotiations' with cotton employers about joint rules governing the settlement of industrial disputes.[7] And during the summer, he had a major part to play in an intensive series of meetings with employers, Board of Trade officials, and the workers involved, as the result of a highly significant local strike in the Ashton mills at Hyde.[8] His strictly 'trade' responsibilities, moreover, had an international dimension which took him to Vienna for the seventh congress of the International Textile Workers, and to other continental cities for meetings of the International's executive committee.[9] Beyond the cotton industry, in a year when the general level of 'industrial disturbance' was higher than it had been for a decade,[10] he also had a hand in attempts to resolve a major shipbuilding lockout on the north-east coast during April and May.[11] His involvement in this dispute arose from the intervention of the Joint Board, one expression of the drive to harmonise the roles of the TUC and the Labour party (see Chapter 4).[12]

5.   *Colne & Nelson Times*, 12 June 1908.
6.   The Departmental Committee on Humidity and Ventilation in Cotton Weaving Sheds met on 44 occasions (mostly in Lancashire, but also in Glasgow and Bradford), visited 121 weaving sheds, and heard 96 witnesses before reporting on 7 January 1909, some 13 months after its first meeting. *Parl. Papers* [Cd. 4484, 4485], 1909, vol. XV, pp. 635–922.
7.   Hopwood, *History of the Lancashire Cotton Industry*, p. 76; see also Clegg et al., *History of British Trade Unions*, vol. 1, p. 458.
8.   *Cotton Factory Times*, 19 June 1908; 3 July 1908. The Ashton weavers had earlier agreed to a maximum of 20 of the new automatic (Northrup) looms per weaver, as against 4 standard Lancashire looms. They struck when the management sought to increase the maximum to 24 looms. See Singleton, *Lancashire on the Scrapheap*, p. 10.
9.   Beginning with a second visit to the United States at the end of 1907 (to attend the annual convention of the American Federation of Labor on behalf of the TUC), his international commitments were unusually heavy during this period – for they also included attendance at an 'Inter-Parliamentary Congress' in Berlin, which he visited again (along with Dresden, Leipzig and Frankfurt) as leader of a TUC mission to look into the working of German social insurance schemes.
10.   Askwith, *Industrial Problems and Disputes*, p. 126.
11.   *Colne & Nelson Times*, 17 April 1908. And beyond the industrial field altogether, during the second half of the year he was on a royal commission, with the agreement of the parliamentary Labour party, inquiring into the working of the Land Transfer Acts. Labour party, *Minutes of Parliamentary Meetings*, 25 June 1908.
12.   Shackleton was made chairman of the Joint Board in February 1908, and remained chairman until he left the labour movement at the end of 1910.

Repelling the Party

In September 1908, Shackleton presided over the TUC's annual Congress. The occasion, once again, attracted Socialist declarations that the TUC was redundant 'now that the Labour Party has become the political organ of Trade Unionism'.[13] Once again, his reply emphasised the TUC's 'distinctive place in the Labour movement, apart from the Socialist or political side'.[14] This exchange occurred during a long lull in the dispute about 'overlapping' which had soured relations with the party during the previous year. The lull ended when the Liberal government moved to establish a system of state labour exchanges.

Two months after the Congress, Winston Churchill, President of the Board of Trade, and Lloyd George, Chancellor of the Exchequer, broached this proposition at a breakfast meeting attended by the two leading office-holders of the TUC, the Labour party and the General Federation of Trade Unions, respectively.[15] But when a government-supported delegation left London a fortnight later, to investigate state labour exchanges and health insurance in Germany, it was led by Shackleton and included only members of the TUC's Parliamentary Committee. The delegation reported its findings in March 1909 to a conference of TUC affiliates. In June, at the request of the Board of Trade, five members of the Parliamentary Committee discussed draft labour-exchange regulations with the board's three senior officials. Churchill himself met the full Parliamentary Committee the following month, and asked for 'a small sub-committee ... which would be handy at any time for him to confer with'. He was informed that 'this had already been appointed' in the form of the five who had met earlier with his officials.[16]

Three days after Churchill was told this, there was a highly unusual joint meeting of the full executives of the three Joint Board partners, the TUC, the Labour party and the General Federation of Trade Unions. The meeting had been called for by the party. Shackleton, presumably because he was chairman of the Joint Board, was in the chair. Henderson, for the party, led the attack. He argued that the TUC leaders should not have met Churchill before the Joint Board had settled on 'the policy of the movement', and charged them with being. 'both unfair and unwise' in suggesting amendments to the government's Labour Exchanges Bill, then before parliament, without informing the party.[17] When he formally moved that the Joint Board look into the question of

13. *Labour Leader*, 4 September 1908.
14. *Colne & Nelson Times*, 18 September 1908.
15. Also present, along with Board of Trade officials, were Sidney and Beatrice Webb – 'Winston', as Mrs Webb put it, 'using us to explain the theory of Labour Exchanges to the Labour men'. *Diary of Beatrice Webb* (MS), 15 November 1908: Passfield Coll., vol. 26, fols. 2574–5.
16. TUC, PC, *Minutes*, 8 July 1909.
17. Ibid., 11 July 1909. In the course of discussion, Shackleton remarked from the chair that the party itself frequently found it necessary to act without consulting its Joint Board partners, and the TUC did not complain of that 'because [we] understood the exigencies of the situation'.

avoiding 'separate action' on legislative matters, Shackleton brusquely retorted that if the motion meant the TUC leaders 'had … to consult the Labour Party before taking any action, they were not going to do it'. He was apparently reassured on the point, because the motion was carried unanimously.

A long discussion then followed. Agreement was reached on a number of issues concerning the administration of labour exchanges. Then it was suggested that the Joint Board should send a deputation to Churchill. C. W. Bowerman, of the TUC, reminded the meeting that the Parliamentary Committee already had a sub-committee 'in readiness to meet [Churchill] at a moment's notice'. That was not acceptable to the party. The present meeting, Philip Snowden argued, had already 'taken the negotiations [with Churchill] out of the hands of the Parliamentary Committee', and it was now up to the Joint Board to continue them. A motion to this effect was moved. Shackleton's response – in sharp contrast to his earlier retort – was a model of diplomatic circumlocution. Remarking that 'his own position was a delicate one', he accepted that the motion represented 'the logical conclusion' of their deliberations. Accordingly, he 'desired to be able to go to [Churchill] and say that all future negotiations must be with the Joint Board, and that other bodies would approach him [Churchill] without the official sanction of the Labour movement'.[18] Henderson accepted this formulation. The motion was carried without opposition.

Shackleton's apparent capitulation was utterly hollow. Ten days later, the Joint Board met under his chairmanship and decided to press the government on a number of matters concerning labour exchanges. Then, as its minutes record, it resolved without opposition that 'the Standing Sub-Committee be the Committee to present these points to [Churchill], and that [Shackleton] endeavour to arrange an interview as soon as possible'.[19] What this meant was that Shackleton and the Parliamentary Committee were confirmed as the sole, legitimate representatives of the labour movement in dealings with the Liberal government on the labour exchange issue. For the 'Standing Sub-Committee' was the five-member body which Bowerman had spoken of, and which Snowden had rejected, at the meeting of the three executives ten days earlier.[20]

18. Ibid.
19. Ibid., 21 July 1909.
20. In the Parliamentary Committee's report to the Ipswich Congress in September, history was rewritten in the references made to this 'Standing Sub-committee'. First, Churchill's request for such a body (made at the 8 July meeting with him) is recorded in the report, but not the fact that he was told it was already in existence. Second, the report asserts that the sub-committee was set up at the 11 July meeting (misdated 9 July in the report) of the three executives: 'On 9th [sic] July a meeting of the three full Committees forming the Joint Board was held to discuss the common action to be taken in regard to the measure, and a Sub-Committee was appointed, as had been requested by Mr Churchill … on the 8th July.' TUC, *Report*, 1909, p. 59. In fact, as we have seen, the meeting of the three executives was told (like Churchill the day before) of the existence of the TUC's standing sub-committee, but chose quite deliberately not to use it and instead, in an ultimately futile gesture, hand matters over to the Joint Board.

Churchill, it seems, refused to discuss the labour exchanges with a negotiating body that included representatives of the Labour party. The party's representatives on the Joint Board were thus forced to accept an arrangement giving the TUC exclusive access to the minister on the issue. Shackleton's leading role in this connection was made publicly evident when Churchill appointed him to the three-man committee which selected most of the staff of the new labour exchanges.[21]

Churchill imposed the same condition on later negotiations to do with unemployment insurance (as also did Sidney Buxton, his successor at the Board of Trade).[22] The Labour party returned to the attack. At the Joint Board's October meeting, Henderson accused the TUC of acting in the matter 'without placing any information before the Joint Board', and claimed that this contravened 'the spirit of the resolution' adopted at the meeting of the three executives three months earlier.[23] Shackleton's response, this time, was brutally uncompromising: 'it was true that the Parliamentary Committee was acting in this matter, but he had no authority to lay any information before the Joint Board'. Keir Hardie then appealed to him, speaking of the 'misunderstanding and friction' that the TUC's behaviour might engender. Shackleton's recorded response is contemptuously repetitious. 'Mr Shackleton said that the Parliamentary Committee had been dealing with the matter for some time, but he was not empowered to make any statement to the Joint Board.'[24] The meeting ended on that note.[25] The party's representatives raised the issue again at the Joint Board's next meeting a month later. Shackleton was as curt and unyielding as before.[26] And that, for the moment, was that.

But the Shackleton who, as TUC leader, thus humbled the Labour party's heavyweights was himself on the eve of being humbled, as leader of the Weavers' Amalgamation. It happened because of the 'half-timer' problem.

---

21.   His appointment was announced at the TUC's annual Congress of 1909 which had, as usual, occasioned Socialist assertions of the TUC's diminishing relevance. Thus: 'The fortunes of Labour are more and more wrapped up in those of the Labour Party, and men are ceasing to look to the Trades Union Congress for a special lead on Labour matters.' *Labour Leader*, 10 September 1909. This is unlikely to have been the perception, at least, of the great many trade unionists among the applicants ('already over 3,000' at the time of the Congress) for labour-exchange positions. TUC, *Report*, 1909, p. 169.

22.   It was thus to the TUC alone that William Beveridge, the civil servant responsible for formulating policy on unemployment insurance, submitted his draft scheme for comment. See Martin, *TUC*, p. 128.

23.   TUC, PC, *Minutes*, 6 October 1909.

24.   Ibid.

25.   The same note of contempt had been there five weeks earlier, too, when the Parliamentary Committee responded to a letter from the Joint Board asking for help in organizing a meeting about old-age pensions. Without directly answering this request, the committee resolved to hold a public meeting of its own on the issue – with the condescending proviso that 'should the Joint Board decide to co-operate ... the Committee will welcome such co-operation'. Ibid., 30 August 1909.

26.   Ibid., 4 November 1909.

The morality of employing school-age children in cotton mills had been hotly contested in labour circles for many years. Since the time Shackleton first worked in a weaving shed at the then minimum age of nine, the minimum statutory age for half-timers had been raised progressively to 12. On each occasion, the higher age-limit had the general support of the labour movement, with the notable exception of the cotton unions. And so, in 1900, when Shackleton was vice-president of the Weavers'Amalgamation, he had vigorously lobbied against the 12-year minimum legislation.[27] In 1907, however, as president of the amalgamation, he spoke out in favour of raising the minimum age to 13 years.[28] His apparent conversion, though he denied it was such,[29] was widely interpreted as a signal that the cotton unions were about to change their traditional position on the issue. And indeed, 18 months later, the Textile Factory Workers' Association resoundingly adopted the 13-year minimum, by 186 votes to 27, and decided to put the matter to a ballot of union members. Shackleton said at the time that those voting for the motion believed they were 'voicing the opinion of the [cotton] workers generally'.[30] The ballot proved him, humiliatingly, wrong. The rank-and-file majority against changing the minimum age of half-timers was a massive 82 per cent.[31] A few days after the publication of this result, the Labour party's annual conference had before it a resolution urging abolition of the half-time system. Shackleton told the conference that the cotton union delegates, while duty bound to vote against the resolution, were nevertheless determined 'to go on educating their people against the [half-timer] system'.[32]

The Party Man

Shackleton's sharply diminished parliamentary involvement and his hard line on the TUC's dealings with Churchill could have reflected a turning

27.   As one parliamentary observer recalled eight years later, Shackleton 'did everything he could from the Lobby and the Gallery to prevent the passing of the Robson Bill'. *Colne & Nelson Times*, 16 October 1908.

28.   *Cotton Factory Times*, 26 April 1907. In the same speech, he also expressed agreement with the 'sentiment' that the general minimum school age should be raised to 16 years, but said that if he 'proposed it ... [he] would be called upon to resign his position as member for Clitheroe' because his union, he knew, would be against it.

29.   See Chapter 10 below.

30.   *Nelson Leader*, 16 October 1908.

31.   Thus in a total of 184,691 votes, only 33,968 were cast in favour of raising the minimum age to 13. See *Cotton Factory Times*, 26 February 1909.

32.   *Labour Leader*, 5 February 1909. And they did, with a campaign of meetings on the issue which, as he told an interviewer, involved the officials 'taking this stand for the first time'. Ibid. 18 June 1909. But it did not work in the short term. Confronted by an identical resolution at the TUC's Congress in 1910, Joseph Cross, for the Weavers' Amalgamation, could say no more than Shackleton had 18 months before at the party conference: 'Some progress has been made in the education of our people on this question ... [but we] shall have to vote against it.' TUC, *Report*, 1910, p. 165.

away from the Labour party, a lack of belief in its future.[33] But it seems unlikely that this was his frame of mind – at least before the general election of January 1910. And so he did not respond to suggestions, encouraged by his renunciation of the party chairmanship and the Hull conference's socialization resolution, that the time was ripe for 'a new ... non-Socialist Labour Party' under his leadership.[34] Nor did he respond to renewed Liberal feelers about a place in the ministry that Asquith formed on succeeding the dying Campbell-Bannerman as Prime Minister.[35]

If anything, Shackleton seems to have been quite optimistic at this time about the Labour party's prospects. Thus he told the Hull conference that, if the party played its cards right, the next general election would see 'the return of 100 Labour members'.[36] And he remained deeply embroiled in the negotiations which eventually brought the bulk of the parliamentary Lib-Labs into the Labour party.

At 25, the number of Lib-Lab trade unionists elected in 1906 came close to matching the successful LRC candidates. Of these, 14 (one of whom quickly defected to the new Labour party) were sponsored by miners' unions. The Lib-Labs set themselves up as the 'Trade Union Group' with their own chairman and whips.[37] The parliamentary Labour party, while declining to form 'a separate section in the House' with them, was willing to co-operate on 'purely Trade Union objects'.[38] In the event, it was the TUC's Parliamentary Committee (three of its MP-members being senior Lib-Labs) which provided such co-ordination as there was between the Lib-Labs and the Labour party

In 1907, under instructions from the previous year's Congress to seek 'perfect political unity of action ... in the House of Commons',[39] the Parliamentary Committee had secured the formation of a 'sub-committee on Unity', on which it was represented along with the two parliamentary groups.[40] The sub-committee quickly reached an impasse on the issue of regular joint meetings

33. It might be thought, too, that his standing in the parliamentary party would have been substantially diminished for the same reasons. This seems unlikely. For example, in 1909 when MacDonald wanted it known on the trade union side of the party that he was (reluctantly) ready to succeed Henderson as chairman, it was to Shackleton that he wrote. See Elton, *Life of James Ramsay MacDonald*, p. 189.

34. *Colne & Nelson Times*, 31 January 1908.

35. As one report put it: 'if the Member for Clitheroe Division had been open to accept an appointment, nobody would have been better pleased than the Prime Minister'. Quoted, 'from a [London] contemporary', in ibid., 17 April 1908. Shackleton, when asked later at a public meeting whether he had been invited by Campbell-Bannerman and Asquith to join their ministries, 'said it was a matter for himself, and ... refused to answer the question'. *Nelson Leader*, 29 January 1909.

36. *Labour Leader*, 24 January 1908.

37. *Cotton Factory Times*, 23 February 1906.

38. Labour party, *Minutes of Parliamentary Meetings*, 12 February 1906.

39. TUC, *Report*, 1906, p. 124.

40. *Labour Leader*, 6 September 1907.

of the MPs. The Lib-Labs wanted attendance confined to bona fide trade unionists, thus excluding a number of the Socialists. The party, with two of the Lib-Labs in mind, wanted to make attendance conditional on withholding support from Liberal candidates when the party had a candidate in the field. The issue gave rise to a heated debate at the TUC's next annual Congress. Shackleton, while reportedly pouring 'large barrels of oil on the troubled waters',[41] declared that it was 'absolutely impossible' for the party to accept the Lib-Labs' condition.[42]

The Parliamentary Committee tried again to heal the breach in April 1908. It was Shackleton, as one of two TUC representatives, who introduced 'the question of united action' at a meeting with the leaders of the two parliamentary groups.[43] This time agreement was reached, and on terms which acknowledged the central interest of both groups. Monthly joint meetings would be held while parliament was in session, and no sitting member of either group, nor any candidate endorsed by the TUC or the party, was to be opposed in any way at elections. The TUC's mediating role was acknowledged at their first joint meeting. For, instead of Henderson or the Lib-Labs' chairman, it was Shackleton, 'as chairman of the Parliamentary Committee, [who] took the chair'.[44] By this time, in any case, the days of the Lib-Lab 'Trade Union Group' were known to be numbered. Beforehand, in a May ballot, the members of the Miners' Federation had finally chosen to join the Labour party.[45] The federation formally affiliated early in 1909, and all but three of their MPs accepted the party's whip. The Lib-Labs were finished as a force in the labour movement.

Throughout these dealings, there was never any doubt about Shackleton's commitment to the alliance with the Socialists which the Labour party involved. By 1909, indeed, it is even possible that his attitude towards the Socialists had softened. Certainly, Bruce Glasier thought so, as the result of a train journey to London which he shared with Shackleton and two other trade union MPs. As he told his sister, 'I ... found them much more friendly towards I.L.P. than they used to be.'[46] Shackleton himself provided qualified confirmation of Glasier's discovery when (after defensively remarking that from 'every point of view the Alliance is perfectly satisfactory') he drew an implicit distinction between Socialists within and without parliament. 'If the Party outside were as anxious to do good work as we are inside, things would be all right', he said. 'Inside the Parliamentary Party there is no trouble whatever. The trouble lies outside with the carping critics.'[47]

41. *Clarion*, 6 September 1907.
42. TUC, *Report*, 1907, p. 146.
43. Labour party, *Minutes of Parliamentary Meetings* ('Report on Labour Unity'), 2 April 1908.
44. *Labour Leader*, 10 July 1908.
45. Arnot, *Miners*, pp. 365–6.
46. Glasier to 'Lizzie', 19 February 1909: Glasier Papers, I.1.1909/20.
47. *Labour Leader*, 18 June 1909.

Six months later, however, it was clear that the greatest 'trouble' confronting the parliamentary Labour party had to do, not with the critics among its supporters, but with its electoral acceptance. By January 1910, it numbered 45 (as against 30 in 1906) as a result of by-election wins and the accession of the miners' MPs. But the general election of that month reduced it to a disheartening 40.[48] Locally, on the other hand, the election was a triumph for Shackleton.

In the Clitheroe Division

Shackleton's local opposition had three principal sources: Conservatives, still-disgruntled Liberals, and Socialists identified with the Social Democratic Federation.[49] He seems to have had no major difficulties with the Socialists of the local ILP branches.

In 1906, three months after the general election, the Clitheroe Division LRC (as it continued to call itself) appointed its first full-time 'registration and election agent', W. H. Boocock.[50] Shortly afterwards, its Nelson branch took the more surprising step of accepting the affiliation of the local Social Democratic Federation branch.[51] In the course of the election campaign, the SDF leadership had publicly accused Shackleton of 'political buffoonery', and other sins, because he had remarked that 'he wanted to do some practical work in this world, for he did not believe in thinking in the clouds'.[52] Unsurprisingly, this affiliation lasted less than a year. Following an episode in which SDF spokesmen openly savaged a newly elected Labour Mayor and most Labour councillors for refusing to municipalize public houses, a massive special meeting of the LRC politely resolved (by 881 votes to 327) that 'the S.D.F. be asked to withdraw from affiliation with us'.[53] The local SDF secretary was reported as snarling: 'If they [the SDF] could not permeate the LRC within, they would fight them from without.'[54]

And fight they did, with Shackleton a particular target, especially during 1909 when a general election loomed. In 'a gross insult to Mr Shackleton', as the editor of the *Nelson Leader* judged it,[55] they brought in Ben Tillett to

---

48.   Shackleton, as we have seen, had spoken hopefully of 100 seats only two years earlier. In the event, the party fielded no more than 78 candidates. See McKibbin, *Evolution of the Labour Party*, pp. 11–12, 51; and 'James Ramsay MacDonald and the Problem of the Independence of the Labour Party', pp. 217–19.

49.   The 'federation' was officially changed to 'party' in 1908, but the former continued to be used locally for some time afterwards.

50.   *Cotton Factory Times*, 27 April 1906.

51.   *Nelson Leader*, 15 June 1906. The ILP was already affiliated.

52.   Ibid., 23 February 1906.

53.   Ibid., 31 May 1907.

54.   Ibid.

55.   Ibid., 26 March 1909. Tillett, in a notorious pamphlet (*Is the Labour Party a Failure?*), had in 1908 attacked Shackleton for supporting the government's Licensing Bill.

deliver a vituperative speech before a Nelson audience. There were even 'threats ... about opposing Mr Shackleton' with an SDF candidate'.[56] But they turned out to be hollow.

For a while, too, there were similar threats from the Liberal side. In February 1909, a former Mayor of Nelson, Alderman A. Nelson, called for a Liberal candidate, adding that he 'would work and vote for a Conservative rather than Mr Shackleton'.[57] The Liberals' sense of grievance was sharpened by perceived injustices in the way Labour had used its majority on the Nelson Town Council in the case of honorific appointments.[58] But, again, no serious challenge eventuated.

It was left to the Conservatives to rise to the occasion. They began looking for a candidate in September 1909, and eventually selected Tom Smith, of Burnley, a salaried lecturer employed by the Tariff Reform League. Smith, a former 'clogger' (boot and clog maker), described himself – with reference to the Irish question – as 'Unionist Labour'.[59] In a campaign that lasted the better part of two months, he posed a much more serious threat to Shackleton in the 1910 general election than had Belton in 1906.[60]

Shackleton's campaign meetings were not only enthusiastically supportive, but were attended by prominent local Liberals, who both spoke for him and made their cars available.[61] Smith, on the other hand, encountered what one journalist euphemistically described as 'the strongest opposition' at his meetings.[62] On polling day, 21 January, an astonishing 92 per cent of those registered in the Clitheroe division cast a vote. Before this was known, Smith toured the constituency in a Daimler car, while Shackleton drove around it in a 'decorated four-horse conveyance'[63] – he had not forgotten the death of the young father four years earlier. The result, announced the following afternoon, was Shackleton by 13,873 votes to 6,727. His majority of 7,146 was exceeded, so far as Labour candidates were concerned, only in the three Welsh mining seats of Merthyr Tydfil (where Keir Hardie's majority was 10,712), West Monmouth (Thomas Richards: 10,250) and the Rhondda (William Abraham: 8,965).[64]

Shackleton admitted that the Clitheroe majority was 'well over 2,000 more' than he had expected.[65] The official Conservatives were also surprised, but

56. Ibid., 11 June 1909.
57. Ibid., 26 February 1909.
58. The publicized cases: one Liberal was removed from the chairmanship of the Finance Committee without being given another committee to chair; and three other Liberals were 'thrown off the Aldermanic Bench'. Ibid., 20 August 1909; 20 November 1909.
59. *Cotton Factory Times*, 10 December 1909.
60. This explains why Shackleton's campaign expenses of £1,160 were almost double his expenses in the 1906 election. *Parl. Debs.*, 13 April 1910, vol. 16, col. 1360.
61. *Labour Leader*, 7 January 1910; 18 November 1910.
62. *Colne & Nelson Times*, 28 January 1910.
63 . Ibid.
64. *Cotton Factory Times*, 28 January 1910.
65. *Colne & Nelson Times*, 28 January 1910.

argued that the result was 'not nearly as bad as the figures would, at first blush, appear to show' because their candidate, despite his late entry, had reduced Shackleton's 1906 majority of 8,207.[66] It was a doleful argument, given their claim in 1906 that, on the showing of 'a weak candidate like Mr Belton', an official Conservative would press Shackleton hard.[67] For Smith, in a poll almost one-third larger than in 1906, could shave no more than 13 per cent off Shackleton's majority. A Liberal assessment was certainly closer to the mark.

> Four years ago ... the contest ... was a farce ... Mr Shackleton's majority was regarded as a purely fictitious one. This year the Tories have worked their very hardest all through the Division ... and ... were sanguine that they would reduce the majority to a very small figure ... A majority ... of over 7,000 is a staggering blow to Tory hopes in the Clitheroe division.[68]

It was a hugely popular victory. In the town of Clitheroe, and at Colne and Nelson, 'the scenes of enthusiasm', according to a Conservative newspaper, 'were beyond description'.[69] Outside the Clitheroe Weavers' Institute, 'the cheering continuing in greater and greater volume', it was almost 10 minutes before Shackleton was allowed to speak. After addressing excited crowds in Padiham and Brierfield, he drove in his coach and four (with a 'huge card' on the back proclaiming his majority) through 'a double line of cheering people' to the Nelson Weavers' Institute for 'a magnificent reception'. His speech outside the Colne Weavers' Institute was not recorded because, owing to 'the cheering, his remarks were not audible to our reporter'. In Sabden, there was a chilling edge to the crowd's enthusiasm: 'An effigy of Mr Tom Smith was hung on a pole and marched around the village, and then set fire to in front of Victoria Mill.'[70]

66. *Burnley Express*, quoted in ibid.
67. *Colne & Nelson Times*, 26 January 1906.
68. *Burnley Gazette*, quoted in ibid., 28 January 1910.
69. *Colne & Nelson Times*, 28 January 1910.
70. Ibid. Another report of the Sabden celebrations, noting 'several free fights', expressed the view that 'the rowdy character of the crowd was due more to women than men'. *Cotton Factory Times*, 28 January 1910.

7

Leaving the Movement

Shackleton probably meant what he said when he assured the Nelson crowd, cheering his re-election in January 1910, that as 'only a young "lad" yet ... he was looking forward to a renewal again of their confidence'.[1] Nevertheless, before the year was out, he had become a permanent civil servant and Clitheroe was being contested by a new Labour candidate in the next general election.

For a time, following his re-election, it was business much as before. A fortnight afterwards, he was in Newport for the Labour party's annual conference. From there he wrote words of comfort to a grieving Ramsay MacDonald (with a recently dead six-year-old son and a dying mother), and asked him to stand for the parliamentary chairmanship.[2] MacDonald agreed, and Shackleton duly nominated him; but caucus preferred G.N. Barnes.[3]

The 'overlapping' issue was again to the fore. Keir Hardie told the Newport conference of his hope that the problem might shortly be solved.[4] But the TUC's Parliamentary Committee, after a formal review of its dealings with the Board of Trade, subsequently refused to alter its practice of entering consultations about unemployment insurance – explaining once again to its Joint Board partners that 'the Board of Trade are unwilling to deal with the Joint Board [because it] has affiliated to it an independent and possibly opposing political party'.[5] The matter was to rest there until after Shackleton's departure from the labour movement.[6] Meanwhile, on a different policy issue, he turned the tables on the party's leaders when they unilaterally arranged a deputation to the Prime Minister. He refused their invitation to

1.   *Colne & Nelson Times*, 28 January 1910.
2.   Shackleton to MacDonald, 8 February 1910: MacDonald Papers, PRO 30/69/3354 69951.
3.   Labour party, *Minutes of Parliamentary Meetings*, 15 February 1910.
4.   His preferred solution, he remarked in distinctly undiplomatic terms, was that 'the Trades Union Congress should discuss trade questions, and the Labour party conference should discuss bigger questions of general order and greater importance'. *Cotton Factory Times*, 18 February 1910.
5.   TUC, PC, *Minutes*, 23 February 1910.
6.   See Martin, *TUC*, pp. 119–27.

join it, saying it should have been arranged by the Joint Board; and the Parliamentary Committee formally endorsed his refusal.[7]

In the same month, he introduced a private member's bill proposing an extension of the parliamentary franchise to women already eligible (as householders or owners of business premises) to vote in local government elections. It was, on one view, a distinctly 'unheroic' bill, as an ILP commentator described it.[8] Shackleton himself undoubtedly agreed with that description, for he had threatened to vote against the third reading of a similar bill three years earlier because it was too 'limited in character'.[9] On the other hand, in the context of the mounting campaign for women's suffrage, his bill was particularly significant. Not only had it been drafted by a large all-party committee of MPs, but it was backed by both the National Union of Women's Suffrage Societies and by Mrs Emmeline Pankhurst and her Women's Social and Political Union. Its second-reading debate occupied a full two days in July, and provided the occasion for a big demonstration in Trafalgar Square by suffragists ('suffragettes' were still to come). Although both Churchill and Lloyd George spoke against it, and Asquith, the Prime Minister, was known to be opposed, the second reading was carried by a majority of more than a hundred.[10] But the bill was then referred, by an even larger majority, to a committee-stage procedure which left it at the mercy of the government. As a result, it proceeded no further.[11] At the time, however, 'Mr Shackleton's Bill' (as press reports constantly described it) was widely seen as bringing women's suffrage to the forefront as a political issue.[12]

The week before the second reading of his bill, London dailies reported a rumour that Shackleton had been offered a post as 'labour adviser' to the

---

7. TUC, PC, *Minutes*, 15 June 1910. The policy issue had to do with the Osborne judgement (see below), and Shackleton refused to join the deputation in his capacity as chairman of the Joint Board. He argued that the judgement, 'being [already] under the consideration of the Joint Board', was a matter for the board to deal with in this way, not the party alone.

8. *Labour Leader*, 10 June 1910. It would, nevertheless, have added one million women to the existing electorate of almost eight million men.

9. *Parl. Debs.*, 8 March 1907, vol. 170, cols. 1146–8. In the meantime, however, he said he would vote for earlier readings because the bill at least affirmed 'that women were entitled to have a share in the government of the country'.

10. Unlike Asquith, neither Churchill nor Lloyd George was opposed to female enfranchisement as such. Their opposition to Shackleton's bill sprang from the belief that it would add many more Conservative than Liberal voters to the electorate. See Jenkins, *Asquith*, p. 248.

11. For a lively interpretation of this episode, and an account of its sequel, see Dangerfield, *Strange Death of Liberal England*, pp. 134–40. See also Liddington and Norris, *One Hand Tied Behind Us*, p. 246. The predominance of women in cotton weaving and the strength of the suffragist movement in north-east Lancashire ensured that Shackleton was under continual pressure from 1902 on the franchise issue. See ibid., pp. 156–9.

12. Thus, from the Liberal side: 'a turning point in the course of our politics, and marks the final emergence of a great issue'. *Manchester Guardian*, 13 July 1910. From the Conservative side: 'Mr Shackleton brings the movement for the enfranchisement of women into the "range of practical politics".' *Colne & Nelson Times*, 15 July 1910. And from the Labour left: 'Women's enfranchisement has been made a vital issue in politics.' *Labour Leader*, 15 July 1910.

Home Office, now headed by Winston Churchill, as Home Secretary. The parliamentary correspondent of the *Pall Mall Gazette* believed the rumour to be true.[13] So did the Press Association's representative, but cautiously added (in telegramese): 'doubtful of acceptance'.[14] The *Cotton Factory Times,* for its part, reckoned that he had not been 'definitely approached'.[15] The Home Office, most awkwardly, simply denied that he had been 'appointed'.[16] Shackleton himself, responding to letters of inquiry from local weeklies, was less equivocal: 'The reference in the Press is the only information I have on the matter you mention.'[17] This was good enough for the ILP's *Labour Leader* which accused the daily press, in reporting the rumour, of 'trying to sow suspicion and mistrust among the adherents of the Labour and Socialist movement'.[18]

Shackleton's statement would have been written on 7 July, and his assertion that he knew nothing beyond what the papers reported was almost certainly the truth. It was some time later in July when he was, apparently, approached by a Liberal familiar and given to understand that he should get in touch with C. F. G. Masterman, Churchill's under-secretary, if he was interested in the possibility of a job as labour adviser to the Home Office.[19] He wrote to Masterman early in August; and he was eager, with the result that the two met – probably as early as 11 August – at Selsey, in Sussex, where Masterman was holidaying.[20] A few days after the Selsey meeting, however, he raised the stakes in a letter which caused Masterman to comment: 'Alas! this change makes things difficult!'[21] Another meeting followed, this time in London, before Masterman left for a Continental tour on the 19th. Shackleton wrote again on the 26th. He had consulted the executive of the Weavers' Amalgamation in the interim and, with their agreement, was now prepared to accept the appointment subject to certain conditions – but wanted no publicity until after the TUC's annual Congress in mid-September. Masterman

13. *Colne & Nelson Times,* 8 July 1910.
14. Quoted in *Cotton Factory Times,* 8 July 1910.
15. Ibid.
16. Ibid. This response, it is to be noted, was forthcoming in the light of a rumour that specified the actual appointment was not to be made 'till the autumn'.
17. *Colne & Nelson Times,* 15 July 1910.
18. *Labour Leader,* 15 July 1910.
19. The following account of Shackleton's dealings with Churchill and Masterman is derived almost wholly from a set of correspondence, in the Shackleton Papers (SP), which is incomplete in that during the crucial period it consists almost exclusively (the single exception being his letter of 26 August) of letters *received* by Shackleton.
20. Masterman first suggested a meeting on the 19th, the day of his return to London, then raised the possibility of an earlier meeting in a postscript: 'If you prefer a day at the seaside, you can come down here by a "Rest All" Excursion every Thursday for some very small fare – and I can give you bathing, boating, lunch and a good talk!!' Masterman to Shackleton, n.d. [6–10 August 1910]: SP. Shackleton chose to make a special trip to Selsey in advance of the 19th.
21. Ibid., 'Wed. 17th 1910' [August]: SP. Masterman's letter provides no clue to the nature of 'this change'.

was back in London by early September. He told Shackleton that he would inform Churchill of 'your decision', and enjoined secrecy; but also made it clear that the appointment could no longer to be regarded as a foregone conclusion.[22] A day or two after reading Masterman's response, Shackleton took the train to Sheffield.

The TUC's Sheffield Congress was to be the last he attended as a trade union official. Once again, he played a larger role than any of his colleagues. But there were aspects of the Congress proceedings that might well have sharpened his hope of a favourable response to the proposition that Masterman had passed on to Churchill. A first, ominous note was struck on the second day by the relatively weak rejection of a resolution which, in effect, urged the TUC to amalgamate with the Labour party and the General Federation of Trade Unions. Shackleton, opposing the resolution, once more affirmed the advantage of having a 'Trade Union body distinct from a political body' so that the unions could negotiate with the government of the day regardless of 'the fight that goes on ... between the three parties'.[23] Two years earlier, a similar resolution had been easily defeated, but this time the majority was a paper-thin 779,000 card votes to 750,000. Worse was to come.

On the afternoon of the fourth day, Thursday, he was massively defeated on a resolution specifying that a state labour exchange should be prohibited from directing workers to employment outside its own district except to jobs known to offer trade union rates. He was the last to speak in a debate in which every other speaker had condemned the labour-exchange system that he had done so much to bring into being. In his speech, he strongly defended the system, and opposed the resolution's requirement concerning trade union rates because it would 'tie the hands of the [Parliamentary] Committee', and make its negotiating position with government 'most difficult'.[24] The vote went against him to the stunning tune of 1,147,000 to 272,000. Nor was that the end of it. The following day, 'Mr Shackleton and the Parliamentary Committee', as the *Cotton Factory Times* put it,[25] were humbled once again when Congress rejected (by 824,000 to 501,000) a resolution that he moved in relation to the election of the Parliamentary Committee.[26]

There were, as well, two other episodes that would have jarred. The first occurred on Thursday morning, prior to the labour exchanges debate. Congress had before it a resolution dealing with the Osborne judgement of December 1909, in which the House of Lords had ruled against union expenditure for political purposes. Shackleton wound up a long debate on this resolution by appealing for a unanimous vote, and effectively got it.[27] But

22. Ibid., 8 September 1910: SP.
23. TUC, *Report*, 1910, p. 121.
24. Ibid., 1910. p. 164.
25. *Cotton Factory Times*, 23 September 1910.
26. TUC, *Report*, 1910, p. 182.
27. 1,717,000 votes in favour, 13,000 against.

underlying the solidarity were deep divisions about tactics and about the authority of the labour movement's official leaders. For most of the speakers preceding him had been highly critical of the Labour leadership and the Liberal government, and called for more aggressive action to gain remedial legislation. Shackleton defended the leadership's efforts, which he claimed had been critically hampered by the public expression of dissident personal views from 'prominent men in the Labour movement'. In any case, he said, remedial legislation could come only by way of a government bill – not a private member's bill – and only a Liberal government was likely to concede that. He poured scorn on the idea that the Labour party could insist on such legislation ('40 [parliamentary] members cannot demand in that sense'). The task before them was to win over, not antagonize, Liberal ministers.[28]

Shackleton spoke with a vigour that attracted a number of interjections and, as one report put it, was 'provocative of two "scenes"'.[29] The 'scenes', the interjections and his responses all bespeak anger. In the case of the first 'scene', Shackleton's anger was focused on one man, Stephen Walsh. Walsh was a fellow Labour MP, a Miners' Federation official from Lancashire, who had spoken earlier in the Osborne debate. Shortly before he did so, Shackleton had passed a note asking him either to explain or deny press reports of a speech in which Walsh was said to have disavowed the principle of compulsory political levies, a central pillar of the labour movement's official policy which the Osborne judgement attacked. In his subsequent speech, Walsh echoed the militant approach of most other speakers and expressed total support for the official policy on political levies, but made no reference whatever to the other speech cited in Shackleton's note.[30] Shackleton, when his turn to speak came, was obviously intent on flushing Walsh out. He referred three times to Walsh's reported remarks, before telling Congress of the note he had sent him. It was at this point that Walsh finally took the bait, and interjected.[31] Shackleton, in magisterial fashion, then wrenched publicly from him a lame, but politically adequate, explanation.[32]

The second 'scene' owed less to Shackleton's deliberate intent. 'Our duty', he said towards the end of his Osborne speech, 'is to win [Liberal ministers] to our side.'[33] There was derisive laughter from some delegates. He snapped

---

28. Ibid., pp. 155–7.
29. *Labour Leader*, 23 September 1910.
30. Walsh was later to excuse this omission by explaining that he had received Shackleton's note only 'three minutes before I was called on'. TUC, *Report*, 1910, p. 156.
31. Walsh, it seems, was accident-prone. Lloyd George, in another (but parliamentary) tense situation, also 'trapped Stephen Walsh into allowing a joke to be made at his expense'. Braithwaite, *Lloyd George's Ambulance Wagon*, p. 192.
32. Walsh is reported (though not in the official Congress minutes) to have shouted at Shackleton that he was 'a swashbuckler' – a charge serious enough at the time to draw a defensive comment from the journalist reporting it: 'That is not David's role at all. He had to defend the Parliamentary Committee in his speech.' *Cotton Factory Times*, 23 September 1910.
33. TUC, *Report*, 1910, p. 157.

back: 'Was it wrong when we won the Government to our side on the Taff Vale question, Old Age Pensions, or the Workmen's Compensation Act? We must deal with the opportunities of the moment.' Then, still nettled, he dwelt on the issue of Liberal goodwill: 'I cannot say all that has been said to me privately, but I do know that there is no one who regrets the [Osborne] decision more than prominent members of the Government.' At this point, there was a loud interjection ('Oh, oh!' according to the minutes). 'Ah,' Shackleton retorted, 'that is the scorn of the man whose daily life is spent in vilifying those who do the work.' This remark prompted one delegate, J. Gribble, to seek an explanation as to whether he, Gribble, was the man accused of vilification. When the chairman refused to hear him, Gribble's fury took him down from the gallery of the hall and on to the platform to confront Shackleton, according to the minutes, 'amid the angry cries of Congress in protest at the disorderly scene'.[34] Gribble was suspended from the Congress.

Gribble may not have been the intended target of Shackleton's retort. But his reaction suggests an acute awareness of the implications of one remark in the speech he made earlier in the Osborne debate. For Gribble had accused the Labour parliamentarians of putting more effort into Shackleton's bill on women's suffrage than they did into rectifying the Osborne judgement.[35] This would certainly have stung Shackleton. Even before he made the jibe that triggered the Gribble incident, there had been flashes of testiness in response to doubts cast on the earnestness, experience and knowledge of the Labour parliamentarians.[36] And immediately after making the jibe, he insisted, pointedly, that 'those who do the work' should be trusted.

> The Parliamentary Committee and the Members of the House of Commons know the situation; and ... knowing as much about it as anybody in [this] hall, I say if you will be united and less discourteous than some of you are – you cannot hit a man [the Liberal government] on the face and then ask him to grant you a concession – we shall have more hope of success ... I want you to realise that we are doing our best for you, and [to] give confidence to the men whom you have placed on your Parliamentary Committee and upon your Joint Board.[37]

This issue of leadership authority was raised in a more personalized form by Ben Tillett, the Dockers' Union leader, at a public meeting on the evening following the Osborne debate and Shackleton's defeat on labour exchanges.

---

34.   Ibid.
35.   He also said they had been 'too mild' in their approach to the Liberals, whom they should, instead, have been telling that 'their political carcases would be exterminated' if they did not act on Osborne. Ibid., p. 154.
36.   Thus, to an interjector denying that Labour MPs had done their best, he lashed back with: 'Here is a non-Member of Parliament who knows what is going on better than we do.' To another, whose comment implied that the Conservatives (in government) would be no less likely than the Liberals to concede remedial legislation, he replied: 'Every man in the House of Commons knows it is moonshine to think about it.' Ibid., p. 156.
37.   Ibid., p. 157.

Tillett's career, marked by extreme ideological oscillations, had entered a new phase when he joined the Social Democratic party (formerly 'federation') in 1908. He quickly became one of that party's leading publicists, and the official leaders of the labour movement were his frequent target.[38] At the previous year's Congress, he had crossed swords with Shackleton (then in the chair), who had sent him back to his seat, with his speech undelivered.[39] He spoke in the labour exchanges debate at the 1910 Congress, and would scarcely have endeared himself to Shackleton with his 'I look upon the Labour Exchange as the greatest evil that has befallen us.'[40] At the evening meeting, he condemned Shackleton for being an executive member of the National Chambers of Commerce.[41] His attack was featured in the local newspapers the next day, one report alleging that Tillett had described Shackleton as 'a traitor to the cause of Labour'.[42]

The Congress ended the day after these reports. But instead of being wound up, as usual, by a few remarks from the president, there was a lengthy statement from C. W. Bowerman, the acting secretary, on the subject of Tillett's evening speech. Bowerman described it as 'a vicious and uncalled for attack … upon our good friend Shackleton', an attack which 'I know Mr Shackleton has taken … very much to heart'.[43] Will Thorne, of the Gasworkers' Union and a fellow-member of the Social Democratic party, sprang to Tillett's defence, denying that he used the word, 'traitor'. Bowerman politely pressed the point that a denial from Tillett himself was required. Tillett,

38. In a 1908 pamphlet he described them variously as 'toadies', 'betrayers', 'sheer hypocrites', 'Press flunkeys to Asquith' and 'liars at five and ten guineas a time'. Schneer, *Ben Tillett*, p. 136; Tsuzuki, *Tom Mann*, p. 143.
39. Tillett had interrupted Shackleton's explanation of an assurance from R. B. Haldane, Secretary of State for War, with a shouted: 'Then Mr Haldane is a liar!' Asked to withdraw this remark, Tillett replied: 'I believe that all Cabinet Ministers are liars. They have proved it up to the hilt.' TUC, *Report*, 1909, p. 128.
40. TUC, *Report*, 1910, p. 162.
41. Shackleton's executive membership was not denied. He probably represented the Blackburn chamber, with which he had been associated for some 14 years. This kind of linkage seems to have been common practice in Lancashire (at least in the case of cotton unions), where the chambers appear to have been less decisively employers' organizations than was elsewhere the case. The Blackburn chamber, at the time, had eight unions and one co-operative affiliated to it. Philip Snowden was also a member. See TUC, *Report*, 1910, p. 205; TUC, *Quarterly Report*, December 1910, pp. 59–60.
42. *Sheffield Independent*, 16 September 1910. The other Sheffield daily's report did not include the word, 'traitor', and otherwise provided a more extended account of Tillett's remarks about Shackleton: 'One of the most prominent men in the Trades Union Congress – a member of the [Parliamentary Committee] and associated with a hundred and one "goody-goody" things – was also on … the Executive of the National Chambers of Commerce … It was unfair to the [trade union] movement. Mr Shackleton ought either to declare himself for the working-class movement or to openly and honestly declare himself a masters' man, as he could only be by remaining on the Executive of the National Chambers of Commerce. (Applause.).' *Sheffield Daily Telegraph*, 16 September 1910.
43. TUC, *Report*, 1910, p. 205.

apparently, was not there to give it. Shackleton then made a short speech, his last at a TUC Congress. There was a farewell air about it.

> I have to thank my colleagues personally for the kind things they have said of me … I say unhesitatingly that a gentleman [Tillett] who says I have to choose between the employing class and my own class is making a most unwarrantable statement. I think my own life shows which side I have chosen. Surely a question of this kind ought not to be used to blur the life-work of a man like myself. I know I have the confidence of the Parliamentary Committee and the delegates; and I sincerely hope that what Mr Thorne says is correct, and if it is so, the whole thing is banished from my mind as an unpleasant recollection.[44]

The Congress ended on that note, but not the Tillett incident. The Parliamentary Committee formally asked him for an explanation. After an exchange of correspondence, he explicitly, if grudgingly, denied saying 'traitor'. The committee judged his final response 'not satisfactory',[45] but decided to close the matter and publish the correspondence.[46]

In the week following the Congress, when Tillett and the Parliamentary Committee were having their first exchange of letters, Winston Churchill wrote to Shackleton. Masterman's news, he said, 'makes me anxious to see you'.[47] He suggested an early meeting, but that proved impossible; and they did not meet until 12 October.

Churchill's letter indicated that the minister was prepared to consider the 'change', in the terms of the original offer, which had so dismayed Masterman when Shackleton put it to him in August. Again, the change was not specified, but there can be no doubt of the importance attached to it. For a start, it required the personal attention of the Home Secretary, and would have been the main topic of conversation at the 12 October meeting. More than that, it also required consultation with Lloyd George, Chancellor of the Exchequer, before the matter could be settled.[48] The second letter Churchill wrote to Shackleton was in his own hand. 'I have now seen the Chancellor of the Exchequer & am in a position to offer you definitely the appointment we talked over last week on terms which will I am sure be satisfactory to all parties.'[49]

Shackleton's reply to Churchill, accepting the position, is dated 23 October.[50] For another three weeks, overtly at least, he remained as deeply

---

44. Ibid.
45. TUC, *PC Minutes*, 13 October 1910.
46. See TUC, *Quarterly Report*, December 1910, pp. 58–60.
47. Churchill to Shackleton, 22 September 1910: SP.
48. The most unusual aspect of Shackleton's appointment (see below) was the size and personal nature of his salary. This would certainly have required special dispensation from the Treasury; and who best to obtain that from than a supple Chancellor?
49. Churchill to Shackleton, 22 October 1910: SP.
50. There is a copy of this letter, and of each of Shackleton's subsequent letters – all of them highly formal – relating to this appointment, in the Shackleton Papers. But there are no copies of his earlier letters, apart from the one of 26 August. In particular, there is no copy of the criti-

immersed as before in the affairs of the labour movement.[51] His appointment as Senior Labour Adviser to the Home Office was announced on 12 November, two days after the Liberal Cabinet opted for a December general election. He took up the post on 1 December.

Public Reactions

Appointing a trade union official to a permanent government post was not in itself unusual. There was a 30-year history to such appointments,[52] and the Asquith government had already made many, especially in the course of staffing the new state labour exchanges.[53] But Shackleton's was a special case because of his eminence. No previous appointee had come anywhere near matching his credentials as a senior member of the parliamentary Labour party and acknowledged leader of the trade unions at large. His prominence ensured that the appointment was the source not merely of interest, but of lively controversy within the labour movement – and not only in Britain. On the Continent, Eduard Bernstein was among those who entered into the discussion.[54]

Labour sensitivities on the general issue had been exposed a year or two earlier, following widespread press reports that Arthur Henderson, then chairman of the parliamentary party, had accepted a civil service post. According to the *Labour Leader*, these reports generated 'deep anxiety' in the party and the unions, and Henderson had been 'besieged with telegrams of inquiry'.[55] When the July rumour of a Home Office appointment for

cal letter he wrote in mid-August proposing the 'change', as Masterman called it, which brought Churchill into the negotiations. Shackleton, a most methodical man, would certainly have kept copies originally.

51.   As is suggested by Ramsay MacDonald's diary entry for 27 October 1910: 'The Joint Board launched its resolution on Osborne ... The manifesto ... was drafted by me at an Express Dairy & read to Shackleton & Henderson. They made suggestions & then we took it & got it unanimously ... carried'. *Diary*, vol. 1, p. 4, PRO 30/69/1753/1. On 31 October, Shackleton wrote to MacDonald about the parliamentary party chairmanship, advising a more cautious approach than he had adopted in February, and suggesting a 'quiet chat' on the matter. He also suggested the Joint Board should meet about Osborne on 9 November. PRO 30/69/1154 69951. On 10 November, he occupied the chair at a conference on Osborne in the Caxton Hall, Westminster, and the following day led a deputation to the Prime Minister on the issue. See *Daily News*, 11 November 1910; *Cotton Factory Times*, 11 November 1910.

52.   See Martin, *TUC*, pp. 31, 61, 105.

53.   See Halévy, *Rule of Democracy*, pp. 446–7. Shackleton, as already mentioned, was a member of the committee that made the bulk of these appointments; but that position had been 'of an honorary and temporary' nature. TUC, *Report*, 1909, p. 169.

54.   In an article entitled 'The Democratization of England and the Shackleton Case', Bernstein seems effectively to have supported Shackleton's decision. See *Labour Leader*, 30 December 1910.

55.   *Labour Leader*, 3 April 1908. Shackleton himself, fighting his last general election, was the subject of a similar rumour about 'an important post in connection with the proposed Labour Exchanges'. *Lancashire Daily Post*, 23 December 1909. But this story, probably inspired by Clitheroe Conservatives, appears to have had a relatively restricted circulation.

Shackleton was confirmed in November, such 'anxiety' might well have turned to anger, especially given the identity of the Home Secretary seen as suborning the lost leader. For November 1910 was the month in which Churchill, in the context of a Rhondda Valley coal strike and a riot or two in the village of Tonypandy, first entered Labour mythology as a minister eager to use troops against strikers.[56]

Unsurprisingly, official and public reactions to Shackleton's appointment were mostly supportive. Congratulatory resolutions were carried on appropriate trade union bodies, such as the executives of the TUC and the Weavers' Amalgamation. Outside the labour movement, the *Northern Daily Telegraph* struck a common editorial note by citing the advantage of having a 'practical' man as Home Office adviser, and describing Shackleton as 'the ideal man for the post'.[57]

Unsurprisingly, too, the most vigorous public condemnation came from the neighbourhood of the Social Democratic party. One spokesman, professing to be 'absolutely paralysed' at the news that Shackleton had 'gone over to the enemy', predictably charged him with 'betraying the trust of the workers'.[58] Another, more thoughtfully, said Shackleton had 'deserted the Labour party at its most troublesome moment'.[59] Ben Tillett, however, capped them both with a remarkably venomous article, entitled 'The Passing of David Shackleton'.[60]

Among leading members of the ILP, recorded reactions were more mixed and, when critical, more restrained. Keir Hardie, in response to an interjection ('What about Shackleton?'), held the line at an Accrington meeting. He argued that the administration of factory laws was better done by a man who had worked in the mill, rather than 'some duke's son from Oxford', and described Shackleton as 'just the man that was wanted for the job'.[61] Philip Snowden, strongly supportive in a column he wrote for the *Nelson Leader*, was privately so, as well, in a warm letter responding to Shackleton's congratulations on Snowden's re-election.[62] J. R. Clynes, responding to a similar letter of congratulation, simply said that 'I do not share the view some few have expressed re your acceptance.'[63] Bruce Glasier, on the other hand, was one of the 'few'. 'The acceptance by Shackleton', he wrote to a confidant, 'wont [sic] help our Party. Tis not playing the game.'[64] Glasier's successor in the editor's chair at the *Labour Leader* aired his disquiet more publicly.

56. But, on this occasion at least, Labour plainly got Churchill wrong. See Gilbert, *Churchill*, pp. 219–21; Pelling, *Winston Churchill*, pp. 136–7.
57. *Northern Daily Telegraph*, 12 November 1910.
58. *Nelson Leader*, 18 November 1910.
59. *Colne & Nelson Times*, 25 November 1910.
60. See *Justice*, 19 November 1910.
61. *Northern Daily Telegraph*, 14 November 1910.
62. *Nelson Leader*, 9 December 1910; Snowden to Shackleton, 15 December 1910: SP.
63. Clynes to Shackleton, 12 December 1910: SP.
64. Glasier to Anderson, 16 November 1910: Glasier Coll., I.1.1910/4.

Churchill's offer was undeniably a tribute to both Shackleton and the Labour party, but Shackleton's acceptance of it was a different matter. For 'the test of Labour stalwarts' was that they recognized the gulf between Liberal and Labour, 'in action as well as in thought', and at the end of the day were 'prepared to remain in the firing line and stick to their guns'.[65] The editor of the *Socialist Review*, the ILP's theoretical journal, had less reason to pull his punches. Shackleton's acceptance not only limited his ability to help 'his people' and ignored his 'obligation to the Party', but 'impoverished the movement' and 'cheapened the dignity of the working-class leader'.[66]

Others in the labour movement, outside the Socialists' ranks, tended to be a little more forgiving. In Lancashire – as Peter Clarke has observed, with specific reference to Shackleton's case – the general rule was that 'the ethic of the cotton unions accepted such defections without bitterness'.[67] Certainly, among the party faithful in the Clitheroe division, Shackleton seems to have had a good deal of support. On the day of the official announcement, he was 'heartily cheered and congratulated' as he entered the hall at a Labour party social in Padiham;[68] and similar responses were reported at other gatherings he attended in the fortnight or so before taking up the post.

The opposition, actual or foreseen, was nevertheless weighty enough to persuade Shackleton's supporters that a formal defence was advisable. On the heels of the official announcement, the Clitheroe Labour party executive made three points in a statement designed, it said, to avoid 'misunderstanding'. First, the office was 'not a political one'; second, it was 'infinitely better' to have it filled by a man of Shackleton's background rather than 'a University man, or the son of a Peer'; and, third, Shackleton's 'usefulness' in the position 'will be so great to the country that it would be selfish to study the interests of the [Clitheroe] Division before those of the general community'.[69] A week later, it was the turn of the Weavers' Amalgamation executive. The chairman of a public meeting, organized by the ILP's Nelson branch, delayed introducing the guest speaker in order to enable F. Constantine 'to make an explanation' on the executive's behalf. Constantine began by saying there was a need to correct 'certain statements' that were circulating, and then he put the responsibility for Shackleton's decision squarely on the shoulders of the weavers' executive:

> Some four or five months ago, Mr Shackleton had [been asked] to take up this office. For some time [he] considered the matter privately, but eventually ... decided to leave [it] in the hands of the Amalgamated Society of Weavers. For two months the executive ... had known of the offer ... After seriously considering the matter, [it] decided that Mr Shackleton could continue his work in a broader

65. *Labour Leader*, 18 November 1910.
66. Quoted in unknown newspaper, n.d.: SP.
67. Clarke, *Lancashire and the New Liberalism*, p. 94.
68. *Northern Daily Telegraph*, 14 November 1910.
69. *Colne & Nelson Times*, 18 November 1910.

sphere and to better advantage by accepting the position ... [The executive wanted the members of the audience] to explain to their friends that Mr Shackleton had been straight and above-board, and if he had done wrong he had done what the committee of the Amalgamation had told him.[70]

Shackleton himself, in the speeches that he made at this time, was equally defensive. More than once, he begged his audience 'to disabuse their minds of any idea that he had gone over to the enemy'.[71] His sympathies, he reminded them, were 'entirely with the working people because he was one of them',[72] and he spoke of 'the useful work ... [for] the working people' that the new post would enable.[73] He also described the job offer as 'an honour ... to the cotton trade', as well as to himself.[74] Above all, however, he echoed and re-echoed Constantine's point: 'it was only upon the advice of the Executive of the Weavers' Amalgamation that he decided to accept the post'.[75]

Shackleton's Motives

The public record sheds little direct light on the reasons Shackleton had for preferring the obscurity of a civil service career to his fame as the leading trade union official-cum-parliamentarian of his day.[76] The only motives implied in his own public statements were totally worthy – an open desire to be more 'useful', than he already was, to the workers' cause, and a half-hinted

70. *Nelson Leader*, 25 November 1910. In this report of Constantine's address, to 'a large audience', 'hear, hear' and 'applause' are frequent interpolations, especially towards its end – and especially in relation to remarks in praise of Shackleton.
71. *Colne & Nelson Times*, 2 December 1910.
72. Ibid.
73. *Cotton Factory Times*, 2 December 1910.
74. *Ibid*. Much later, he was reported as saying that he 'would have wronged ... the textile operatives if he had declined the honour'. Ibid., 4 August 1911.
75. *Colne & Nelson Times*, 2 December 1910. The Clitheroe Labour party executive, significantly, was altogether ignored in this respect. The bad taste this left is indicated by a resolution of the Clitheroe party's 1911 conference which specified that if the local MP was offered 'an appointment as a Civil Servant or a Government official, he should be asked to consult the Labour party in the division before accepting'. *Cotton Factory Times*, 24 February 1911.
76. Churchill's motives are less problematic. As President of the Board of Trade in 1908–09, he had acquired a taste for highly publicized interventions in major industrial disputes (see Gilbert, *Churchill*, pp. 195, 199–200, 205) – an area in which Lloyd George, who had acquired the same taste at the Board of Trade, was his principal ministerial competitor. Churchill's creation of the labour adviser post could be represented (as it was, for example, in the *Nelson Leader* of 18 November 1910) as a reclaiming of the Home Office's original jurisdiction which had been eroded in favour of the Board of Trade and the Local Government Board. Recruiting Shackleton, given his prominence, would have been a great coup in this connection. In addition, it had the advantage of weakening the Labour party's parliamentary presence. One indication of the importance Churchill attached to recruiting him is the unusual salary settled on (see below). Churchill, in any case, appears to have thought highly of him. See Gilbert, *Evolution of National Insurance in Great Britain*, p. 256n.

belief that he should bow to the will of the Weavers' Amalgamation executive. But neither carries much conviction, especially given that the potential
for 'useful' work was confined to a quite limited, and mostly technical, area
fixed by the nature of the Home Office's jurisdiction.

His enemies, of course, saw money as the motive. He expressly denied this,
as Constantine carefully recounted in his defence at the Nelson public meeting: 'Mr Shackleton had pointed out [to the weavers' executive] that he had
had many tempting offers before, more tempting from a financial standpoint
than the present one, but he had always tried to consider the workers first.'[77]
There is, however, no doubt that money was of great importance. Following
his appointment, and after 'much speculation',[78] it was revealed that his starting salary amounted to £500 a year, rising to £700 by annual increments of
£20. These were princely sums by the standards of Shackleton's people.[79] The
terms were also well in advance of those offered previous union appointees.[80]
But what was even more remarkable was a fact not publicly revealed until
four months later, when the Home Office estimates were tabled in parliament. For the terms were personal to Shackleton. Any subsequent occupant
of his position would receive an initial salary of just £300, rising to £400 by
increments of £15. There was a 'good deal of curiosity', one journalist noted
at the time, 'as to the reason for fixing Mr Shackleton's salary at such a ...
high figure'.[81] The surviving correspondence with Masterman and Churchill
suggests that this figure, or something like it, was probably Shackleton's
price – a price that he put on himself in the demand which upset Masterman,
and required the personal attention of both the Home Secretary and the
Chancellor of the Exchequer.[82]

---

77. *Nelson Leader*, 25 November 1910. Interestingly, Philip Snowden expressly and publicly
rejected this motive as well. 'It is no financial consideration which has induced a man like Mr
Shackleton to leave the attractions of a political career for the obscurity of an official position ...
Mr Shackleton's motives ... are that he believes he can be more useful than in the position he
has filled so ably in the past.' Ibid., 9 December 1910.
78. *Colne & Nelson Times*, 2 December 1910.
79. They put him, according to a contemporary study of income and social class, into the cat-
egory of those heading business firms, filling the professions, and occupying administrative
positions, who were usually the product of secondary or public schools and the universities. G.
F. D'Aeth, 'Present Tendencies of Class Differentiation', *Sociological Review*, October 1910, cited
in Waites, *Class Society at War*, pp. 77–8.
80. At the time, it was thought that, at the Board of Trade, C. J. Drummond might earn as
much as £500, and I. H. Mitchell and D. C. Cummings between £300 and £400. Richard Bell, as
head of the state labour exchange system, certainly had a salary of £400. *Northern Daily Telegraph*,
12 November 1910; see also Halévy, *Rule of Democracy*, p. 446.
81. *Blackburn Times*, 25 March 1911.
82. One of Churchill's letters to Masterman provides the most suggestive indication of this
(though it also implies that there was more to it that just the money): 'You [Masterman] should
tell Lloyd George what you have told me about Shackleton ... [It] is very hard that a man's own
virtues and qualities should ... condemn him to the sordid anxieties of Labour politics ... The
incident is one of the strongest practical arguments for payment of Members [of parliament] that
I have ever seen.' Churchill to Masterman, 10 September 1910: Masterman Papers.

If the money was important, so would have been the security associated with it. Shackleton is unlikely to have felt insecure about his tenure of either the union presidency or the parliamentary seat, on which his income (total unknown) then depended. Moreover, unlike most other Labour MPs,[83] his financial position was not threatened by the Osborne judgement because the Clitheroe party had already accumulated sufficient funds 'to support a member for years to come'.[84] On the other hand, at the age of 47, a prudent Shackleton could not have failed to consider the future security promised by an appointment which (in the word of the formal letter of offer) was 'pensionable'.[85] It was to be all of three decades before the cotton unions began to 'provide reasonably' for their retiring officials.[86]

It is possible that money and security are all there was to Shackleton's decision. There were many, like Ben Tillett, who had no doubt about it. But that seems a little too simplistic an explanation in the case of someone who gave every sign of relishing his public position as a man of affairs, a notable in the land.[87] Moreover, the circumstances of the time – as they touched Shackleton's concerns – suggest two other considerations that may well have influenced his decision. One has to do with the way the future presented itself to him; the other with his valuation of the life he was living.

By August 1910, when the negotiations with Masterman opened, the labour movement was widely seen as facing a tempestuous and uncertain future. The glow of the Labour party's early successes had long since faded. Shackleton's personal triumph in the January elections served only to highlight the poor showing of the party at large. There was not the slightest sign of the parliamentary advance he had spoken of so hopefully in 1908, let alone of Labour supplanting the Liberals.[88] In the bleak political climate of 1910, it is possible that he ceased to believe in the party as a credible electoral alternative to the Liberals – perhaps even to have doubts about it as a tolerable ideological alternative.

The industrial prospect was, if anything, worse for a man who had preferred leadership of the TUC to leadership of the parliamentary party.

---

83. By October 1910, some 20 major unions (as well as the railways union, Osborne's original target) were subject to injunctions debarring expenditures and compulsory levies for political purposes, including the Weavers' Amalgamation and all but one of the other cotton amalgamations. *Cotton Factory Times*, 21 October 1910. The Labour party claimed to be 'severely handicapped' by these injunctions in the December general election. Clegg et al., *History of British Trade Unions*, vol. 1, p. 419. See also Wrigley in Brown, *First Labour Party*, pp. 146–7.

84. *Nelson Leader*, 18 November 1910. Shackleton, in any case, was publicly confident that state payment of MPs was 'coming ... very soon'. *Labour Leader*, 28 October 1910. He was right. Legislation providing an annual salary of £400 for MPs was enacted in 1911.

85. E. Troup to Shackleton, 7 November 1910: SP.

86. Turner, *Trade Union Growth, Structure, and Policy*, p. 322.

87. See Chapter 10.

88. See Brown, *First Labour Party*, pp. 1–2, 29–30; McKibbin, *Evolution of the Labour Party*, p. 13; Wilson, *Downfall of the Liberal Party*, p. 17.

Stoppages, on the rise since 1907, soared during 1910. It was the start, and widely seen so at the time,[89] of the 'storm of strikes' that raged up to the outbreak of the Great War.[90] And the cotton industry was not immune. The weavers, later to play a prominent part in the storm,[91] were already showing signs of being 'infected with the labour unrest'.[92] Moreover, while the swelling tide of worker militancy was largely a response to declining real wages,[93] it embodied as well an anti-leadership element, fostered by a surge in the popularity of syndicalist ideas, which often prompted strikes in defiance of union officials. A 'good part of the trade union world', as a contemporary journalist put it, 'deserted its chiefs' in this sense during 1910.[94] It was a trend that Shackleton certainly detested. For he had a thoroughly elitist vision of the relations that ought to exist between union leaders and their members.[95] And underlying his disquiet on this score, in 1910, there would have been the humiliating memory of the way his own members had earlier rejected him in the ballot on the half-timer issue.[96]

With deeply troubled times ahead, the party at its lowest ebb, and trade union officialdom plagued by revolts from below, it may well have seemed to Shackleton that the labour movement was going to the dogs. In these circumstances, his frame of mind would not have been improved by an unremitting workload.

House of Commons business, and related meetings, still took up much of his time after 1907. He maintained close touch with the party faithful in his electorate, and that required some effort because the Clitheroe Labour party boasted no less than 19 branches by 1909.[97] Another local responsibility that

89.   Thus James Cornthwaite, writing in the *Sunday Chronicle* (18 September 1910) about leading trade unionists – including Shackleton – under the headline of 'Some of the Men Who Will Figure in the Coming Industrial Strife', ended with a reference to 'the great Labour war which is threatening the land'.

90.   Cole and Postgate, *Common People*, p. 486.

91.   See White, *Limits of Trade Union Militancy*, p. 34.

92.   Price, *Labour in British Society*, p. 145.

93.   See Clarke, *Lancashire and the New Liberalism*, p. 98.

94.   Unknown newspaper, n.d. (November 1910): SP. This was arrestingly demonstrated in the first big strike of 1910 (it opened the year) when more than a third of the coalminers in Northumberland and Durham went out in the face of their union leadership's vehement opposition, many staying out for three months. See Dangerfield, *Strange Death of Liberal England*, p. 195.

95.   Thus the first principle of collective bargaining, he told the TUC's annual Congress, was that the rank and file should 'place confidence' in their officials, as the 'best informed' about bargaining possibilities, and allow them 'plenary powers'. TUC, *Report*, 1908, p. 53.

96.   His sensitivity on the point was exposed at the 1909 Labour party conference. George Bernard Shaw called out 'Shame!' when Shackleton referred to the half-timer ballot. Shackleton snapped back: 'Those of us who are doing our best to educate the workers ought not to be sneered at.' *Labour Leader*, 5 February 1909. Shaw later claimed his target had really been 'the parents' who voted against Shackleton's advice. *Cotton Factory Times*, 5 February 1909.

97.   *Ibid.*, 10 December 1910.

114   The Lancashire Giant

ate into his time was his membership of the magistrates' bench.[98] He often spoke (outside as well as inside Lancashire) on temperance, free trade and other platforms – as at the Co-operative movement's national 'festivals' and London meetings of the Labour Co-partnership Association, whose platform he usually shared with Arthur Balfour. But his core responsibilities arose from the leading role he played in the TUC, the Weavers' Amalgamation and the Textile Factory Workers' Association – which involved, as well as more solitary administrative activities, a continual round of meetings with other union officials, dealings with employers, deputations to ministers, and addresses to local gatherings of union members. Ancillary responsibilities took their toll. There was government work, like the time-consuming Home Office inquiry into humidity in weaving sheds, and the three-man selection committee that was 'stormed and inundated with applications' for posts in the new labour exchanges.[99] On behalf of the British Cotton Growing Association (see Chapter 4), of which he was president by 1910, he regularly attended monthly meetings at the Colonial Office.[100] And two significant sources of responsibility had to do with working women and working-class education.

Shackleton remained treasurer of the Women's Trade Union League (see Chapter 4) until he left the labour movement, chairing the league's annual conference, and speaking at its major demonstrations. During this time, while he often took pride in the early and distinctive achievement of equal pay for female cotton weavers,[101] the organizational standing of women did not noticeably improve within either the Weavers' Amalgamation[102] or the

98.   In 1906 (having resigned from the Accrington bench on entering parliament in 1902) he was appointed to the Darwen bench. He resigned from that when he shifted his family to Manchester in 1908, but was reinstated when they moved back to Darwen in 1910. From 1908, as well, he was 'a county J.P.'. Ibid., 10 April 1908.

99.   *Labour Leader*, 24 September 1909.

100.   *Cotton Factory Times*, 9 December 1910. *Nelson Leader*, 6 May 1910.

101.   Thus, from an Ipswich platform, he said: 'Some of the girls in the Ipswich factories would be astonished that in ordinary times in Lancashire girls from 18 would be earning anything from 18s. to 30s. a week – (murmurs of surprise).' *Nelson Leader*, 10 September 1909.

102.   When two women were elected to the Blackburn weavers' executive in 1911, the *Cotton Factory Times* (22 September 1911) recalled that the Oldham weavers 'for years' had a woman as president and others on its executive, while the executives of the Bolton, Stockport, Glossop and Manchester unions, for 'many years', had also 'to a certain extent, [been] "manned" by women'. A 1914 survey seems to have uncovered other cases, but produced the 'almost certain' conclusion that most weavers' executives consisted wholly of males. White, *Limits of Trade Union Militancy*, p. 53. There seem to have been no full-time women officials, with a possible exception in the case of an exclusively female weavers' union, founded in Salford in 1902, as an offshoot of the radical wing of the suffragist movement. See Liddington and Norris, *One Hand Tied Behind Us*, p. 241 It persistently refused to join the Weavers' Amalgamation, which set up a rival, mixed union in 1907. Both local unions seem to have collapsed during the war. See White, *Limits of Trade Union Militancy*, pp. 53–5. In the meantime, for example, a 1905 meeting of the amalgamation's general council was reported to consist of 'some 480 delegates from the various districts (including half-a-dozen lady representatives)'. *Cotton Factory Times*, 26 May 1905.

TUC.[103] On the other hand, it was only after he became president of the amalgamation that it took two decisions of considerable importance to the Women's Trade Union League. First, it wholly financed an extra league organizer to work in the sweated trades, outside cotton manufacturing.[104] Then it abandoned the policy of local union affiliation to the league, and formally affiliated on its own account – with the result that the league could claim, for the first time, to represent 'practically all the organised women workers in the country'.[105]

Shackleton's commitment to working-class education cut more deeply into his time. Early links with the Workers' Educational Association (see Chapter 4) were strengthened when he became the association's national vice-chairman, and chairman of its Lancashire-based branch. He joined the governing body of Ruskin College[106] – and on its behalf negotiated with discontented students in 1908, and again in 1909 when they declared a 'strike' in protest at the dismissal of the Marxian college principal, Dennis Hird.[107] In 1907, Shackleton was appointed both to the central Board of Education's national consultative committee, and to the vice-chairmanship of an Oxford-established 'joint committee' investigating university-level courses for working people.[108] Subsequently, he was vice-chairman of the Oxford body administering a scheme of 'tutorial classes', and chairman of a similar body

103. At the 1908 Congress, attended by 518 delegates, the number of women delegates was unusually large – at seven. *Cotton Factory Times*, 11 September 1908. Not one of the seven was from the Weavers' Amalgamation, the union with the largest female membership in the country. Between 1901 and 1906, the weavers sent, all told, just six women delegates to Congress. They did not send another until 1910, and one more in 1912 – a grand total of eight for the period 1901–14, in which there were a total of 125 male weavers' delegates. See White, *Limits of Trade Union Militancy*, p. 233.
104. *Cotton Factory Times*, 26 October 1906.
105. Women's Trade Union League, *34th Annual Report*, 1909: Tuckwell Coll. Shackleton's strong support is at least partially explained by the fact that the league and its secretary, Mary MacArthur, were often at odds with the radical wing of the suffragist movement which was particularly strong in Lancashire. See Liddington and Norris, *One Hand Tied Behind Us*, pp. 240–1.
106. Originally known as Ruskin Hall, the college was set up in Oxford, but outside the university's structure, by an American philanthropist on the occasion of John Ruskin's eightieth birthday in February 1899, with the aim of catering for resident working-class students. After the desertion of its founder and benefactor in 1902, the college survived on contributions from trade unions, co-operative societies, and a variety of private donors, many of them noble. See Yorke, *Ruskin College*; and Craik, *Central Labour College*. Shackleton was instrumental in ensuring that the Weavers' Amalgamation provided, from 1906, three annual college scholarships. See *Cotton Factory Times*, 26 October 1906.
107. See Yorke, *Ruskin College*, p. 31; Simon, *Education and the Labour Movement*, pp. 318ff. The strike leaders were reported as saying that Shackleton was 'as much out of sympathy with [their] educational views … as with their views on political questions'. *Colne & Nelson Times*, 9 April 1909.
108. The joint committee's report drew heavily on pioneering courses taught in Rochdale and Longton by a young R. H. Tawney, under the auspices of the WEA and the Oxford University Extension. See Stocks, *Workers' Educational Association*, pp. 38–41.

at the University of Manchester when that university, along with others, followed Oxford's example.[109]

It is most unlikely that the weight of this workload was, in itself, a factor in Shackleton's decision to go to the Home Office. He was not one to shy away from work, his health was excellent, his stamina considerable, and he paced himself (see Chapter 10). But the workload might have been a consideration if he had come to re-evaluate its worth – if, in other words, he had begun to sense less reward and more frustration in it, and so lost zest for the fight intrinsic to his life as politician and trade union leader.

S. G. Hobson, a contemporary, had Shackleton specifically in mind when he subsequently wrote on the question of union officials accepting civil service appointments.[110] Although no friend of 'the official Labour leader' (as he described Shackleton's kind),[111] and especially contemptuous of those who accepted government preferment,[112] Hobson nevertheless displayed some understanding of their world when he referred to 'the strenuous impotence of Labour politics',[113] and acknowledged that they suffered from 'too many goads and too little security'.[114] By mid-1910, with the heady, hopeful days of 1906 long gone, Shackleton may well have felt something like a sense of impotence, especially when confronted with the swelling tide of rank-and-file disaffection. Perhaps, too, the 'goads' became less tolerable than they once were. Certainly, in September, his Congress demeanour suggested, on past performance, a man who was unusually touchy.[115] Moreover, to judge from his reactions and words at the Congress, what riled him had mostly to do with a feeling that his and his colleagues' efforts, judgement, experience and integrity were not being fairly appreciated.

The workload, in these circumstances, could well have become irksome, a source of resentment. If so, that would certainly have enhanced the attraction of the Home Office option. For Shackleton, more likely than not, would have shared Hobson's commonplace view that it was an option offering 'the ordered ease of the Civil Servant'.[116] The contrast was with 'the uneasy life of

109.   See Mansbridge, *University Tutorial Classes*, p. 35. Shackleton, revealingly, ended his presidential address to the TUC's 1909 Congress with a lengthy and enthusiastic account of his work with 'the University men at Oxford' on the tutorial classes scheme. TUC, *Report*, 1909, p. 50.

110.   Hobson did not actually name Shackleton in an early treatment of the topic, which first appeared in a 1912 article and was republished in a 1914 book. But in a later discussion, published in 1920, he cited Shackleton's as the major case. See Hobson, *National Guilds and the State*, p. 231.

111.   Hobson, *National Guilds*, p. 219.

112.   He referred to them as 'the reactionary or obese Labour officials'. *National Guilds and the State*, p. 232. Shackleton, it is to be noted, was a very large man.

113.   *National Guilds*, p. 219.

114.   *National Guilds and the State*, p. 232.

115.   And not only on the Congress floor, according to Clegg et al., who record that he 'had shown signs of irritation with his colleagues behind the scenes [as well as] publicly with the delegates'. *History of British Trade Unions*, vol. 1, p. 422.

116.   Hobson, *National Guilds*, p. 219.

the politician' which, as C. P. Scott was to tell him years later, Shackleton escaped from when he left the labour movement.[117] The chances are that this is much the way Shackleton himself saw things at the time.

---

117.   Scott to Shackleton, 19 December 1925: SP.

8

The Civil Servant, 1910–1925

The post of Senior Labour Adviser, which Shackleton took up in December 1910, was formally concerned with the administration of the Factory Acts. A Junior Labour Adviser position, concerned with mines, was created at the same time, and was variously reported as having been offered to William ('Mabon') Abraham, William Brace and Thomas Richards, all both MPs and Welsh mining union officials; but no appointment was ever made.[1] As it happened, the investigation of a mine explosion which killed 350 men in Christmas week, at the Pretoria pit outside Bolton, was one of Shackleton's earliest official tasks. Otherwise, his Home Office activities largely escaped the public eye.

Early in the New Year, he was appointed to an interdepartmental committee of inquiry into 'shuttle-kissing' in weaving sheds.[2] The committee issued its report some 15 months later, and then identified him as 'Late Senior Labour Adviser'.[3] In the meantime, he was recorded as being present when the Home Secretary received a TUC deputation, and as playing a mediating role in negotiations about the Brooklands agreement which had governed collective bargaining in cotton spinning since 1893.[4] On the other hand, in all but one of the big strikes that flared during the summer of 1911, he seems to have played no part whatsoever. Government attempts at mediating these strikes, apart from isolated interventions by the Prime Minister and the Chancellor of the Exchequer, were handled almost entirely by the Board of Trade, acting especially through George Askwith, a civil servant. One of the strikes Askwith helped settle was the Liverpool transport strike. This, while not the largest, was the most violent of that summer's disputes. Askwith arrived in Liverpool, however, some days after the most serious incidents occurred, being engaged elsewhere by a national railway strike. He had been

1. See *Cotton Factory Times*, 8 July 1910; *Northern Daily Telegraph*, 17 November 1910. The salary was fixed at the lower rate (£300, rising to £400 by increments of £15) to which the senior post was to revert when Shackleton left it. See Chapter 7.
2. The standard shuttle used in cotton weaving required the weft (thread) to be sucked, by mouth, through the eye of the shuttle, an act which a weaver performed up to 500 times a day. Moreover, each weaver's shuttle was repeatedly 'kissed' by one or more others in the course of a working day.
3. *Report*, 1912, Cd. 6184.
4. *Cotton Factory Times*, 24 February 1911; 15 September 1911.

preceded by a three-man Home Office commission, including Shackleton,[5] which Askwith credited with having done valuable work.[6] But when the strike ended, it was Askwith alone who was celebrated in the slums of Liverpool,[7] in the columns of *The Times*[8] – and later in the account of the historian.[9]

A few days after the Liverpool strike ended, Shackleton was sitting on the platform at the TUC's annual Congress. It was the first time the Home Office had been represented by an official observer, though the Board of Trade had been sending observers since 1893. He heard glowing references to himself in the presidential address, and later witnessed a lengthy and heated debate on a resolution condemning the Parliamentary Committee for inviting the Home Office and the Board of Trade to send observers to the Congress.[10] This resolution, inspired principally by resentment at the outcome of Churchill's recent enthusiasm for deploying troops in strike centres,[11] was defeated (by 262 to 70) on a show of hands.[12] That was in September.

In October, Churchill left the Home Office to become First Lord of the Admiralty. Within weeks, it was announced that Shackleton was moving to the new National Health Insurance Commission for England.[13] Churchill's successor as Home Secretary assured parliament that Shackleton would be replaced, and that there was no intention of allowing the labour adviser position to lapse.[14] Arthur Henderson may have been approached about it, because he went out of his way to make it known that 'he is not a candidate for the office'.[15] Despite the minister's assurance, Shackleton was never replaced.

5.   The other members, both MPs, were T. P. O'Connor and Colonel Kyffin-Taylor.

6.   As he said at the time: 'I came here ... last night, and have had little to do with making peace. I had interviews with the Lord Mayor and ... the chairman of the [employers' body], and afterwards with various representatives of the men ... All the work that may have been done in calming the riots and smoothing the angry feelings among the people has been the work during a long time of the Commissioners appointed by the Home Secretary.' *The Times*, 25 August 1911. He was equally generous in a later, more considered account of this episode. See his *Industrial Problems and Disputes*, p. 171.

7.   '"Askwith!" – the name ran down the streets – "a man from London, sent by the government! He settled it! He told the bosses!" People gabbled it out again and again, overjoyed at the news.' Roberts, *Classic Slum*, p. 73.

8.   *The Times*, 25 August 1911.

9.   See Clegg, *History of British Trade Unions*, vol. II, pp. 36–9.

10.   See TUC, *Report*, 1911, pp. 150–5.

11.   See, e.g., Hikins, 'Liverpool General Transport Strike, 1911', p. 188.

12.   This vote was followed immediately by the passage of a resolution protesting against the Home Secretary's 'unwarrantable use of the military', and demanding an inquiry into 'the excesses committed by the police and military, notably at Liverpool and Llanelly'. TUC, *Report*, 1911, p. 155.

13.   Clegg et al. give no source for their assertion that Shackleton had originally accepted the Home Office post 'with a view to becoming National Insurance Commissioner in the following year'. *History of British Trade Unions*, vol. 1, p. 422. Nor do they indicate why such a stratagem should have been thought necessary.

14.   *Parl. Debs.*, 30 November 1911, vol. 32, col. 588.

15.   *Nelson Leader*, 1 December 1911.

From the first day of 1912, Lloyd George's innovative health-insurance scheme was the focus of Shackleton's working life for the better part of the next three years.[16] His salary doubled, to £1000 a year,[17] which brought him up to the income level of the 'top civil servants' and, decisively, into the ranks of Booth's and Rowntrees' 'servant-keeping class'.[18] He became, as is clear from the surviving minutes of the National Health Insurance Commission (England), the commission's principal liaison with the unions, many of which were directly involved in the scheme's administration.[19] But he also played a very active part in the broader publicity campaign, in dealings with employers, and in general administrative matters such as the formulation of rules and regulations.

The outbreak of the First World War changed his focus but not, initially, his official position. Like most in the labour movement, he was fervently pro-war. At the end of 1914, he visited a number of industrial centres to assess the response of workers to the army recruitment campaign, and reportedly 'found everywhere a fine patriotic feeling among the responsible representatives of the working classes'.[20] Following the momentous 'Treasury conference' of March 1915, at which Lloyd George secured an initial union agreement to the 'dilution' of craft restrictions in munitions production, it was Shackleton who represented the government in negotiations with the cotton unions and employers about steps 'to release more men from the cotton trade' for munitions work and the army.[21] About this time, too, he was on a commission that investigated conditions in French munitions factories. Later in 1915 a journalist, writing for the metropolitan press, provided an indication of an eyes-and-ears-of-government role:

> No man in London is more intimately acquainted with the views ... of the textile workers in Lancashire than Mr D. J. Shackleton ... He has recently revisited the cotton districts of the county ... He tells me he found the operatives very keen for the war. Radicals of former times ... have caught the flame of self-sacrificing enthusiasm for victory ... excepting in the Blackburn district, where some followers of Mr Philip Snowden are the isolated exceptions.[22]

On the other hand, returning from the TUC's annual Congress a little later, he showed he was no jingo when he emphasized 'the strength and sincerity'

16. During 1913-14 he was also a member of a major royal commission into the railways.
17. The position, on the other hand, was for a fixed (but renewable) term of five years and, unlike his Home Office position, 'will not carry any title to a pension'. Treasury to Chairman, Insurance Commission, 30 December 1911: MH 78/37/3846.
18. Perkin, *Rise of Professional Society*, pp. 78, 91–2.
19. This, of course, was his intended role. 'Lloyd George proceeded upon the basis of conciliating the interests; thus there was a doctor to represent doctors, Lister Stead to represent the Friendly Societies, T. Neill to represent Industrial Insurance, D. J. Shackleton for the Trade Unions, Mona Wilson for the women.' Braithwaite, *Lloyd George's Ambulance Wagon*, p. 261.
20. *Nelson Leader*, 11 December 1914.
21. Ibid., 16 April 1915.
22. Quoted in ibid., 13 August 1915.

of the union opposition to military conscription in his report to the government.[23]

In January 1916, while still a health insurance commissioner, he was appointed to a three-man 'dilution commission' in Newcastle, with responsibility for the Tyne district. The commission's function was to promote the policy of having unskilled and semi-skilled workers take over tasks formerly reserved for tradesmen. In mid-year, he figured in the King's Birthday honours list as a Companion of the Bath.

Late in 1916, the Ministry of Munitions created a Labour Enlistment Complaints Section in the hope of dispelling workers' suspicions, often erupting in industrial action, about the granting of exemptions from compulsory military service. It was to be unique among the ministry's sub-units because, after a great deal of soul-searching,[24] the bureaucrats and former 'captains of industry' running the ministry had decided that it should be headed by 'a representative trade unionist'.[25] Shackleton – whose tenure as a health insurance commissioner had recently been extended for another year – was announced as its 'Director' on 6 December. Then the lightning struck.

The Permanent Secretary

That same December, David Lloyd George, lunging for the Prime Ministership, struck a bargain with the Labour party. One item in the bargain was the formation of a Ministry of Labour. The first Minister of Labour (though not Lloyd George's first choice for the post)[26] was John Hodge, acting chairman of the parliamentary Labour party and former leader of the Steel Smelters' Union. Hodge wanted the civil servant heading his ministry to be someone 'who understands Labour'.[27] He chose Shackleton,[28] who thus became the first permanent secretary of the Ministry of Labour shortly before Christmas 1916.

His appointment came at a time when Lloyd George's new broom was beginning to sweep aside civil service conventions on a massive scale, as Beatrice Webb observed:

> The swollen world of Whitehall is seething ... The permanent officials, who in pre-war times lived demure & dignified lives ... are now fighting desperately for

---

23. Wilson, *Political Diaries of C. P. Scott*, p. 174. The Prime Minister, Asquith, in a letter to Balfour on the issue, placed great weight on Shackleton's report. See Wrigley, *David Lloyd George and the British Labour Movement*, p. 167.

24. See Martin, *TUC*, pp. 138–9.

25. *History of the Ministry of Munitions*, vol. VI, part I, p. 49.

26. That was J. H. Thomas, of the Amalgamated Society of Railway Servants, who declined the offer. See Lowe, *Adjusting to Democracy*, p. 28.

27. Hodge, *Workman's Cottage to Windsor Castle*, p. 168.

28. A decade earlier, in the election of the parliamentary Labour party's first chairman, Hodge (by his own reported testimony) voted for Shackleton in the first vote, but switched to Hardie in the second. See Bealey and Pelling, *Labour and Politics*, p. 279.

the control of their departments, against invading 'interests' and interloping amateurs. Under the Lloyd George regimen, each department has been handed over to the 'interest' with which it is concerned ... The Insurance Commission ... is controlled by the great Industrial [Assurance] Companies; the Board of Trade is controlled by the Shipowners; the Food Controller is a wholesale Grocer; the Ministry of Munitions is largely managed by the representatives of the manufacturers of munitions, whilst a Duke's land-agent has been placed at the head of the Board of Agriculture. Finally, a Trade Union official is Minister of Labour and has been given, as the permanent head of his Department, an ex-Trade Union official.[29]

But Shackleton's appointment was not the same as the others. For it broke through a much more formidable class barrier, and was bound to be more controversial.

Before the war, appointments to senior levels of the civil service had been 'the perquisite of the universities'[30] – and the perquisite especially, by a ratio of four to one, of Oxbridge graduates.[31] By late 1916, business (the 'captains of industry') had made substantial inroads into the upper echelons of the civil service, particularly under Lloyd George as Minister of Munitions. Labour, however, was in a quite different position. Hodge, as Minister of Labour, was one of six Labour MPs with ministries in Lloyd George's coalition government; and there was a history – sparse, but a history – of working-class ministers that reached back to 1886 through John Burns and Henry Broadhurst. But Shackleton, Hodge's permanent secretary, stood alone. He had no working-class predecessors in the uppermost levels of the civil service, and no companions. There was no possibility that this breakthrough by a self-educated weaver would go either unremarked or uncontested.

The most direct protest came from William (later Lord) Beveridge, then a senior Board of Trade official who had been lent to the wartime Food Control Board. Labour affairs had been his principal interest, and he had expected eventually to return to the Board of Trade to pursue that interest. He made no bones about his ambition to be permanent secretary of the new Ministry of Labour. 'I had been in charge [at the Board of Trade] of everything that fell to the new Labour Department and I would have liked to be its principal official.'[32] Moreover, it was not only a matter of wanting the job: it was also a matter of regarding the competition as inadequate. 'I did not see Shackleton running a large department.'[33] According to Hodge,[34] Beveridge complained first to Shackleton, who advised him to 'see the Minister', and then arranged an appointment for him. When he saw the minister, as Beveridge recorded it, 'I asked [Hodge] if he would consider making me Joint

29. *Diaries of Beatrice Webb* (MS), 22 February 1917: Passfield Coll., vol. 34, fols. 3492–3.
30. Hobson, *National Guilds*, p. 218.
31. See Lowe, *Adjusting to Democracy*, p. 8.
32. Beveridge, *Power and Influence*, p. 141.
33. Ibid.
34. Hodge, *Workman's Cottage to Windsor Castle*, p. 179.

Secretary with Shackleton.'³⁵ Hodge's recollection of what Beveridge said strikes a less conciliatory note: 'In my [Beveridge's] opinion, I was entitled to be made the Permanent Secretary of this new Department, but in face of the fact that Mr Shackleton has been appointed, the only other course is that I should be made joint Secretary with him.'³⁶ Either way, Hodge rejected the proposition.³⁷

The offensive against Shackleton's appointment then moved to a higher plane. During question-time in the House of Commons, Bonar Law, Chancellor of the Exchequer, invited Hodge back to his room: 'I want to chat with you.'³⁸ There, the preliminaries over, the Chancellor drove straight to the point. 'Do you think you are wise in your appointment of a Permanent Secretary?' Hodge, naturally, said he was. But the Chancellor persisted: 'Are you quite sure that [Shackleton] is capable and has had the experience necessary to organise a new Department?' Hodge, as he recorded it, rejected at length the notion that 'routine organising work' was an appropriate concern for a permanent secretary.³⁹ The Chancellor gave up.

On that day, as it happened, Hodge was under siege from two directions. For pressure was also being applied to Shackleton, who transferred it to Hodge by offering him his resignation. Hodge's reaction, by his own record, was tough and totally supportive. 'I told him he should fight and not cave in; that I would not accept his resignation, and he could make up his mind to this – that if he did resign, Beveridge would not get the job.' Hodge next hurried over to 10 Downing Street, where he was unable to see the Prime Minister but spoke to Arthur Henderson, the senior Labour member in the Coalition, who was then Minister without Portfolio and a member of the War Cabinet. Shortly afterwards, Henderson himself told Shackleton that 'he must not on any account resign, and [Henderson] had Mr Lloyd George's authority to say that he must stick to his guns'.⁴⁰ He did.

Hodge stepped in again to back Shackleton when Sir George Askwith, one of the senior civil servants transferred from the Board of Trade, made what Hodge described as a 'most amazing demand' for direct access to the minister. Hodge interpreted this attempt to by-pass Shackleton as a 'caste

35. Beveridge, *Power and Influence*, p. 141.
36. Hodge, *Workman's Cottage to Windsor Castle*, p. 179.
37. Later, Hodge also decided not to hold open Beveridge's original position (transferred from the Board of Trade) on the ground that 'in face of [his] demand [for a joint secretaryship], it was impossible that he could come back ... to the Labour Ministry. It would have been very awkward for Mr Shackleton, and in my opinion ... equally awkward ... for Mr Beveridge.' Ibid., p. 180. In relation to this decision, Beveridge later said that Hodge 'took umbrage' at his 'suggestion'. *Power and Influence*, p. 141. There is, however, no hint of umbrage in Hodge's letter to Beveridge informing him of this decision. It is, like a second letter responding to Beveridge's carefully redrafted reply to the first, a model of courtesy. Correspondence, 21–22 December 1916: Beveridge Coll., vol. IIb 15.
38. Hodge, *Workman's Cottage to Windsor Castle*, p. 180.
39. Ibid., pp. 180–1.
40. Ibid., p. 181.

difficulty', arising between 'a Knight' and 'a plain secretary'.[41] He solved the problem, to his own satisfaction, by securing a knighthood for Shackleton. And so, in June 1917, 'the first Labour knight' was created.[42]

The Wartime Ministry of Labour

John Hodge was replaced as Minister of Labour, in August 1917, by George Roberts, another Labour MP and a former printers' union official, who held the office until January 1919. Like Hodge, Roberts stood firmly on the conservative side of the labour movement. Shackleton is likely to have found both congenial masters.

The Ministry of Labour had been carved out of the old Board of Trade's sprawling empire, taking over four of its departments. The Employment Department, with a staff of thousands, handled employment exchanges and unemployment insurance. The Chief Industrial Commissioner's Department, headed by Sir George Askwith and concerned with conciliation and arbitration, boasted a staff of less than three dozen. The staff of the Trade Boards Department, concerned with minimum wage regulation in nine trades, and of the Labour Statistics Department, were even fewer. The two principal preoccupations of the ministry's senior officials were industrial relations and planning for postwar demobilisation and industrial reconstruction. Their role in the field of industrial relations, however, was severely constrained because the ministry was 'constantly embroiled in debilitating administrative battles with other departments'[43] – with the result that, in virtually every major industrial sector, it played at best a secondary, backing-up role in determining labour policy or settling disputes about wages and working conditions. Thus, in the industrial relations of civilian munitions industries, the predominant force behind government intervention was the Ministry of Munitions; in coal mining and the railways, it was the Coal Controller and the Railway Executive, both under the Board of Trade; in military industrial establishments, it was the War Office; in naval shipyards, it was the Admiralty; in merchant shipping, it was the Ministry of Shipping; and in a key sector of the building trades, it was the Air Ministry.

Officially, the Ministry of Labour was supposed to play a co-ordinating role, especially in wage disputes with implications extending beyond the province of the ministry immediately concerned. The War Cabinet formally endorsed its co-ordinating role on more than one occasion. But, when it came to major disputes, the ministry's efforts to discharge that role were repeatedly undermined by 'the intransigence of the production departments and the

41. Ibid., p. 182.
42. Unknown newspaper, n.d. (1917): SP; and see Martin, *TUC*, p. 209. He was made a KCB (Knight Commander of the Bath), having been awarded CB (Companion of the Bath) the previous year.
43. Lowe, *Adjusting to Democracy*, p. 53.

prevarication of the Cabinet'.[44] The ministry was handicapped in this context by a relatively lowly status, which was reflected in the salary originally allotted its minister.[45] Its status also made for difficulties in recruiting 'able officials', difficulties that were compounded, according to Rodney Lowe, by having Shackleton ('a trade-unionist, whose expertise lay in an area other than the administrative') as its permanent secretary.[46]

Shackleton, in the event, seems to have played a smaller part than usual in the administration of his department, especially in the first two years, when H. B. Butler was his deputy. Butler, at the urging of Hodge's parliamentary secretary, W. C. Bridgeman, had been brought in from the Home Office for the express purpose of making up for Shackleton's inexperience, and he quickly took on the lion's share of the ministry's administration.[47] That was probably a relief for Shackleton – though he may have been less content with Butler's 'radical enthusiasm' when it came to policy matters.[48] In any case, the signs are that their relationship was at least amicable; and Butler was to remember Shackleton with great warmth.[49]

Outside the ministry, Shackleton had a hand in the conciliation of industrial disputes. This was initially the exclusive province of Sir George Askwith, as Chief Industrial Commissioner. Askwith, however, destroyed himself by making outspoken and unremitting attacks on Cabinet and on the officials of other ministries for their handling of wartime strikes. His ministry functions, as a result, were 'gradually assumed, in long-term planning, by Butler and, in day-to-day conciliation, by Shackleton'.[50] Outside the ministry, too, there were interdepartmental committees that demanded Shackleton's attention,[51] and he remained a health insurance commissioner,

44.   Lowe in Burk, *War and the State*, p. 116.
45.   This was £2,000 a year compared to the £5,000 of an 'established secretary of state'. Lowe, *Adjusting to Democracy*, p. 12. Hodge, the first minister, protested about the salary, alleging 'a degradation of labour'; but Bonar Law, Chancellor of the Exchequer, won him around by proposing that all ministerial salaries be pooled and distributed equally for the duration of the war. Hodge, *Workmn's Cottage to Windsor Castle*, pp. 177–8.
46.   Lowe, *Adjusting to Democracy*, p. 53.
47.   See ibid., pp. 66–7, 87; and Lowe in Burk, *War and the State*, p. 111. Puzzlingly, after repeatedly emphasizing Butler's administrative leadership, Lowe places the blame for the ministry's internal shortcomings almost wholly on Shackleton: 'An unorthodox appointment at an unorthodox time, [Shackleton] had not the administrative ability to establish the Ministry on an orthodox footing; responsibility for the wartime chaos must consequently be placed largely on his shoulders.' Ibid., p. 66.
48.   Ibid., p. 112.
49.   See Butler, *Confident Morning*, p. 116.
50.   Lowe, *Adjusting to Democracy*, p. 78.
51.   Such as a Statutory Committee for Discharged Soldiers; a committee inquiring into the 'labour embargo' scheme regulating the use of skilled labour; a committee exploring ways of bringing more. women into the employed workforce; and a sub-committee (of the Reconstruction Committee) working on postwar demobilization arrangements.

unsalaried, until 1919.[52] But the pinnacle of his wartime activities was his involvement in the War Cabinet, Lloyd George's most striking constitutional innovation.

The War Cabinet initially consisted of the Prime Minister, Lord Curzon, Lord Milner, Arthur Henderson and Bonar Law.[53] Only Law, as Chancellor of the Exchequer, had departmental responsibilities. Balfour, the Foreign Secretary, could attend its meetings 'whenever he chose',[54] but other ministers had to wait on invitations. In a radical departure from tradition, invited ministers were allowed to bring along their senior officials. The War Cabinet, as a result, rarely met on its own. It also met frequently, 'almost daily'.[55] Shackleton attended more than sixty of its meetings between January 1917 and October 1919, most of them before the Armistice. Usually he accompanied his minister, but not always; and he was normally on his own when the minister was absent (otherwise being accompanied by one, or occasionally two, of his departmental colleagues). He was thus the sole representative of the Ministry of Labour at 18 War Cabinet meetings, more than a quarter of all the meetings he attended.[56]

As permanent secretary, Shackleton appears to have been occupied primarily with the kind of advisory role implied in his War Cabinet attendances. He would certainly have found this a more congenial role than the detailed administration of the ministry; and it made way for Butler. It was as the government's chief labour adviser, Butler later recalled, that 'Shackleton's advice was frequently sought and sometimes taken.'[57] In general, however, Churchill and the others in charge of war production were disinclined to pay much attention to the 'still small voice' of the ministry which, accordingly, 'had little part in solving the day to day industrial problems arising from the war'.[58]

The Horace Wilson Years

In January 1919 a Conservative, Sir Robert Horne, became Minister of Labour. Shackleton could no longer count on the sympathetic connection, arising from shared backgrounds, which he had enjoyed with Horne's

---

52.   He also acted as director of the Labour Enlistment Complaints Section of the Ministry of Munitions for three months after becoming permanent secretary.

53.   There were later variations in its size, but it never exceeded seven members.

54.   Hankey, *Government Control in War*, p. 43.

55.   Daalder, *Cabinet Reform in Britain*, p. 51. In 1917, it met 'more than 300 times', according to its secretary. Hankey, *Government Control in War*, p. 41. It met 'over 500' times between its creation and the war's end in November 1918. Mackintosh, *British Cabinet*, p. 348.

56.   The nature of his participation in the proceedings of the War Cabinet is discussed in Chapter 10.

57.   Butler, *Confident Morning*, p. 121.

58.   Ibid.

predecessors, Hodge and Roberts.[59] And only once, towards the end of his career, was he again to serve under a similarly sympathetic minister.[60] Horne's appointment, in any case, brought about a radical change in the general climate of the ministry.[61] But Shackleton might still have survived, better and longer than he did, had it not been for the Horace Wilson factor.

H. J. Wilson, a relatively junior official when he joined the ministry at its foundation, was to rise quickly through it on the way to becoming (as Sir Horace) permanent secretary to the Treasury, personal adviser to two prime ministers (Baldwin and Chamberlain), and one of the 'Men of Munich'. Wilson was a master of bureaucratic politics. Lowe has neatly depicted the stages in his progress up the ministry ladder: 'After the war, from under [Askwith's] tutelage, there ... emerged Horace Wilson to supplant first Askwith himself as head of the industrial relations staff (in November 1918), secondly Butler as strategist (in the autumn of 1919), and finally Shackleton as permanent secretary (in 1921).'[62]

When Askwith transferred from the Board of Trade to take charge of the Ministry of Labour's conciliation service, he took with him the title of Chief Industrial Commissioner, the rank of a permanent secretary, and a salary of £2,000 compared with Shackleton's £1,500. He also took Horace Wilson. Subsequently, as already noted, because of his outspoken views he was progressively bypassed, to Shackleton's advantage. The climax came near the end of 1918 when the ministry moved to absorb conciliation officials attached to disbanding wartime ministries. They were placed, not under the Chief Industrial Commissioner, but in a new department of Wages and Arbitration. Wilson was put at its head, and given effective control of all conciliation work. Askwith was forced into early retirement.

There was an internal reorganization of the ministry in the spring of 1919, after Butler had been seconded to Paris to help found the International Labour Organisation. In the reshuffle, Askwith's old title of Chief Industrial Commissioner was discarded but his position, as head of the industrial conciliation unit, was vested in Shackleton – who also remained permanent secretary of the ministry.[63] Some time after this the title 'Chief Labour Adviser' somewhat mysteriously emerged, and began to be used officially in relation to Shackleton's conciliation responsibilities.

59. A few weeks later, Shackleton suffered what may well have been a similar blow when Butler was seconded to Paris to help found the International Labour Organisation, and became its deputy director.

60. Horne was minister until March 1920. He was followed by Dr T. J. Macnamara, Liberal (March 1920–October 1922); Sir Montague Barlow, Conservative (October 1922–January 1924); T. Shaw, Labour (January–November 1924); and Sir Arthur Steel-Maitland, Conservative (November 1924–June 1929).

61. See Lowe, *Adjusting to Democracy*, pp. 91-2.

62. Ibid., p. 78.

63. As a ministry minute later put it: 'the attempt was made to combine the duties attaching to the two [positions] in one and the same office'. Undated [1923], M.L.2, LAB 2/1804 4896.

The new title, it became clear, was designed to facilitate the edging-out of Shackleton. In April 1920 Sir James Masterton-Smith, from outside the ministry, was appointed joint permanent secretary. Treasury authorized this unusual arrangement on the understanding, first, that the circumstances were 'altogether exceptional'; second, that 'the immediate object ... is to free Sir David Shackleton for the discharge of his increasing duties as Chief Labour Adviser'; and, third, that Masterton-Smith was 'to take administrative charge of the Department as a whole'.[64] Shackleton's formal title now became 'Joint Permanent Secretary and Chief Labour Adviser'. But soon and revealingly thereafter, when ministry files were intended for the joint permanent secretaries, the notation on the forwarding minute was 'Secretary' for Masterton-Smith and 'C. L. A.' for Shackleton.

Shackleton's last link with the permanent secretaryship was finally snapped the following year. Illness forced Masterton-Smith's retirement. His replacement, appointed in September 1921, came from within the ministry. It was Horace Wilson. And there was to be no doubt about his pre-eminence: he 'will be the sole Permanent Secretary, Sir David Shackleton holding only the office of Chief Labour Adviser'.[65]

This time there was no ambiguity about Shackleton's demotion. His salary might be unchanged, and remain higher than Wilson's, but the order in which participants are listed in the minutes of meetings is a surer guide to status in the mandarin-world of the English bureaucracy. Prior to September 1921, Shackleton's name always followed the minister's and preceded Masterton-Smith's. After September 1921, he took third place, and it was Wilson's name that followed the minister's.

Among the ministry's senior officials, it seems, nobody doubted the principal author of Shackleton's demotion. 'Wilson ousted Shackleton', as one of them crisply put it many years later.[66] But the ousting was still less than complete. More than two years were to elapse before Wilson was able to deliver the *coup de grâce*. Ironically enough, his opportunity came at a time when the first Labour government in British history held office, and under a Minister of Labour, Tom Shaw, who was a former cotton union official.

Wilson's initiative in the affair is evident from a personal letter he wrote to Sir Russell Scott of the Treasury.[67]

My dear Russell,
    I have put to my Minister [Shaw] the proposals we have been discussing with a view to the re-arrangements of the top posts here and he agrees ... He said he

64. Treasury (M. G. Ramsay) to Ministry of Labour, 23 April 1920: LAB 2/1727/CEB543 4896.
65. Ministry of Labour (A. W. Watson) to Treasury, 5 September 1921: LAB 2/1727/CEB543 4896.
66. Sir Frederick Leggett, interview, 25 March 1981.
67. Wilson appears to have had a close association with Treasury (which he was later to head) from early in his career. See Lowe, *Adjusting to Democracy*, pp. 56–7.

would like to speak to Shackleton personally and I, of course, agreed ... We will send you the official letter towards the end of next week.[68]

The 'official letter' duly followed, in late April. In it, Shackleton was represented as initiating a move to change the terms of his appointment.[69] The minister, in turn, was represented as having reacted to this initiative by proposing that Shackleton 'vacate his present permanent post', but 'continue to serve as Chief Labour Adviser' on a part-time basis.[70] The minister proposed, as well, two ancillary conditions favourable to Shackleton. The first was that he should hold this part-time position until his sixty-fifth birthday in November 1928. The second, surprising in its apparent pettiness, was that because of his residing in 'the North of England',[71] he should be paid the cost of a first-class railway season ticket to London for the remainder of his time with the ministry. The late April letter also referred to a review of the ministry's senior positions that would be carried out 'at a later date, e.g. on the eventual complete retirement [in 1928] of Sir David Shackleton'.

Nothing came of any of these proposals; and there is no record in the relevant file of a Treasury reply to the late April letter. Instead, in July, the ministry sent a second 'official letter' to Treasury – 'in modification of our original letter of the 28th April'.[72] The 'modification' was radical. This time there was no reference to a part-time position, no reference to a railway season ticket; and the ministry's senior positions were to be reviewed, not in 1928, but 'on the retirement of Sir David Shackleton in December 1925'.[73] Shackleton, in other words, instead of retiring at 65 years of age after four years' half-time employment, was now to retire in 18 months at the age of 62.

Who jibbed at the minister's April proposals? Certainly the Treasury; and probably Wilson as well. Those proposals, especially with the odd season-ticket permutation, smack of a deal worked out between two co-operating ex-union colleagues. Shaw, the minister, Shackleton's junior by nine years, started work as a half-time cotton weaver at the age of ten, and became active in the Colne weavers' union about the time Shackleton won the Ramsbottom

68.   Wilson to Scott, 16 April 1924: LAB 2/1727/CEB543 4896.
69.   'Sir David Shackleton has recently represented to the Minister that, for reasons of health, it would be convenient to him if it were possible to arrange a modification in the existing arrangements whereby he renders a whole-time service.' Ministry of Labour (A. W. Watson) to Treasury, 28 April 1924: ibid.
70.   Ibid.
71.   More precisely, in St Anne's-on-Sea in Lancashire, to which the Shackletons had moved, from Golders Green, after he lost the permanent secretaryship in 1921. See Chapter 9.
72.   'At H. J. Wilson's request', this official letter was 'forwarded under private cover' provided by a 'Personal' letter, of the same date: A. W. Watson signed both. No reason was given for this stratagem. The personal letter noted that 'Wilson would be grateful if you would let me have formal Treasury sanction to the modified proposals as early as possible.' Watson to Sir Russell Scott, 9 July 1924: LAB 2/1727/CEB543 4896.
73.   Ibid.

secretaryship.[74] He knew Shackleton well, and may have looked up to him.[75] He was undoubtedly sympathetic when he discussed Wilson's proposed 'rearrangements' with Shackleton – indeed, the railway season-ticket requirement (which, most certainly, did not come from Wilson) suggests his eagerness to please.

As for Wilson, it is remotely possible, since the files are opaque on the point, that he approved of Shaw's deal with Shackleton. But that interpretation depends upon either (or both) an unlikely sympathy for Shackleton or an equally unlikely preoccupation with a linked proposal for an increase in Wilson's own salary.[76] What is far more likely is that Wilson's proposed 'rearrangements', so far as they affected Shackleton, resembled the eventual (July) outcome; and when he told Scott (in April) that Shaw was going to speak with Shackleton, he either overestimated the strength of Shaw's resolve or mistook Shaw's understanding of the 'rearrangements'.

Two things, at least, are clear. The April deal between Shaw and Shackleton ran into deadly Treasury opposition; and the July arrangement left Shackleton worse off. Like Askwith before him, he was steered into early retirement. On the other hand, he accepted the fact without Askwith's open anger, and possibly with less reluctance. Certainly, Sir Frederick Leggett's recollection was that Shackleton 'retired for his own reasons. He wanted to. He wasn't very happy at the end. He was almost out on a limb.'[77] But none of this reached the public domain.

The Public Face

Published perceptions of Shackleton's first demotion, in April 1920, altogether missed the reality. Masterton-Smith's appointment as joint permanent secretary was interpreted as a compliment, and due recognition of Shackleton's heavy load. 'Even with his passion for work, Sir David Shackleton finds it difficult to discharge the many duties thrust upon him ... Sir David has too much to do ... The appointment [of Masterton-Smith] will have the effect of freeing [him] for his increasing duties as Chief Labour Adviser.'[78]

In the role of Chief Labour Adviser,[79] Shackleton's activities attracted little

74. See Tracey, *Book of the Labour Party*, vol. III, pp. 186–9.

75. He was to write a very warm obituary notice on Shackleton's death. See *Manchester Guardian*, 2 August 1938.

76. Shackleton's deal with Shaw proposed that, as a part-time Chief Labour Adviser, his salary should be reduced to £1,500 (from its current £3,000); and that Wilson's salary, as permanent secretary, should accordingly be increased (from its current £2,200) to £3,000. Labour to Treasury, 28 April 1924: LAB 2/1727/CEB 543 4896.

77. Interview, 25 March 1981.

78. *Nelson Leader*, 23 April 1920.

79. This role was officially described as follows: 'The Chief Labour Adviser is the officer to whom the Minister looks for advice on matters of general Labour policy, including particularly questions concerning relations between employers and employed. He is consulted by all Depart-

public attention, even when relatively public in character[80] – although an investigation of Belgian unemployment policies and administration was noted,[81] and his involvement in the conciliation of industrial disputes occasionally caught the public eye.[82] Instead, what seems to have stirred most public interest in him during these years was the money he earned.

His annual salary of £1,500 was increased to £2,000 with Masterton-Smith's appointment, Treasury deciding that both joint secretaries should receive this amount in the 'special circumstances' of the case.[83] Some time later, the two salaries were raised to £3,000 on the recommendation of a committee which was headed by Asquith, the former Prime Minister, and concerned with the senior officials of all 'first class Departments'.[84] In August 1921, there were parliamentary questions asked about the new salaries, and especially about the fact that, as a Conservative MP put it, Shackleton's had 'lately been doubled from £1,500 to £3,000'.[85] Likely public reactions to this revelation are suggested by a comment, widely repeated in the Lancashire press, which is notable for the absence of the eulogistic note usually found in local newspaper references to Shackleton. 'It is true ... that he once received the modest salary of £250 as a trade union official. He earned it. [But in] raising his stipend as Chief Labour Adviser ... from £1,500 to £3,000 a year, the Government invited the challenge it received the other night.'[86]

The controversy left its mark, but not on Shackleton's salary. This remained unchanged at £3,000, the following month, when he was once again demoted with Horace Wilson's appointment as sole permanent secretary. It was Wilson's salary that bore the brunt. For it was set at £2,200 – though on 'the understanding' that he would nevertheless 'be regarded as Permanent Secretary of a First Class Department'.[87] The extraordinary nature of this

ments on matters involving negotiations, as well as on questions of policy affecting employment and Unemployment Insurance, wages and hours, disputes, Trade Boards, Joint Industrial Councils, and industrial organisation generally.' 'First Report from the Select Committee on Estimates', 10 April 1922, App. II: *Parl. Papers*, 1922, vol. V, p. 305.

80.   As in his attendances at conferences of the International Labour Organisation, and his appointment (in 1924) as the British government's representative on the ILO's Governing Body.

81.   And was taken, locally at least, as evidence of the 'confidence reposed by the Prime Minister [Lloyd George] in the judgement and capacity of Sir David Shackleton in the handling of industrial problems'. *Nelson Leader*, 14 October 1921.

82.   For example, in relation to a cotton dispute in 1920: 'It is possible any other mediation would have failed where Sir David succeeded.' *Nelson Leader*, 24 June 1920. And a printing dispute in 1922: ' one more triumph for the tact, persuasiveness, and the fairness, which commands the respect of both sides, on the part of Sir David Shackleton'. Ibid., 7 July 1922.

83.   Treasury (M. G. Ramsay) to Ministry of Labour, 23 April 1920: LAB 2/1727/CEB543 4896.

84.   'First Report from the Select Committee on Estimates', 10 April 1922, App. II: *Parl. Papers*, 1922, vol. V, p. 306.

85.   *Parl. Debs.*, 10 August 1921, vol. 146, col. 417.

86.   *Blackburn Times*, 13 August 1921; *Nelson Leader*, 19 August 1921.

87.   Ministry of Labour (A. W. Watson) to Treasury, 5 September 1921: LAB 2/1727/CEB543 4896.

arrangement is underlined by two accompanying stipulations: first, that Shackleton's salary was personal to him; and, second, that Wilson's salary was to rise to £3,000 whenever Shackleton ceased to be Chief Labour Adviser.[88]

Six months after Wilson's promotion, the parliamentary Select Committee on Estimates took a close interest in the ministry. As permanent secretary, he endured a grilling that extended over five days. A great deal of the questioning revolved around Shackleton's role and salary as Chief Labour Adviser. Shortly before the committee tabled its report, that salary was again the subject of a parliamentary question from a backbencher who scythed at 'permanent officials and their bloated salaries'.[89] The select committee's report was no kinder. It was particularly critical of Shackleton's salary, expressing the belief that 'a gentleman competent to advise on labour matters could be obtained … at a far less salary than £3,000 a year, which, it must be remembered, carries a pension for life'.[90] This humiliating observation, and related comments, were widely reported. The *Nelson Leader*, for example, quoted most of the committee's comments concerning Shackleton under the headlines: 'Sir David Shackleton's Salary … Is it Too Much?'[91]

It was another three years before his retirement took effect on 18 December 1925. But the money issue dogged him to the end. The mere mention of his salary, at some inquiry, inspired a local reflection that it was an amount a '"bloated capitalist"' might envy.[92] Shortly before he retired, a Cabinet committee decided that the post of Chief Labour Adviser would lapse when he left it. A London daily, noting a saving of 'one and a half times [the salary] paid to the Minister of Labour himself', reported the committee's feeling that 'the present staff was fully competent to advise the Minister … on all questions relating to labour'.[93] It was not an issue that worked in Shackleton's favour where public perceptions were concerned.

The retirement itself stirred some sympathetic press interest. It tended to be attributed to a decision he, not others, had made; and was often described as a 'resignation'. 'Need for rest', one Lancashire paper commented, 'is understood to be the reason for this step.'[94] His own explanation, as recorded in a London daily, stressed formal requirements: 'Simply because I am 62 years of age and over the age limit'.[95] Nothing was said of his preferred option, embodied in the failed deal with Shaw, of retirement at the age of 65.

88.   Ibid. The end of Shackleton's civil service career thus resembled its beginnings in that his original Home Office salary had also been personal to him.

89.   *Parl. Debs.*, 5 April 1922, vol. 152, col. 2215.

90.   'First Report from the Select Committee on Estimates', 10 April 1922: *Parl. Papers*, 1922, vol. V, p. 209.

91.   *Nelson Leader*, 21 April 1922.

92.   Ibid., 11 September 1925.

93.   *Daily Telegraph*, cited in *Nelson Leader*, 20 November 1925.

94.   *Northern Daily Telegraph*, 26 October 1925.

95.   *Evening News*, (January?) 1926: SP.

The chairman at his retirement dinner in the Trocadero, on 22 January 1926, was Horace Wilson.[96] Steel-Maitland, the Minister of Labour, spoke; and so did three ministerial predecessors, but only those from the Labour party. Shackleton was given a grandfather clock; his wife a reading lamp.

Postscript

His professional life was not quite done. Neville Chamberlain (as Minister of National Service, a frequent opponent in War Cabinet debates), as Minister of Health, remembered him in 1928 and had him put on the Industrial Transference Board along with Sir Warren Fisher, permanent secretary of the Treasury, and Sir John Cadman, prominent scientist and businessman. The board, concerned with moving workers – especially miners – from high centres of unemployment, was sufficiently important to engage the attention and attendance of Tom Jones, Cabinet deputy-secretary and confidant of the Prime Minister.[97] In 1934, four years after Wilson had left the Ministry of Labour for higher things, Shackleton was appointed to a standing arbitration board dealing with mining disputes in South Wales.

Throughout, he acted as a Justice of the Peace on the bench at Preston, the county centre: 'His main occupation', as one paper described it.[98] He continued to attend major conferences of the Rechabites and of the cotton unions, where he was always accorded a place of honour.[99] He died at the age of 74, in his home at St Anne's-on-Sea, on 1 August 1938.

96.   It was also Wilson who later wrote the entry on Shackleton in the *Dictionary of National Biography*.
97.   See Jones, *Whitehall Diary*, vol. II, p. 137. Jones's diary entry, moreover, makes it clear that membership of the board was no sinecure.
98.   *Lancashire Daily Post*, 27 May 1935.
99.   Less than three months before his death, 'tall and erect … a striking figure', he attended the conference of the Textile Factory Workers' Association at Blackpool. *Nelson Leader*, 13 May 1938.

Part II

The Man

9

The Private Man

Home and Family

Shackleton's wife, Sarah, was described in her forties as 'a woman below the medium height, but with plenty of timber about her ... a "gradely" [true] Lancashire lass ... who sets to and does her own housework'.[1] At the time that description was published, the house she took care of was the one that she and Shackleton had occupied since he entered parliament some five years earlier. A 'house of the better working classes',[2] two-storeyed, narrow and one of a long row, it stood at 51 London Terrace, Darwen – 'an ordinary street ... dimly lighted, with the grocer's shop in it, and the tripe shop and the clogger's [wooden shoe] shop round the corner ... [and] the clogs of the factory folk ... clattering on the hard pavement'.[3] An interviewer, ushered into the kitchen of 51 London Terrace, observed

> a typical Lancashire kitchen, with a bright fire, a bookcase in the chimney corner, a sofa under the window overlooking the backyard ... a dresser on another side ... [and] pictures on the walls ... such as you see in ordinary workmen's homes – pictures of the family as it was, and of the family as it had been before the parents had cause to weep for those that had been laid in the churchyard.[4]

This was the world familiar to Shackleton's wife, the world where she had friends. Then, some time during 1908, she left its comfort. The Shackletons moved house to Manchester: 350 Great Western Street, Rusholme. There were obvious professional advantages for Shackleton in the shift to Manchester. There were none, two years later, when the family went back to Darwen, in a move that must have been driven by domestic considerations, including Sarah Shackleton's sense of comfort.[5] Within months, however, she was again torn away from Darwen, this time to London, by Shackleton's Home Office appointment. Number 55 Rotherwick Road, Golders Green, was a semi-detached, three-bedroom house, not far from the Underground.

1. *Cotton Factory Times*, 31 January 1908.
2. *Blackburn Times*, 15 February 1908.
3. James Haslam, 'Working Man M.P. at Home', unknown newspaper, 15 February 1908: SP.
4. Ibid.
5. It may also have had something to do with her daughter's love life. Margaret's engagement to W. Scholfield, of Manchester, was announced in August 1908, and broken off some time before December 1910 (the family was then on the point of leaving Darwen for London), when her engagement was announced to a Darwen man, Herbert Catlow.

They christened it 'Sunnyhirst', the name of 'the Darwen beauty spot'.[6] It was a wistful touch. For Rotherwick Road, to the '"gradely" Lancashire lass', was light years away from the comfort of Darwen.

There were, to be sure, comforts of a sort in Golders Green. For one thing, at least from 1912 when Shackleton's appointment as Health Insurance Commissioner doubled his annual salary to £1,000, the family were sufficiently well off to employ a live-in maid. But Sarah Shackleton did not fit in middle-class Golders Green. Unlike her husband, she never lost, in either speech or thought, the marks of her class origins. She often lapsed into dialect (not just broad Lancashire), especially when she became excited.

> Nobody could be in the presence of my aunt more than a few minutes before becoming aware of her background and her mental limitations. She remained in essence a cotton operative. There were unlikely to be in Golders Green any women or group of women with whom she would have felt at home. She would simply not have fitted in. It is difficult to present this picture without appearing snobbish, but somehow the picture is not true if this is not said.[7]

In Darwen, she had been a skilled and devoted card-player, although she never played for money. But in London, there were no card parties; and Shackleton himself did not play. Moreover, as Ernest Wilkinson observed during a six-month stay in the Golders Green house, his aunt seemed to have no London friends whatever. The maid probably provided some company. But, otherwise, the only other regular feminine companion Sarah Shackleton seems to have had in that house was her daughter – and that ceased to be the case from May 1912, when Margaret married Herbert Catlow, a surveyor with the Darwen corporation.

Sarah Shackleton's loneliness probably explains the last shift the Shackletons made. It occurred in 1921, the year he lost the permanent secretaryship to Horace Wilson, and became solely the Chief Labour Adviser. For his wife, the demotion was a blessing in disguise. It tied him less firmly to his London desk, allowing him to commute in much the same way he had done as an MP. So it was back to Lancashire, but not to Darwen. This time Lady Shackleton, as she liked to be known, set up house at St Anne's-on-Sea, a respectable resort town on the coast south of Blackpool. There, on Beach Road, she recovered a comfort that Golders Green had never provided.[8] 'My aunt then had friends whose early days had been like her own. Some ... she had known since they were in the cotton mill together. It was with these friends that she spent so much time playing cards.'[9]

Shackleton and his wife, so far as Ernest Wilkinson's observation goes, 'got

---

6. *Northern Daily Telegraph*, 6 June 1916.
7. Ernest Wilkinson, letter to author, 28 May 1981.
8. At the same time, she also retained one comfort that Golders Green did provide by continuing to employ a maid until early in the Second World War, when she went to live with her daughter's family.
9. Ernest Wilkinson, letter to author, 28 May 1981.

on famously together'. Occasionally, she would say something to him in dialect; he would smile and reply in the same fashion. Their two grandchildren had much the same impression of an easy relationship. In David Catlow's words, Shackleton 'was very good with my grandmother'. All three remarked on the pronounced gap in intellectual capacity and interests.

Wilkinson remembered Shackleton as being 'intensely loyal' to his wife, and connected that with 'his never forgetting how much was owed to her when he was unemployed' in 1884–85.[10] Shackleton himself, on numerous occasions, publicly retold the story of the way his wife took over as breadwinner during those 17 black weeks. But his debt to her involved more than that. In the eight years that elapsed from the time he entered parliament until he went to the Home Office, she would have managed the household (including an infant son, from 1903) on her own for up to six days a week, most weeks. In addition, as the Labour party's records indicate, she helped to arrange his speaking appointments.[11]

Two shifts of house – Manchester to Darwen in 1910, and London to St Anne's in 1921 – suggest that Shackleton was sensitive to his wife's concerns. There is, too, his longstanding practice of spending Sundays quietly at home (see below), which might have been inspired by nothing more than self-indulgence, but also possibly registered a husband's recognition of his wife's needs. Ernest Wilkinson recalled an exchange in the Golders Green house which suggests some such sensitivity. She asked him: 'Aren't you going out tonight?' He replied: 'No, they didn't invite you.'

He did, however, take her out on some other occasions. Before the move to Golders Green, there were press references to a number of them. She accompanied him to at least five of the TUC's annual Congresses (including the two of which he was president), to a royal garden party at Windsor in 1905, and on the six-week trip he made in 1907 as the TUC delegate to the American Federation of Labor. At the local level, in addition to one or two electorate tea parties while he was an MP, she is recorded as attending the formal farewell he was given by the Textile Factory Workers' Association following his departure for the civil service. Fifteen years later, she was beside him at his retirement dinner in the Trocadero. And while he took his daughter to two Rechabite functions in the early 1930s, according to press reports, Sarah Shackleton was beside him when he played a leading role at the Rechabites' centenary conference in 1935.[12] She did not, however, go to his funeral. She said she was too ill. Her daughter and granddaughter did not believe her.

★ ★ ★ ★

10. Ibid.
11. However, as the chaos of the Shackleton Papers suggests (see Chapter 10), it is most unlikely that she performed anything like the complete secretarial role that Martha Burns did for her husband. See Brown, *John Burns*, p. 106.
12. In an interview at the time of her golden wedding, in 1933, she added three royal occasions to this list: King Edward's birthday celebration, the coronation of King George V, and the 'King and Queen's silver wedding festivities'. Unknown newspaper, n.d. (August 1933): SP.

By the time Shackleton's nephew, Ernest Wilkinson, stayed with the family in Golders Green before the war, the surviving children were David, a boy of 10, and Margaret, newly married and living in Darwen. Wilkinson had also seen the family together earlier, on the occasions he was taken with them on holidays. He thought that both children 'got on well' with their father. Margaret was patently 'very proud of him' and his achievements; and later, it was the daughter, not the grandmother, who regaled the grandchildren with memories of Shackleton.

Margaret, according to Wilkinson, tried to 'boss' her younger brother (there were, after all, 15 years between them). She also tried with her mother in matters of grammar and diction, and that often led to conflict. 'Uncle never interfered' when his women were at odds.

David, a 'very happy, carefree' boy, according to Wilkinson, grew into a sociable and popular adult, and 'a bit of a rebel' (to quote Nancy Smith), who was a conscientious objector during the Second World War. His mother evidently doted on him. He was not academically inclined; and that, certainly, was a disappointment to his father. He was sent to a private school: Queen's College at Taunton. Margaret had gone to a Darwen state school.[13]

Wilkinson, the nephew, provided some compensation for the son's academic limitations. He was bookish and won a County Council scholarship in 1909, the only 11-year-old to do so in Accrington that year. Despite the scholarship, he left school at 15 because his parents could not provide the additional financial support required for him to go on.[14] He passed another exam and joined the civil service and the Tax Office, which was the point at which he lived in the Shackletons' Golders Green house for six months. Then the war came. As soon as he was old enough, he joined up. He survived for over a year in the trenches of the Western Front. In April 1918, for the better part of three days, he lay wounded in no man's land near the Belgian village of Ploegsteert. Nine months in a German prisoner of war camp followed. He returned to England, 'in poor fettle' (as he put it), and to an uncle who 'knew how much I'd longed to go to university'. Shackleton 'took him in hand', with the result that Ernest Wilkinson entered Christ's College and, in due course, presented his uncle with a Cambridge degree. Shackleton would doubtless have preferred a degree won by David, the son. But there is no question that Ernest's graduation would have given great pleasure to a man with both a strong sense of family and an intense interest in education.

The pleasure, moreover, would have been sweetened by the fact that the graduate's mother was the sister who was closest in his affections. Nellie (christened Ellen) Wilkinson was Shackleton's illegitimate half-sister, and

13.   Later she started as a pupil teacher, but left that in order to take care of her brother when her parents travelled.
14.   His father was a painter and decorator, and his two sisters and one brother were all put to work as 'half-timers' at 12, the minimum age at the time.

only eight months younger. They had worked in the mill together as young-
sters, running six looms between them, in the days when he always had (as
she told her son) some kind of 'study book' above one of the looms. Ernest
Wilkinson thought that Shackleton was closer to Nellie than anyone outside
his immediate family, an impression confirmed by Nancy Smith, the granddaughter. Shackleton was a frequent visitor to the Wilkinson household
when Ernest was a schoolboy; and appeared to make a point of dropping in
on his sister whenever he was travelling nearby. He also made a point of
going to Accrington to walk in the procession marking the inauguration of
Nellie's husband, Charlie Wilkinson, as Mayor.

Shackleton's five other half-sisters ('our girls', he called them)[15] were much
younger than he and Nellie. The gap ranged from 7 to 18 years. All five
remained in the parental home until their father left it in 1906 (see below).
Three of them never married;[16] and one (Emma Jane, born 1878) married
only 'late in life',[17] after their father's death. Ella ('Cissie', born 1877) alone
joined the rebel, Nellie, by marrying while her father was still alive. Cissie
took that momentous step in 1905. Her mother, it seems, had died some time
before,[18] and Lizzie, the oldest of the five, 'kept house' while the others
worked in the mill and presumably enriched their father. But not long after
Cissie's marriage, the father opted for a third wife and a shift away from the
girls, to Nelson.

When the father left Accrington, the unmarried sisters continued living
together with Cissie and her husband, Absalom Palmer, a dedicated brass
bandsman. Some time after the war, when Absalom retired, Shackleton
bought a house for them all in St Anne's. Cissie was later to commit suicide
in its gas oven, following Absalom's death. That happened a year or two
before the Shackletons celebrated their golden wedding anniversary.

When Shackleton first moved on to the national stage in 1902, his father,
William, was already a public figure in Accrington. A well-known watchmaker, he was associated with the Gospel Temperance Mission, speaking
often at its meetings, and had helped found the Unsectarian Mission in
which he both taught Sunday school and was an active social worker. He was
reputedly diligent in 'promulgating his views through the press', and 'never
slow to express [them] … especially when he considered the moral welfare of
the community was involved'.[19] After leaving his daughters in Accrington for
his new wife in Nelson, he continued both his watchmaking and his good
works, early on taking classes at the 'Salem Sunday School' and reportedly
delivering 'a stirring address' at the Belgian Chapel in Leeds.[20] Years later, in

15.   *Co-operative News*, 18 January 1908.
16.   Sarah Elizabeth ('Lizzie'), b. 1871; Eliza, b. 1873; Ada, b. 1882.
17.   Wilkinson, letter to author, 13 February 1984.
18 .   Shackleton once conventionally recalled his stepmother as 'a second mother'. *M.A.P.*, 26
January 1907, p. 110. There is no other record of her presence. .
19.   *Accrington Observer*, 11 November 1919.
20.   *Nelson Leader*, 30 November 1906; *Cotton Factory Times*, 7 December 1906.

his mid-seventies, he was still 'a working watch repairer', and still 'regularly
... addressing adult classes and temperance gatherings'.[21] That was the public
aspect.

The private aspect completes the Victorian stereotype of lofty public
moralist and domestic martinet.[22] The family memory, in Ernest Wilkinson's
words, is of a father who 'ruled his household with a rod of iron', a man of
whom 'all the single daughters were afraid', and whose opposition to Shackleton's marriage (see Chapter 1) meant that 'no Shackleton would have dared
to attend the wedding'.[23] Nevertheless, his father's approval remained important. On the day Shackleton learned that the seat of Clitheroe was his, he sent
two telegrams: one to his wife ('Returned unopposed'), the other to his father
('Shackleton unopposed').[24] Up to that day, as both Wilkinson and Nancy
Smith were told, relations between the two men had been strained, but thereafter the father basked in the glow of reflected glory and boasted of 'my son,
David'.[25] They became close enough for Shackleton to stay overnight at least
once in his father's house in Nelson, and he is recorded as visiting the house
on other occasions before William Shackleton died in 1917.[26]

It is, however, the paternal grandfather, not the father, whose influence is
emphasized in Shackleton's scanty published recollections. The grandparents, William and Sarah (who gave the same names to their two oldest children), were both cotton-mule spinners, and came originally from
Todmorden, in Yorkshire. Shackleton recalled his grandfather, with high
praise, as 'one of the old-time cotton operatives' who had somehow 'learned
to read, and was no mean student'.[27] It was he who had provided the books
and newspapers that the young Shackleton devoured. And it was he, not the
father (despite a filial obeisance, made when the father was still living, and
the grandfather long dead),[28] with whom the young Shackleton 'often discussed' the political events and personalities that took his interest. Only his
teetotalism was 'thanks in the first instance to my father's example'.[29]

21. *Nelson Leader*, 9 June 1916; 23 March 1917.
22. A man who could write, in a letter to the editor: 'The longer I live the more I feel that
virtue is more than wealth, and character more than creed or cleverness.' *Haslingden Guardian*,
24 December 1898.
23. Letter to author, 13 February 1984.
24. SP; *Blackburn Weekly Telegraph*, 2 August 1902.
25. Thus, after the general election of January 1910, he wrote to his local newspaper as follows: 'Kindly allow me, through your columns, to express the thanks of my heart for the grand
result of the Clitheroe election. The support given to my son in the division has made me a proud
father.' *Nelson Leader*, 28 January 1910.
26. *Colne & Nelson Times*, 9 October 1908. *Nelson Leader*, 5 August 1938.
27. *M.A.P.*, 26 January 1907, p. 110.
28. 'From my father and my grandfather ... especially the latter, I ... inherited the interest in
things political.' Ibid.
29. Ibid., p. 111.

Interests

Tom Shaw, thinking back as a former Minister of Labour and cotton trade union leader, believed that Shackleton had virtually no non-professional interests. 'Outside his own immediate work he did not seem to have any hobbies, if one excepts his religious interests and connection with the "Rakkabites" (Rechabites)'.[30]

His religious interests, in fact, seem to have been quite slight once he left Accrington and the immediate neighbourhood of his father. In his youth he was a Sunday-school teacher, like his father, and later he and his wife seem to have regularly attended a Wesleyan chapel in Accrington, along with the rest of the Shackletons. In Ramsbottom and in Darwen, however, his wife and children were reported as having 'gone to the Primitive Methodists', and he as 'occasionally' going with them.[31] In London, according to Ernest Wilkinson, he encouraged his wife and son to attend chapel, but never went himself. The evidence suggests that he tended to steer clear of organized religion and attended chapel rarely, if at all, but pragmatically accepted the Methodist label.[32] In retirement, if the information available to the clergyman who officiated at his memorial service is to be believed, he regularly tuned in to the BBC's 'daily service' at 10.15 a.m.[33]

Sunday was sacrosanct throughout his time as a parliamentarian. He was well-known for his general refusal either to preach or to address meetings on that day. But religion was not the issue. He spent the day at home. 'One rule I shall do my best to stick to, and that is not to take any Sunday engagements, unless in very exceptional circumstances. I am determined to give that to my wife and family.'[34] The only 'very exceptional circumstance' reported in a local newspaper involved a meeting about the half-time system, which Shackleton said he agreed to speak at 'when he knew that Sir John Gorst was prepared to give up a Sunday night' for the occasion.[35]

30. *Manchester Guardian*, 2 August 1938.
31. *Colne & Nelson Times*, 11 July 1902. The Primitive Methodists were an independent, evangelistic offshoot of Wesleyan Methodism. See Thompson, *Cambridge Social History of Britain*, vol. 3, pp. 326–7. There was from early on a close connection with trade union organization (see Hobsbawm, *Uncommon People*, pp. 46–7), and the social correlation this implied persisted into the twentieth century, as the Rev. Arthur G. Gray observed at Staveley, north-east Derbyshire, in the 1920s: 'It was a strange social phenomenon that while the officials of local industry attended the Parish Church with its High Anglican Vicar, and the local business people were associated with the Wesleyan Church, the miners and their leaders were connected with the Primitive Methodist Church.' Quoted in Harold Miller, *Growing Up with Primitive Methodism*, p. 35.
32. In 1906 he was one of 18 Labour MPs who claimed to belong to a nonconformist church. But only eight of them, and he was not one those, were claimed as church members in relevant denominational publications ('all of which took great pride in listing "their" MPs'). Brown, 'Nonconformity and the British Labour Movement', pp. 116, 120–1.
33. John S. Walsh, 'Memorial Service Address': SP.
34. Unknown newspaper, 4 March 1905: SP.
35. *Nelson Leader*, 16 October 1908.

The connection with the Rechabites, to which Tom Shaw referred, was maintained to the end of Shackleton's life. He ceased to play an active part in the organizational side of the Order once he entered parliament. But as an MP, and later a retired civil servant, he spoke often at Rechabite ceremonies and at public meetings in the cause of temperance.

Shackleton was widely known not only as 'a teetotaler', but also as a 'non-smoker, and non-swearer'.[36] He once admitted to having smoked 'for twelve months' as a young man, and giving it up 'simply because I wanted the money for something else'; but later, non-smoking became 'a matter of principle'.[37] Nancy Smith, his granddaughter, remembered him as 'hating tobacco'. Her father, Herbert Catlow, smoked. That, she was told, was the only thing that her grandfather 'disliked' about his son-in-law.

Her grandfather also hated gambling. It was the reason for one of his more excitable parliamentary interventions, and led his opponent of the moment to describe him as 'one of the ablest and best, but ... most Puritanical of the Labour men'.[38] As a magistrate, he was reputed to have 'influenced his colleagues on the Bench to successful vigilance against street betting'.[39]

He was not, however, the complete puritan. Nor, as one journalistic speculation suggests, did he always come across as such: 'I have never heard that Mr Shackleton is an admirer or a frequenter of what are called "music" [music halls?], but judging from his geniality, one would rather fancy that the wit and humour of those institutions would be acceptable to him.'[40] The speculation was well judged. Following the 1909 Congress of the TUC in Ipswich, Shackleton and his wife spent the weekend in Felixstowe, a resort town on the East Anglian coast. 'On Saturday night they were to be seen laughing at the clever foolery of the White Coons.'[41] His appreciation extended to 'light classical' music, as Ernest Wilkinson described it. On prewar holidays, he took his young nephew to concerts on the pier at St Anne's, and regularly attended them after he retired. Nancy Smith also recalled him playing the piano at home in St Anne's, while the family sang hymns from the Methodist hymn book. His favourite was 'The Lord is My Shepherd'. In the Golders

---

36. *Blackburn Times*, 15 February 1908.

37. Unknown newspaper, 4 March 1905: SP.

38. Bottomley, *Bottomley's Book*, p. 71. See Chapters 5, 10, and below, concerning the Bottomley incident.

39. *Preston Guardian*, 12 November 1910.

40. *Colne & Nelson Times*, 1 November 1907.

41. *East Anglian Daily Times*, (September) 1909: SP. 'White Coons' were white performers (usually with blackened faces) of the 'coon' songs and jokes which were highly popular in the music halls of English-speaking countries from the mid-1890s and up to the eve of the First World War. The 'coon' song succeeded the minstrel-show song, and was to give rise to the ragtime era in popular music. Both 'coon' and 'minstrel' depicted black Americans in derogatory terms; but whereas the minstrel stereotype was happy, lazy and foolish, the coon stereotype was aggressive, dangerous and over-sexed. See Waterhouse, *From Minstrel Show to Vaudeville*, pp. 90–1; Schafer and Riedel, *Art of Ragtime*, pp. 24–8.

Green house before the war, according to Wilkinson, only young David played the piano; and there was no singing.

Shackleton evidently saw some plays. In retirement, he told a journalist that his favourite 'opera or play' was 'The Passing of the Third Floor Back', a hugely popular play in the years immediately preceding the war.[42] He also nominated cricket as his favourite sport;[43] and the 'Wireless' as his favourite 'amusement'. He had one of the first radio sets that Nancy Smith could remember, and she recalled him wearing its earphones 'for hours' at a time. He was particularly fond of radio talks. In retirement, he planned his day around the BBC's programmes, with the help of *Radio Times*.

Before the war, as well as spending some weekends, initially, at Blackpool and later at St Anne's, Shackleton took his family on brief summer holidays to the same place.[44] Ernest Wilkinson was often taken along to provide company for the younger David. Otherwise, it was those precious, strictly guarded Sundays at home (see above) which accounted for the bulk of Shackleton's leisure time. Wilkinson remembered Sunday in the Golders Green house as a day his uncle spent reading (and slowly eating a whole coconut that his wife had cut up for him). He read on holiday, too, and always took a book with him when he went to concerts on the pier at St Anne's – indeed it was on the pier that the permanent secretary of the future Ministry of Labour first read a copy of William Beveridge's *Unemployment*, lent to him by his young nephew.

Reading was clearly important to Shackleton; but what it was he read is less clear. In 1906, W. T. Stead, editor of the *Review of Reviews*, wrote to 51 Labour party and Lib-Lab MPs in the new parliament, asking them about the books they found 'most useful to you in the early days when your battle was beginning'.[45] Stead published all 45 responses in full. Shackleton's was one of the half-dozen briefest. It was also the only one to make no mention of specific authors or books (such as the Bible); and, unlike almost all the rest, it made no reference to adult reading. 'In regard to your letter, I cannot say that any particular book influenced me in my youth or early manhood. The

---

42. *Blackpool Gazette & Herald*, 30 June 1928. This play, written by Jerome K. Jerome, opened on 1 September 1908 at the St James's Theatre, London, to critical condemnation and resounding popular acclaim which ensured the contemporary fame of Johnson Forbes-Robertson, its lead actor, in both London and New York over the following seven years. It was twice translated into film, first in 1918 and again in the 1930s. It embodied a familiar theme: a Christlike stranger enters a distrustful and grasping world (in this case a seedy lodging-house in Bloomsbury Square) inhabited by corrupt souls. All are eventually purified by the words and presence of the stranger, who leaves as mysteriously as he arrived, and at his leaving is recognized only by the meanest in that place – in this case, Stasia, 'a slut'. See Connolly, *Jerome K. Jerome*, pp. 144–9. I am indebted to Vivienne Martin for first identifying the author and circumstances of a play that remains unacknowledged in standard histories of English theatre.

43. According to David Catlow, his grandson, he regularly attended games at St Anne's; and his son played for St Anne's.

44. *Colne & Nelson Times*, 14 September 1906.

45. 'The Labour Party and the Books that Helped to Make It', p. 568.

Manchester Guardian was my chief instructor on political and social questions, and the practical experience gained since I was twenty of official trade
union work has been my chief guide.'[46]

A year later, as we have seen (Chapter 1), he was to remember being influenced as a youth by William Cobbett's *Advice to Young Men* and the more
obscure *Hugh Wellwood's Success: or, Where There's a Will There's a Way*, by
Anne Jane Cupples.[47] He also mentioned then, with reference to his paternal
grandfather, that 'I used to pore over his books and newspapers.'[48] The extent
of his adult reading is uncertain. Tom Shaw thought it was limited: 'No one
could accuse him of being very widely read', although he remembered him
habitually coping with travel delays by 'reading a book or a paper' in a railway waiting-room.[49] Shackleton himself once implied some breadth of reading in the course of an interview when, after citing his lack of formal
education, he spoke of 'passing the threshold of a liberal education' by way of
'continual reading and private study over a course of many years'.[50] Two more
precise, though in one respect contradictory, indications of a wider reading
range may reflect the opportunities that retirement provided. Asked about
his 'favourite novelist', on one occasion, he named Dickens.[51] Seven years
later, it was reported that he 'has not been a reader of fiction, his chief literary interest being centred on biography and autobiography'.[52]

Nevertheless, whatever the scope of his reading, Shackleton is clearly
one of the 'earnest minority' of the working class, as defined by Richard
Hoggart.[53] For he was, as he made clear in his response to W. T. Stead's
inquiry, an inveterate reader of a 'quality' newspaper, the *Manchester
Guardian*. Shackleton's devotion to the paper is conveyed in a personal letter
he wrote to its longstanding editor, C. P. Scott, on leaving the Ministry of
Labour in 1925.

> Dear Mr Scott,
>   On my retirement from the position of Chief Labour Adviser to the Ministry of
> Labour I should like to tender to you my sincere thanks for the great help the
> 'Manchester Guardian' has been to me during the 41 years I have been, in various
> capacities, interested in Trade Union and Labour questions. In the early days my
> income and responsibilities would not allow of an expenditure of one penny
> per day on a newspaper, but I was enabled through the Co-operative Society

46. Ibid., pp. 579–80.
47. *M.A.P.*, 26 January 1907, p. 110. In the Stead survey, A. H. Gill, another Lancashire cotton
unionist, also cited Cobbett's book as the only one he remembered from his youthful reading:
Stead, 'The Labour Party and the Books that Helped to Make It', p. 574.
48. *M.A.P.*, 26 January 1907, p. 110.
49. *Manchester Guardian*, 2 August 1938.
50. *Northern Daily Telegraph*, 20 May 1920.
51. *Blackpool Gazette & Herald*, 30 June 1928.
52. *Lancashire Daily Post*, 27 May 1935.
53. Hoggart, *Uses of Literacy*, pp. 260–1. Surprisingly, the examples Hoggart himself gives of
this minority are limited to those on the Socialist side of the labour movement.

Newsroom to see the 'Guardian' daily and for many years purchased it for 6d. per quarter and was able to read it a day late. Whether as an operative Cotton Weaver, or Trade Union Official, Member of Parliament and later as a Civil Servant, I have received the greatest help from the paper. During the past nine years at the Ministry of Labour its guidance has been particularly helpful ...
I am deeply grateful for this assistance, and would like you to know of it.[54]

Friends

Shackleton does not seem to have had a great deal of time for friends; or they for him. Ernest Wilkinson, whose experience in his parents' Accrington home had been very different, was struck by the absence of visitors to the Golders Green house during the six months he lived there. Shackleton, like his wife, may have left friends behind when they moved from Darwen to London in 1911. But London would not have been the alien place to him that it was to her. For he had spent a large part of the previous eight years living and working there. However, if he had friends in London, he chose (on Wilkinson's evidence) not to invite them to his home. That may have been because – although now a well-paid civil servant, living in a middle-class suburb – he clung to a common working-class disinclination to entertain in the home.[55] The character and interests of his wife would have worked in the same direction. On the other hand, as Wilkinson also observed of Shackleton: 'He never went out'. Time free from work was spent at home, reading. Nor, in the family context at least, was he an eager conversationalist. 'If you spoke of something that interested him', Wilkinson recalled, 'he'd chat about it; but otherwise he'd nothing much to say.'

In general, it seems that Shackleton was not a very sociable being. Even in retirement, according to Nancy Smith, he declined a great many invitations. Towards the end of his life, after many refusals, he finally bowed to family pressures and took his wife, and then his daughter, to successive royal garden parties.[56] But David Catlow, the grandson, did not think of him as a 'loner'. His morning routine, in retirement, was to read the *Manchester Guardian* and then go for a walk. This usually took him to the pier, 'one of St Anne's' most select rendezvous',[57] where he met with a number of other retired men. They talked over coffee, and called themselves 'the seabirds'. Catlow had the impression that his grandfather was responsible for forming 'the seabirds'.

Shackleton is recorded as speaking of some men (and only men) as friends. With one exception, they were all parliamentary colleagues. In 1905 he was interviewed in the 'cosy little parlour', at the front of his house in London Terrace, Darwen. The interviewer noticed two photographs, one on either

54. Shackleton to Scott, n.d. (1925): SP.
55. See McKibbin, *Ideologies of Class*, p. 61.
56. His granddaughter was to have gone with him to the next one, but he died beforehand.
57. Parry, *Resorts of the Lancashire Coast*, p. 74.

side of the parlour window, opening directly on to the street. Each was of a man in mayoral robes. '"My friend Arthur Henderson," remarks Mr Shackleton, pointing to one, and "My friend Will Crooks," pointing to the other.'[58] Both Henderson and Crooks, of course, had followed Shackleton into parliament in 1903; and, together with Keir Hardie, comprised the independent Labour group until 1906. A second interviewer entered the house in London Terrace, three years after the first. This time, he was ushered past the parlour and into the kitchen at the back, where the walls held only family photographs. But an album was to hand. It was 'an album of photographs associated with [Shackleton's] Parliamentary career', and figuring in it were 'his favourites', three fellow-MPs, Henderson, Crooks and A. H. Gill: 'More than once he laughingly referred to them as "my pals, Arthur and Bill and Alf"'.[59]

Arthur, Bill and Alf were all there four years later at his daughter's wedding, when Shackleton was a civil servant. Another photograph was taken, and published under the headline: 'Labour M.P.s at a Wedding'. Bill missed the photo opportunity, but Arthur and Alf were in it, alongside the bridal party and Shackleton (but not his wife), together with two other Labour parliamentarians, G. J. Wardle and C. W. Bowerman, then secretary of the TUC.[60] The meticulous listing of 'presents' added to the parliamentary echoes with entries relating to Mr and Mrs Richard Bell, who gave a cheque, and to Mr and Mrs Philip Snowden, who gave a 'case of silver dessert knives and forks'.[61]

Arthur Henderson was certainly the closest of Shackleton's parliamentary associates. They shared the same lodgings from mid-1903 until the beginning of 1906, when Henderson brought his family to London. 'Alf' Gill and his wife also shared lodgings with Shackleton, for a time, after Gill entered parliament in 1906; but he, in any case, was a cotton trade union official with whom Shackleton was long familiar. Will ('Bill') Crooks was a Londoner with a London electorate, and so at home from the start.

Henderson, like Shackleton, was a teetotaller and non-smoker, as was Crooks. Keir Hardie, the fourth member of the pre-1906 LRC group, was also a non-drinker but loved his pipe. Like Shackleton, too, Henderson was a northern trade union official and had been a strong Liberal. Ideologically and, it seems, temperamentally sympathetic, they spent many hours alongside each other in the House of Commons; and chatted often in the parliamentary tea room over glasses of milk.[62] In the early days especially, they also appear to have spent appreciably more time, than either Crooks or Hardie, in speaking at local meetings on the other's behalf.[63] They also appeared together on non-Labour platforms – and, as a result, were joined as the target

58. Unknown newspaper, 4 March 1905: SP.
59. Ibid., 15 February 1908: SP.
60. Ibid., n.d. (May 1912): SP.
61. *Blackburn Weekly Telegraph*, n.d. (May 1912): SP.
62. Hamilton, *Arthur Henderson*, p. 47.
63. See, e.g., *Nelson Leader*, 2 December 1904.

21   Shackleton at 29.
*Lindsey, Duckworth-street,
Darwen*: SP.

22   Sarah Shackleton at 26.
*Harrison, Abbey-street,
Accrington*: SP.

23 On the left, Shackleton, at 50 years of age. Margaret, his daughter, displays her infant son, David, alongside the great-grandfather, William.
M.A.P. (*Mainly About People*), 22 November 1913: SP.

24 This photograph, taken probably in 1925, shows (left to right)
Ernest Wilkinson (nephew); David Shackleton (son); Gladys Pearce (maid);
Sarah Shackleton; David Catlow (grandson); and Shackleton.
SP.

25 Shackleton and his wife at the time of their golden wedding
in 1933.
Geo. Lord, St Anne's-on-Sea: SP.

26 Shackleton, with his son-in-law, Herbert Catlow, and (largely obscured) his grandson, David Catlow, watching the cricket at Blackpool, probably about 1928. His son, David, played for St Anne's.
SP.

27 Shackleton's daughter, Margaret, married Herbert Catlow in the Wesleyan
Church, Hampstead, in May 1912. The top photograph shows (left to right) Arthur
Henderson, MP; G. J. Wardle, MP; R. S. Catlow (best man); the bridegroom and
bride; Miss Haw (bridesmaid); Shackleton; A. H. Gill, MP; and C. W. Bowerman,
MP. Those in the front rank of the bottom photograph, partially obscuring the best
man and the bridesmaid, include (left to right) Shackleton; the bridegroom's
mother; Shackleton's son, David; and Sarah Shackleton.
Unknown newspaper, May 1912: SP.

28   Ben Turner, on the left, posing for the camera with Shackleton, in 1908, when the latter was at the height of his authority in the labour movement. Turner headed the Yorkshire-based Textile Workers' Union and had a reputation as a Socialist (though he accepted a knighthood in 1931). He publicly laid claim to Shackleton's friendship more than once, but altogether ignored him in an autobiography with a chapter devoted to 'Folks I Have Known'.
Unknown newspaper, September 1908: SP.

29   The platform style of Shackleton (left) and Keir Hardie (right). The inset
shows their amusement at a Philip Snowden joke. The occasion was an Independent
Labour Party 'demonstration' held, with permission, on the estate of Lord
Ribblesdale, whose son was well known for his 'pronounced Socialistic views'.
Daily Sketch, 27 June 1910: SP.

A caricature by Matt of some leaders at to-morrow's Trades Union Congress.

30 Left to right: J. E. Sutton, J. R. Clynes, Shackleton, Will Thorne and C. W. Bowerman. This caricature emphasizes the physical discrepancy between Shackleton and his fellows in the labour movement. His height and bulk, especially in the light of his beginnings as a nine-year-old 'half-time' weaver, were a constant source of comment throughout his career.

Ideas (September 1907?): SP.

SIR
DAVID
SHACKLETON
K·C·B·, J·P·

31   This sketch, published when Shackleton was 71, accompanied a long
newspaper article about him entitled 'The Lancashire Half-Timer Who Became a
Leader Among Men'.
Lancashire Evening Post, 27 May 1935: SP.

of the Socialists' fury in the Devonport affair (see Chapter 4). Henderson's
first biographer claimed that, from early in their parliamentary association,
they 'had become and were to remain, close friends'.[64] A letter from Henderson's son to Shackleton's widow in 1938 (Henderson had died three years earlier) seems to confirm that judgement. 'As you know, the friendship between
your husband and my father was deep and sincere, and we all remember him
as a good friend of the family.'[65] Nancy Smith, the granddaughter, recalled
being told that the Hendersons and the Shackletons were very close. She also
recollected that Henderson's was the only 'political' wife with whom Sarah
Shackleton was friendly.[66]

There was one other man – not a parliamentarian – whom Shackleton was
reported in 1935 to have regarded as a friend: 'He acclaims the late C. P. Scott
as his greatest teacher, his best friend.'[67] If the report is accurate, the friendship was not of many years standing to judge by the formality of the letter
Shackleton wrote to Scott, editor of the *Manchester Guardian*, in 1925 (see
above) – unless, of course, it was a letter designed to support an ageing friend
in the face of challenges to his position.[68]

Shackleton's surviving papers suggest that he took pains to maintain
formal contact through letters of congratulation, on such things as election
results, and commiseration in cases of illness and death. Thus, in relation to
John Burns, with whom he had had a flaming public row in 1904 (see Chapter 4), Shackleton wrote courteously in 1908 expressing the hope that Burns's
health was improving; and almost thirty years later (when the 'Dear Mr
Burns' of 1908 had become 'Dear John'), he offered Burns condolences on the
death of his wife.[69] It may well be that Shackleton regarded Burns, and the
others to whom he wrote in similar vein, as friends – although, in the particular case, the style of Burns's later years seems to have admitted little in the
way of friendship.[70]

Then there are those who claimed friendship with him. One was Lord
Shuttleworth, the Liberal who (as Kay-Shuttleworth) stepped down from the
Clitheroe seat in 1902 at the age of 58 and, despite persistent ill health, lived

64. Hamilton, *Arthur Henderson*, p. 46.
65. W. W. Henderson to Lady Shackleton, 2 August 1938: SP.
66. Philip Snowden, hearing of the Shackletons' imminent move to Golders Green where he
already had his home, wrote that his wife would be 'delighted to make friends with Mrs Shackleton when you come down here'. Snowden to Shackleton, 15 December 1910: SP. Ernest
Wilkinson, aware that the Snowdens lived nearby during his stay at 55 Rotherwick Road, said
that they never visited. They were invited to Margaret's wedding in May 1912, and sent a gift
(see above), but did not attend. On the other hand, Nancy Smith recalled that Snowden's wife,
by then Lady Snowden, once stayed in her parents' Blackpool home.
67. *Lancashire Daily Post*, 27 May 1935.
68. Scott, after 57 years as editor, retired in 1929. He died in Manchester on New Year's Day
1932.
69. Shackleton to Burns, 2 June 1908; November 1936: Burns Coll., vol. XX, BM Add. MS
46300, fol. 84; 46304, fol. 242.
70. See Brown, *John Burns*, p. 202.

long enough to write to Shackleton's widow: 'Sir David was a very good friend to me.'[71] Ernest Wilkinson thought of his uncle as 'a close friend' of Shuttleworth;[72] and Nancy Smith remembered her grandparents visiting Shuttleworth and his daughter, Rachel, whom Nancy's mother, Margaret, knew well. A second aristocratic claim of friendship was made in more flamboyant fashion by Lord Derby, who had been a member of the House of Commons during Shackleton's early years as an MP. In 1933, as Nancy Smith recalled, Derby, then Lord Lieutenant of Lancashire, drove to St Anne's in a car laden with 50 yellow roses from his country seat to celebrate the Shackletons' golden wedding.[73]

From two trade unionists, Ben Turner and Margaret Bondfield, there were claims of friendship which were followed by strange autobiographical silences. Turner, a Yorkshire textile union official, boasted in 1925 that 'I have had the friendship of David Shackleton for over 30 years.'[74] Sixteen years earlier, indeed, he had given unusual expression to the friendship in the form of a warmly supportive four-stanza poem, published in the *Cotton Factory Times* as a 'tribute to Mr Shackleton from a worker'.[75] But his autobiography, published in 1930, does not so much as mention Shackleton's name – even in an 18-page chapter on 'Folks I Have Known'. Similarly, Shackleton is altogether passed over in the later autobiography of Margaret Bondfield, a union official and parliamentarian, who told his widow of a 'kindly friendship', stretching back to 1899, and of his 'most precious ... capacity for making and keeping friends'.[76] According to Nancy Smith, moreover, Bondfield had stayed overnight at the Shackletons' house in St Anne's at least once; and at Shackleton's request, she came to his granddaughter's school speech-day and presented the prizes. Her autobiography is certainly a raw and formal work, concentrating very much on the public record and the political testament, but – while ignoring Shackleton – she still found room in it for three warm personal references to Arthur Henderson.[77]

Finally, there are the friendships attributed, mostly casually, by others. One press report described Tom Shaw, a newly appointed Minister of Labour, as Shackleton's 'old friend'.[78] Again, after a newspaper photographer snapped Shackleton talking with Ramsay MacDonald outside the Blackpool hall where the Labour party's 1927 conference was held, the photo was published

71. Shuttleworth to Lady Shackleton, 2 August 1938: SP.
72. Letter to author, 17 July 1979.
73. The same Lord Derby was claimed as a generous and courteous friend by James Sexton, the dockers' leader. See Sexton, *Sir James Sexton Agitator*, pp. 290–2.
74. Unknown newspaper, n.d.(1925): SP.
75. *Cotton Factory Times*, 31 December 1909.
76. Bondfield to Lady Shackleton, 10 August 1938: SP.
77. Bondfield, *Life's Work*, pp. 253n, 262n, 316–17.
78. Unknown newspaper, n.d. (1924): SP.

over a caption which began: 'Old Friends ...'.[79] And, more than twenty years earlier, there were rumours that linked Shackleton with the notorious Countess of Warwick, erstwhile mistress of the Prince of Wales, and subsequently a devotee of left-wing causes and the men who promoted them. Nancy Smith was told of a poison-pen letter sent to Shackleton's wife that alleged a liaison. There was also a story, part of the Catlow family lore, which had the Countess offering Shackleton (with his wife nearby) the remaining seat in her carriage; he accepted, but took his wife on his knee. This could have occurred during one of the TUC's annual congresses at which Shackleton was a leading figure. The Countess is recorded in the official Congress minutes as attending the opening ceremony at six of the seven congresses held between 1904 and 1910.[80] But her two autobiographical works, like those of Turner and Bondfield, make no mention of him.[81]

Feelings

What kind of person was David Shackleton? In the recollections of his nephew, Ernest Wilkinson, and his grandchildren, Nancy Smith and David Catlow, there is one feature of Shackleton's conduct in the family circle that stands out. It is the calm face he turned to those around him. Nancy Smith remembered him as softly spoken and 'very, very gentle', and could not recall him ever losing his temper. When she was a child, he was the kind of grandfather who took his granddaughter, on his own, for quiet walks through the park, and then to a café for ice-cream. The grandson, David Catlow, similarly remembered him as 'very kindly, placid' and 'very tolerant'. Ernest Wilkinson, more familiar with him before retirement, remembered him as 'very sober', 'always calm', 'a very peaceable man: I've never seen him roused in any way at all'. Nor did he laugh much.

No emotion and little humour: that seems to be the impression in the family. It was often the public perception as well. 'There is no sentiment in Shackleton, neither is there much humour', wrote James Cornthwaite.[82] And Alfred Kinnear, in a passage much quoted by other journalists, underscored the lack of humour in a comment about Shackleton at Westminster. 'His addresses have been usually couched in the graver moods of debate. He does not suggest humour at sight, and his character has been unflecked by jest or frivolity.'[83]

---

79. *Northern Daily Telegraph*, n.d. (1927): SP. The MacDonald Papers contain two letters Shackleton wrote to MacDonald after 1910 (one in 1914, the other in 1937), both mainly to do with the latter's state of health. PRO 30/69/759 and 1158 69951.

80. At the 1905 Congress, she put her 'motor car ... at the disposal' of the TUC's Parliamentary Committee. TUC, PC, *Minutes*, 1 September 1905. On two other occasions, in 1904 and 1909, the committee accepted an invitation to take afternoon tea with her. Ibid., 25 October 1904; 7 July 1909.

81. Warwick, *Life's Ebb and Flow*; *Afterthoughts*.

82. *Sunday Chronicle*, 18 September 1910.

83. *Lancashire Daily Post*, 17 June 1908.

There is, nevertheless, clear evidence of frivolity. One interviewer was taken with 'his broad smile ... his hearty laugh'.[84] An observer at the TUC's 1906 Congress saw him 'convulsed with amusement at [a delegate's] transparent tactics'.[85] Following the 1909 Congress, he was seen laughing at the antics of the 'White Coons' on the Felixstowe pier (see above). And later, an enterprising *Daily Sketch* photographer at a Labour party demonstration not only snapped the orators about their business, but also caught Keir Hardie smiling and Shackleton plainly laughing at a remark of Philip Snowden's.[86]

However, the most trenchant evidence of Shackleton's sense of humour comes (*pace* Kinnear) from the House of Commons. One parliamentary observer described him as 'Breezy, full of fun'.[87] Another, recounting an episode in which Ramsay MacDonald's 'usual corner seat' in the House was usurped in his absence by a certain Henniker Heaton, contrasted the reactions of MacDonald's immediate neighbours. 'Shackleton took the invasion jauntily, and apparently made jokes with the invader. Henderson was much more solemn over the act of sacrilege, and once ... gave the offender a good hint by sitting down in the gangway, as if deprived of a regular seat.'[88] And then there is the way Shackleton dealt with some opponents of the Trade Disputes Bill: 'now and then as a Tory speaker gets tedious, Shackleton turns to him a laughing face which simply disarms all opposition'.[89] In addition, he made at least one deliberate attempt at humour in a parliamentary speech. He had intervened in an Estimates debate to attack regulations excluding 'hired cabs', but not private motor cars and carriages, from Hyde Park. The joke: 'He did not keep a motor-car or carriage, and the only thing of that kind he ever owned was a perambulator.'[90] This 'amusing sally', according to one observer, 'put the House of Commons in a roar'.[91] Capping it all is a newspaper sketch entitled 'Mr Shackleton, the Champion Chuckler', which depicts a huge-bellied, hands-in-pockets Shackleton lounging on a parliamentary bench, with the notes of his last speech scattered about him. A brief article by an anonymous journalist follows.

> Mr Shackleton, the member for Clitheroe, is the champion chuckler. You remember the Mephistophelian laugh at the close of 'Faust.' Well, if you can conceive Mephistopheles as a broad, big man, who takes 47's in waistcoats, and then imagine him laughing, you will have a good idea of the Shackletonian mirth. When he laughs heavily, the centre of the bench swings like a man walking on the plank. It

84.   Unknown newspaper, 4 March 1905: SP.
85.   *Cotton Factory Times*, 7 September 1906.
86.   Unknown newspaper, (27 June 1910): SP. This is the only light-hearted photograph among some 150 (almost all from newspapers) included in the Shackleton papers. In the style of the times, photographing and being photographed was normally a serious business.
87.   *Colne & Nelson Times*, 22 March 1907.
88.   *Labour Leader*, 26 October 1906.
89.   Ibid., 9 November 1906.
90.   *Parl. Debs.*, 21 February 1907, vol. 169, col. 1062.
91.   Unknown newspaper, February 1907: SP.

is delicious to hear. Many a time, when I have finished my article for the night, and am snoozing in the Gallery, paying little more attention to the babble downstairs than one does to the murmur of a brook ... Mr Shackleton's laugh breaks the happy rhythm of my dream, and I get the idea ... that the entire building is shaking.[92]

The public man could laugh. Could he show anger? It seems so, although the evidence provided by observers is sketchier. He is described as attacking, 'with some heat', Quelch's resolution proposing a Labour party programme at the party's 1907 conference.[93] At its 1908 conference, when he rose to oppose yet another socialization resolution, the 'big Lancashire man, who is generally quiet and self-restrained, was quivering with excitement'.[94] At the next conference a year later, with Ben Tillett as his target, he 'spoke with unwonted fire, and his arms swung around him as if he would fain have used them in a more potent fashion upon his adversary'.[95] And in 1910, at his last TUC Congress as a unionist, there was palpable anger in his words and the exchanges he was involved in as the Osborne debate ended (see Chapter 7). There was, too, at least one matching parliamentary occasion. It had to do with Bottomley's bill to legitimate street betting. As reported, the 'usually genial and placid Member for the Clitheroe Division displayed unwonted heat, and ... indignantly demanded where the Member for South Hackney [Bottomley] got his mandate to speak, on behalf of the working-man'.[96] Bottomley himself had a more vivid recollection: 'Shackleton was white with indignation.'[97]

So much for anger; but what of sorrow? There is no evidence that Shackleton ever wept, either in public or in private. He may well have wept when his sons died. He may even have done so following the young Burnley man's death under the wheels of the car he was in on polling day in January 1906. Certainly, thereafter, he avoided cars when he could. Nancy Smith said he 'hated' them; and, in his retirement, he never travelled in one unless it was driven by either Herbert Catlow, his son-in-law, or the police sergeant who regularly took him to the County Court at Preston, where he sat as a Justice of the Peace.

There is a similar suggestion of deep feeling in the reports of two speeches on the issue of temperance.[98] One included a moving (if, to modern ears,

92.   Ibid., n.d.: SP.
93.   *Cotton Factory Times*, 1 February 1907.
94.   *Daily Chronicle*, 23 January 1908.
95.   *Labour Leader*, 5 February 1909.
96.   *Colne & Nelson Times*, 6 April 1906.
97.   Bottomley, *Bottomley's Book*, p. 71.
98.   On this issue, there was a connection with personal experience. Sarah, his wife, came from a drunken home. She had a sister who remained in that environment, and put in an occasional appearance. Nancy Smith, at the tail-end of it all in the years when the widowed Sarah was living with her daughter's family, remembered the sister's visits as 'dreaded occasions'.

faintly priggish) recollection of agonising insecurity, in the face of 'the temptations that beset public men'. He told his audience that 'on more than one occasion he had had to upset his glass in front of him, and it had required a strong nerve to refuse to touch it when he had been the only one who would not have it round a table of 20 or 30 men holding official positions'.[99] In the other speech, he struck a truly chilling note in the course of commenting on the employment of barmaids in public houses. It has to be remembered that he spoke as a man who not only had a 15-year-old daughter and a newborn son at the time, but had suffered the deaths of two sons (aged 4 and 11) within the previous five years.

> During his work he had occasionally to go to these places [public houses] and it was a sad sight for him to see girls behind the counter ... He thought sometimes when he saw them what he should think of his girl behind that counter. *He would sooner bury her.* No one knew the loss of a child unless they had lost one, but to him the sight of a young girl behind the bar of a public-house was very serious.[100]

There were one or two other occasions, too, when his choice of words betrayed deep feeling – as in the uncharacteristic extravagance of 'workmen slain by the way' in strikes, of employers as 'the man with the money-bags',[101] of landlords living 'their life of pleasure and luxury',[102] and of Britons as 'semi-slaves' because of the House of Lords.[103]

★ ★ ★ ★

Shackleton clearly possessed a strong sense of honour, a feeling of right and of the need to stick to it. That is not to say he always acted with complete propriety. For one thing, there was the lie he certainly told about his age when he married Sarah Broadbent in 1883 (see Chapter 1). He may have lied again 27 years later, when he denied knowledge of a Home Office job offer, but probably not (see Chapter 7). In the intervening years, he was once publicly accused of sharp practice as chairman of the TUC's annual Congress;[104] and, less plausibly, of unfair tactics as a Congress speaker.[105] It may be, too, that he privately accused himself of an unworthy action when he discarded

99. *Nelson Chronicle*, 3 October 1902.
100. Ibid., 2 October 1903. Emphasis added.
101. *Cotton Factory Times*, 30 July 1909.
102. TUC, *Report*, 1909, p. 48.
103. *Cotton Factory Times*, 4 December 1908.
104. The Salford Catholic Federation complained – with some justification, it would seem – about his refusal to put a resolution on secular education to a card vote at the 1909 Congress. See Chapter 10.
105. Some time after his exchange with Shackleton in the Osborne debate at the 1910 Congress (see Chapter 7), Stephen Walsh wrote a long letter to the *Manchester Guardian* in which he detailed his complaint that Shackleton had breached the principles of 'fair argument and decent regard for the rights of others' – and also charged him with 'a domineering attitude, a strident voice, and a sledge-hammer style'. Quoted in *Nelson Leader*, 4 November 1910.

(assuming he was the discarder) his copies of the three hard-bargaining letters he wrote to Masterman about the Home Office job (see Chapter 7).[106]

Overwhelmingly, however, what others observed in Shackleton, and remarked on, were the traits of an honourable man. In Conservative journals, for example, he was described as 'a thoroughly honest man',[107] whose parliamentary successes were due to 'his force of character and evident sincerity'.[108] On the Labour left, Blatchford's *Clarion* said he was 'trusted by his fellows [in the labour movement] because of his honesty and sincerity';[109] and Bruce Glasier thought his first presidential address to the TUC (while 'no ... great utterance' – for it lacked even 'an atom of Socialism') 'plain and straightforward, and ... Mr Shackleton meant every word that he said'.[110] A Liberal journalist also opted for 'straightforward': 'Of the numerous candidates and M.P.'s that one has heard, Mr Shackleton bears the palm for straightforwardness.'[111] Even Keir Hardie, in an atypically generous comment, once reached for the same term. 'He [Shackleton] is very loyal and straightforward and were I in heaven [he] wd. feel happier and give I believe a very straight lead. As it is he does his best to control the feeling of personal dislike which he has imbibed from his surroundings & is by far the best of the lot.'[112]

Hardie's depiction of Shackleton as 'loyal' is significant, especially given his recognition of the absence of fellow-feeling between them. Loyalty and obligation are twins. And around about the time that Hardie expressed this opinion, Shackleton demonstrated his sense of obligation in relation to three men who were much more remote from his immediate interests. They were the three who had most to do with his unopposed win in the Clitheroe by-election: Philip Snowden of the ILP, and the Liberals, Philip Stanhope and Franklin Thomasson. Shackleton publicly thanked Snowden in several speeches after the by-election,[113] and later chaired a meeting in support of Snowden's campaign for the Blackburn seat, explaining that he did so 'because he desired to reciprocate that good feeling which Mr Snowden showed towards himself and the Labour party in the Clitheroe Division'.[114] In Stanhope's case, Shackleton wrote to the Liberal party authorities in the Cleveland electorate warmly supporting his selection: 'His action during the Clitheroe by-election has earned for him our [those in the cotton trade] lasting gratitude.'[115] Thomasson's case provided the sterner test. It involved a

106. It is possible, of course, that they were discarded, deliberately or accidentally, by another hand.
107. *Pall Mall Gazette*, quoted in *Nelson Leader*, 26 January 1906.
108. *Colne & Nelson Times*, 9 February 1906.
109. *Clarion*, 11 September 1908.
110. *Labour Leader*, 11 September 1908.
111. *Nelson Leader*, 26 January 1906.
112. Hardie to Glasier, n.d. (1903): Glasier Coll. I.1. 1903/40. Arthur Henderson and Will Crooks comprised the rest of 'the lot' that Hardie had in mind.
113. See, e.g., *Nelson Chronicle*, 8 August 1902.
114. Ibid., 26 December 1902.
115. Ibid., 17 October 1902.

by-election in Accrington in which Thomasson, standing as a Liberal, was opposed by an LRC candidate, T. Greenall. Both the local LRC leaders and Ramsay MacDonald, national LRC secretary, repeatedly pressed him to speak in support of Greenall and against Thomasson. But he steadfastly refused, despite damaging rumours about a prior deal with the Liberals, and a formal appeal by the Accrington LRC to the national executive (see Chapter 4).

The better part of a century after these events, Shackleton was described by Frederick Leggett, who worked under him at the Ministry of Labour, as a 'very upright man ... He couldn't do a dishonourable thing.'[116] Leggett, of course, may have been tempted into eulogizing the dead. On the other hand, he spoke far less kindly of other deceased colleagues. In addition, there is an incident which tends to support Leggett's opinion about Shackleton's sense of fair play. It concerned William Beveridge's protest against his appointment as permanent secretary. Beveridge, after talking with Shackleton, asked him to arrange an appointment with John Hodge, the Minister. Shackleton fixed a time for the next day, and then told Hodge of the appointment. When Hodge asked him what Beveridge wanted, he would say no more than that 'Mr Beveridge will tell you when he comes.'[117] After his meeting with Beveridge, Hodge queried Shackleton about the lack of warning. As he recalled it, the reason Shackleton gave was that 'I did not want to prejudice the position, preferring that you should make your decision with an unprejudiced mind.'[118] According to Frederick Leggett, it was precisely this penchant for straight dealing which was Shackleton's Achilles' heel as a senior civil servant: 'He wasn't really equipped to be permanent secretary of a government department ... He wasn't up to the scheming.'[119]

★ ★ ★ ★

The Beveridge episode reveals, as well, a sense of humility. This seems to have had its main source in Shackleton's feelings about education. His lack of formal education was an acutely sensitive issue: hence the apologia at a prize-giving for Nelson evening class (technical education) students.

> Mr Shackleton said that of all the meetings he had to attend up and down the country, [this] class of meeting was to him the most satisfactory in one sense, and not in another. He liked to be at [these] meetings, but he liked to be there as a listener. Of all the subjects he was least competent to speak about was that of education of the character they were met to celebrate that night. He had no opportunity such as the boys and girls had to-day. He was limited to his three R's, half-time at 9, full-time [employed] at 13, and a little night school in the ordinary elementary

116. Interview, 25 March 1981.
117. Hodge, *Workman's Cottage to Windsor Castle*, p. 179.
118. Ibid., p. 180.
119. Interview, 25 March 1981.

subjects. Therefore any of the educated ladies and gentlemen there that night would have some sympathy for him when he spoke on education.[120]

Even speaking to his own people, the nerve could be exposed, as in his response to a Congress vote of thanks: 'We do our best ... with the education we have had.'[121] And a decade later, as an extremely senior civil servant, he could still reflect wistfully on the difference that, as he saw it, a university education made.

> I realise now, as I realised many years ago, how great is the help to a man engaged in public work of a University training. I have often regretted that such an opportunity did not come to me ... Often, in my early days in the House of Commons, in the presence of gifted men of affairs in different parties, whose intellects have been trained and specialised before they really started life, have I wished for their advantages.[122]

His sense of disadvantage, of being under-qualified, could only have intensified once he entered the civil service, especially at the Ministry of Labour. There he was surrounded by men, technically his subordinates, who possessed not only university degrees but years of senior bureaucratic experience. His early reaction to Beveridge's onslaught bespeaks a man who suspected he was not up to the job. On the day Bonar Law pressed Hodge to drop him as permanent secretary, Shackleton himself said he *wanted* to be dropped, and backed down only after Hodge brought in Arthur Henderson and the Prime Minister (see Chapter 8).

He may have been sufficiently reassured for the moment, but there is no doubt that a feeling of inadequacy lingered. Others would have masked the fact with bluster and assertions of seniority, or worse.[123] But Shackleton was capable of something else. He showed this when he chaired a departmental committee investigating the organization and staffing of the Ministry of Labour. He had been permanent secretary for over a year, and all the other committee members were his subordinates. But he chose to open the first meeting with a self-effacing confession.

> His own experience in the Civil Service had not been such as to give him much opportunity of forming a judgement as to the proper organisation of Government Departments. Although he had served in two Government Departments prior to his appointment as Permanent Secretary of the Ministry, he had been an Advisory Officer and not responsible in any way for the administration of the Department. He would be glad, therefore, to hear the views of the Committee.[124]

120. *Nelson Leader*, 28 September 1906.
121. TUC, *Report*, 1908, p. 199.
122. *Northern Daily Telegraph*, 20 May 1920.
123. Josef Stalin, it seems, turned the same feeling into a source of resentment and advantage. See Bullock, *Hitler and Stalin*, pp. 34–5.
124. Departmental Committee on the Organisation and Staffing of the Ministry of Labour, *Minutes*, 19 April 1918, p. 1: LAB 2/274/372/2 4000.

There was humility, too, in Shackleton's reaction when Hodge suggested a knighthood as a way of overcoming the 'caste difficulty' created by Askwith (see Chapter 8). Hodge said he was 'very reluctant' to accept the offer, 'but I insisted'.[125] Hodge's recollection is confirmed, in significantly greater detail, by the panegyric which the Reverend John Walsh delivered at Shackleton's memorial service: 'He *twice* refused his Knighthood.'[126] That precise information must have originated with Shackleton. Exit humility; enter pride.

Shackleton was unashamedly proud of a number of things. One was his physique. In an interview he recalled himself as a youth, 'unusually big and strong for my age'; and as a young married man, 'a great, hulking fellow'.[127] He also took pleasure in the advantages it had given him. Thus, when he was a half-timer, despite the demands of the mill, the school and his father's business, he still managed to play cricket and football – 'and, being unusually big and strong for my age, was something of a champion at them, as I continued to be throughout my youth'.[128] He was also proud of his good health, looking back to early days as 'a strong, "robustious" lad', and regarding his good health as an 'inestimable blessing [which] has ... had a great deal to do with my getting on'.[129]

Above all, of course, there was the 'getting on' itself to take pride in. His major formal achievements were usually well known to those who interviewed him; but he was not above reminding them of lesser ones. Thus, as a freshly elected parliamentarian and a JP of ten years' standing, he could not repress a small boast: 'I believe I am the first man ever made a Justice of the Peace while still an operative.'[130] Nor, like so many of his kind,[131] was he immune from the pride that comes with ostensible social acceptance by the great. In the summer of 1905, three of the four LRC parliamentarians (Keir Hardie, predictably, was the absentee) took their wives to a royal garden party at Windsor Castle. The following account is attributed to Shackleton.

> We three ... and our wives formed our own little party ... Towards the evening our party had a pleasant little surprise. We were just about to reach a gate by which to leave the grounds, when the King and Queen and Royal party appeared on the terrace ... Our party stepped back for the moment, and I noticed that the Marquis of Hamilton had seen me from the distance, and I also saw him go to speak to the King. Immediately afterwards his Lordship came to me and said the King desired to be introduced to me and my friends. Therefore, myself and Messrs. Crooks and Henderson stepped forward, and the King, leaving the rest of his party, shook hands with us and had a short chat. But that was not all. His Majesty noticed the

125. Hodge, *Workman's Cottage to Windsor Castle*, p. 182.
126. 'Memorial Service Address': SP. Emphasis added.
127. *M.A.P.*, 26 January 1907, p. 110.
128. Ibid.
129. *Pearson's Weekly*, 15 March 1906. Later in life, however, he contracted diabetes; and (refusing insulin injections) maintained a very strict diet. He died of cancer, probably of the throat.
130. Unknown newspaper, 5 September 1902: SP.
131. See, e.g., McKibbin, *Ideologies of Class*, pp. 18–19, 25–6; Martin, *TUC*, pp. 39–40; Michels, *Political Parties*, p. 319.

ladies in the rear, which we considered very kind indeed, and he said, 'Are those your wives?' We answered in the affirmative, and he then asked if he might have an introduction to them, and consequently our wives were then introduced to the King, and after his Majesty had shaken hands with them and had a further little chat, he bade us good afternoon. It was absolutely a surprise to us, and we were glad to see the free and friendly manner in which His Majesty spoke to us.[132]

Thirty years later, in his St Anne's home, Shackleton had the symbols of his success on display for a passing journalist to admire: 'Photographs ... medallions ... Golden keys ... The Star of the Order of the Bath ... the collar and jewel of a Past Chief Ruler of the Order of the Rechabites'. And in addition, there was a recent 'tribute': 'In his retirement, he was not forgotten by the King, who caused him to receive a special Jubilee medal. "It was nice of him not to forget me – very nice, indeed," comments Sir David.'[133]

Between these two events, there was the continuing accumulation of the newspaper clippings which comprise the great bulk of the Shackleton papers. Although most lack notations, there are many with handwritten dates and/or newspaper titles; and usually the handwriting is Shackleton's. Those with which he can be firmly identified in this way range from 1902, the earliest date in the collection, to 1938, the year of his death. The selection of clippings is slanted in the sense that it has been confined wholly to the mainstream, non-Socialist, press – which means, in particular, that neither the ILP's *Labour Leader* nor Blatchford's *Clarion* figure in the collection. But there is no sign that the clippings have been culled with an eye to their being either uncritical or significant. Not all are supportive, and the simple mention of his name (or his presence, however dimly, in a photograph) seems to have been enough to ensure inclusion. On the other hand, heavy culling has undoubtedly occurred in the case of the 50 or so letters, preserved from a lifetime, which the Shackleton papers contain. These letters are overwhelmingly concerned with appointments, honours, congratulations and condolences, most of which were either received from notable names or are copies of letters Shackleton sent to notable names.[134] The letters, that is to say, reflect a pride in official, formal associations and achievements.[135]

★ ★ ★ ★

132. *Cotton Factory Times*, 23 June 1905.
133. *Lancashire Daily Post*, 27 May 1935.
134. One noteworthy exception is a letter that Shackleton neither wrote nor received. It is a handwritten *copy* of a letter from Stanley Baldwin, then Prime Minister, to his Minister of Labour agreeing to Shackleton's appointment as the British member of the ILO's governing body. The body of the letter consists of just four words: 'I agree to Shackleton.' The copy is in Shackleton's hand.
135. That, too, seems to be central to the value that Shackleton attached to the clippings as well. This is suggested by a handwritten cut-out which has been pasted into the scrapbook. It reads as follows: 'Extract from Lytham St. Annes Express, 1.12.33. Many happy returns to Sir David Shackleton, J.P., K.C.B., who has celebrated his 70th birthday. "A man he seems of cheerful yesterdays and confident to-morrows." Factory Times, Nelson Leader, Accrington Observer.' The hand, again, is Shackleton's.

Striking though his achievements were, and proud of them as he was, Shackleton was nevertheless not the kind of man that people generally thought of as ambitious, in the hard, burning, unpleasant sense of the term. Thus, when he was close to the peak of his parliamentary and trade union career, it could be said of him that 'every distinction has come to him unsought. He is the antithesis of the "pushful" politician'.[136] Of course, he was certainly 'pushful' in that he actively sought union office: the young man with the book of 'sorts' above the loom was nothing if not ambitious. And once launched on this career path, he certainly *wanted* such step-ups as the Clitheroe candidacy, the presidency of the Weavers' Amalgamation, membership of the TUC Parliamentary Committee and, initially, the parliamentary Labour party's chairmanship. But what is not clear is whether, and to what extent, he actively *sought* any of these positions.

Frederick Leggett, who knew Shackleton in the final phase of his career, echoed the earlier judgements of others when he remarked: 'He wasn't an ambitious man, you know.'[137] Of course, when Leggett knew him, Shackleton had his permanent secretaryship and his knighthood, and was approaching retirement. It was probably a matter of the pinnacle reached, and all ambition spent. But that conclusion misses the extent to which achievement had outstripped ambition. For it is in the highest degree unlikely that a younger Shackleton, with his perceptions of class, education and opportunity (see Chapter 10), ever seriously imagined himself either heading a government department – at least as a civil servant – or becoming a knight.

What has to be remembered is that, by 1910, Shackleton has achieved a quite considerable public eminence. He is the subject of innumerable newspaper stories, many newspaper photographs and sketched portraits, and even attracts the attention of the cartoonists whose work is beginning to figure on an increasingly regular basis in the metropolitan daily press.[138] As one journalist puts it: 'he holds a position in the country to-day which must be the envy of many a more ambitious man'.[139] But this high profile depends upon the political and trade union fight in which he is involved. And, late in 1910, he opts out of that fight. Others, like Arthur Henderson, soldier on and achieve the kind of political fame which, at the time, was seen as Shackleton's destiny, too, before he opted out. 'It is to be regretted that the post he has accepted must necessitate his removal from Parliament, where he could not have failed ultimately to attain high political office.'[140] But high political office is no longer his ambition. Perhaps it never was. He settles, instead, for the obscure life of a middle-level, pensionable civil servant.

136. Unknown newspaper, December 1906: SP.
137. Interview, 25 March 1981.
138. See Geipel, *Cartoon*, p. 41.
139. *Nelson Leader*, 10 January 1908.
140. *Manchester Guardian*, 12 November 1910.

Then six years later the lightning strikes. David Lloyd George negotiates a wartime coalition. The Labour party demands, and wins, the creation of a Ministry of Labour. Its minister has to be a Labour man, a trade unionist; and John Hodge is the man. He, in turn, looks for a permanent secretary he can trust – and, perhaps even more important, feel comfortable with in the alien world of university-educated civil servants. Shackleton is there, ready-made, a former trade union colleague, already a civil servant; and, in terms of the old game, a plainly able man. So you get him; and then you have to struggle to keep him as the pressures mount against such an outlandish appointment, a struggle made more difficult because Shackleton's ambition and self-confidence had never stretched so far. In the end, to make assurance double sure, you cement him in with a knighthood, an audacious stroke made possible (given ministerial determination) by the tradition of knighting permanent secretaries.

If Shackleton's ambitions for place were over-fulfilled, the same is likely to be true of his ambitions for wealth.[141] To the end, as Tom Shaw remarked, he remained 'extraordinarily modest in his tastes',[142] and he was careful about money in a way that betrayed his upbringing.[143] He was capable, too, of driving a hard bargain on his own account, as shown by the special nature of the salary he secured as Senior Labour Adviser at the Home Office, in 1910, and as Chief Labour Adviser at the Ministry of Labour in 1921 (see Chapter 8). On the other hand, he seems to have been neither avaricious nor mean. An avaricious man would not, as Nancy Smith affirmed, have 'invariably' rejected lucrative invitations to directorships and 'sleeping partnerships'. A mean man would not have bought a house in St Anne's for four of his half-sisters, and the husband of one, to live in.

141.   He died a wealthy man by the standards of a Lancashire weaver, leaving an estate of £7,288. On the other hand, this amount was exceeded in the case of nine other members of the original, 30-member parliamentary Labour party of 1906. Arthur Henderson and Ramsay Mac-Donald, for example, each left an estate that was well over three times as great. See table in Martin and Rubinstein, *Ideology and the Labour Movement*, p. 128.
142.   *Manchester Guardian*, 2 August 1938. Ernest Wilkinson, who accompanied the Shackletons on prewar holidays, recalled that even when Shackleton was a very well-paid civil servant, the family continued to avoid staying at a boarding-house, choosing instead the cheaper option of 'apartments' which allowed them to supply their own food for the landlady to cook.
143.   Thus the will he left was home-made, handwritten on a form bought from the local newsagent, and witnessed by the Shackletons' live-in maid and the housemaid from next door, at Lytham St Anne's in February 1931.

10

The Public Man

Appearance

At the age of 39, Shackleton was described as 'a big, burly fellow, with kindly brown eyes, and ... 6 feet 1½ inches' in height.[1] He was thought to weigh 'somewhere about 17 or 18 stone'.[2] Ernest Wilkinson, his nephew, recalled his heavy tread. His size, the first thing to be mentioned in the recollections of slighter colleagues ('a genial giant'; 'over six feet'),[3] was frequently referred to by parliamentary observers. Thus, when he first entered the House of Commons after the Clitheroe by-election: 'In contrast with Mr Bell and Mr Hardie [his formal sponsors], Mr Shackleton seemed some Gulliver among the Lilliputians.'[4] Similarly, in the totally different environment of a Berlin conference hall, packed with 6,000 people and thousands more outside: 'The announcement of the well-known name of Mr Shackleton evoked loud cheers, which grew into a wild demonstration of admiration when this splendid specimen of a Briton, with his black beard and fine physique, advanced to the front of the platform.'[5] There were many journalistic variants on this theme of an arresting physical presence,[6] but by far the most common were of the giant variety – 'the giant M.P.' (once delicately elaborated as 'the giant M.P. with his little good wife'),[7] 'the Labour giant', 'the Clitheroe giant' and 'the Lancashire giant'.

Much of the wonder at his size stemmed from the contrast with the stunted growth characteristic of his class and occupation. 'One could hardly believe', as one commentator put it, 'that he had begun life as a half-timer in a Lancashire cotton mill.'[8] An elderly working-class Conservative made the same

---

1. *Co-operative News*, 31 January 1903 (6 feet 1½ inches equal 184 cm).
2. *Colne & Nelson Times*, 11 July 1902 (18 stone equal 252 lb or 114 kg).
3. Clynes, *Memoirs*, p. 126; Snowden, *Autobiography*, vol. I, p. 105.
4. *Cotton Factory Times*, 8 August 1902.
5. *Colne & Nelson Times*, 25 September 1908.
6. Though that of the *Tailor and Cutter* was unique: what 'a pity', it commented on his entry into parliament, 'that such a fine, large fellow should be wasted on such clothes'. *Daily Dispatch*, cited in unknown newspaper, n.d. (December 1916): SP.
7. *Cotton Factory Times*, 12 September 1902.
8. *Nelson Chronicle*, 8 August 1902. This was a reaction on which Shackleton seems to have capitalized before he changed his public position on the half-timer issue in 1907 (see Chapter 6 and below). He was remembered for light-heartedly presenting himself as a former half-timer in

social point in a different way, on first seeing him as a new MP: 'What a fine-looking chap he is. He owt [ought] to be a Tory!'⁹ At the opposite end of the political spectrum, the supercilious Henry Hyndman used Shackleton's bulk to make a painfully weak pun about the Labour party.¹⁰

There was one incongruity. After Shackleton's death, John Burns was asked what he remembered most about his former parliamentary colleague. 'His hands', Burns replied. 'Shackleton's hands were as handsome as a woman's that are carefully manicured. They always drew your attention when he put them on the table in committee. They were not the hands you look for in a workman – a weaver.'¹¹

The hands might be a mismatch, but the voice was not. In conversation, as Ernest Wilkinson remembered, it was deep and without a pronounced accent – although 'a Lancashire man' would have picked him. Another observer, at an earlier stage of Shackleton's career, descried only a 'slightly Lancashire accent'.¹² On the platform, it was a 'big strident voice'.¹³ Indeed, with the

response to arguments about the physical damage inflicted on children by the half-time system, a tactic which 'usually created great amusement because ranged alongside Mr Shackleton there were many puny specimens of other men who had been half-timers'. Hodge, *From Workman's Cottage to Windsor Castle*, p. 157; see also Snowden, *Autobiography*, vol. 1, pp. 5–6. A *Yorkshire Post* journalist, recalling an occasion in the House of Commons lobby, gave a less charitable account of this tactic by describing Shackleton as 'sneering at those who said that half-time labour injured the physique of the children. "Look at me," he said to one member, "I went to work at ten [*sic*]." And as Mr Shackleton is a giant among men, the argument told.' Quoted in *Colne & Nelson Times*, 16 October 1908. In 1907, when he changed his public position, Shackleton himself spoke of the tactic as a jest made by others. 'My physique affords an excuse for joking amongst our people in Lancashire ... and my acquaintants frequently point to me and say "Mr Shackleton's not a bad sample of a half-timer, is he?".' *Cassell's Saturday Journal*, quoted in *Colne & Nelson Times*, 22 March 1907. Fom that time on, he made no attempt to play down the general physical difference between former half-timers and other workers: 'the latter', he said, 'were inches taller'. *Cotton Factory Times*, 12 March 1909.

9.   Unknown newspaper, n.d. (August 1902): SP. Biographic studies occasionally touch on the issue of leadership and physical size. See, e.g., Brett, *Robert Menzies' Forgotten People*, pp. 226–7; Bullock, *Hitler and Stalin*, pp. 13, 948; Tuchman, *Practising History*, p. 84. Systematic studies of the linkages between leadership and physical qualities have tended to focus on the broader attribute of 'attractiveness'. See, e.g., Cherulnik, 'Physical Appearance and Leadership'. There are nevertheless a number of early studies – mainly dealing with student leaders – which indicate 'a low positive relationship' between both greater height and leadership, and heavier weight and leadership. Stogdill, 'Personal Factors Associated with Leadership', p. 41. In Shackleton's case at least, there is little doubt that he was greatly advantaged by his size.

10.   'The total victories of the Labour Party were ... a good deal more than respectable, showing a solid body – Shackleton, Will Thorne, and Hodge justify the epithet – of more than thirty members.' Hyndman, *Further Reminiscences*, p. 272.

11.   Unknown newspaper, n.d. (1938?): SP. Many years earlier, too, Burns had been reported as saying Shackleton's hands were 'the most beautiful in the House'. *Lancashire Daily Post*, 17 June 1908. Burns had a point, as the portrait providing the frontispiece above indicates.

12.   *Clarion*, 6 April 1906.

13.   James Cornthwaite, *Sunday Chronicle*, 18 September 1910.

death of Pete Curran in 1910, it was judged 'the strongest voice' in the labour movement 'since Curran has left us'.[14] In the chapel, it was 'that fine bass voice' recalled by the minister at Shackleton's memorial service.[15] As one account of a Labour party conference suggests, the voice and the size were a powerful combination. 'Raising his huge form like a mountain and his huge voice like a brass band, Mr Shackleton compelled the attention of the conference.'[16]

Working Style

No one, at least among those who wrote about him, thought of Shackleton as clever or imaginative. When the mind was touched on, the picture invariably given was one of sober common sense. 'Solidity', as an anonymous journalist put it, 'is the note. One expects [from Shackleton] no flighty speculation, little ingenuity of resource, but simply the square and level application of good, well-tried principles.'[17]

There was general agreement, too, on the qualities which – in the absence of cleverness – best explained his achievements. In Hesketh Pearson's words: 'Possibly the finest example in our political and industrial world of a man who has got on in life by sheer hard work and dogged perseverance is Sir David Shackleton.'[18] His dedication to his work was supported by 'a constitution of iron', according to one observer, and 'inexhaustible energy', according to another.[19] But he was no frenetic workaholic. Sunday was sacrosanct, a day for rest and reading; and he took regular annual holidays in peacetime (see Chapter 9).

An emphasis on order was part of his working style. He ran a tidy, well organized union office: 'Its interior appearance is enough to satisfy anyone that order is Mr Shackleton's supreme law.'[20] It is highly probable that, like Arthur Henderson, he 'always kept a clean desk ... answered letters at once, and then put them in the waste-paper basket', disposing of notes for speeches and reports in the same way.[21] Everything, in other words, was discarded once it had been acted upon, or the event it related to had passed – unless, rarely, it happened to have a very special personal significance. That is at least the most likely explanation of the fifty or so letters surviving in Shackleton's sparse papers (see Chapter 9).

In another respect, however, those papers fly in the face of an orderly

---

14. *Labour Leader*, 16 September 1910. Curran was a prominent trade union official and Labour MP.
15. John S. Walsh, 'Memorial Service Address': SP.
16. *Nelson Leader*, 24 January 1908.
17. Unknown newspaper, 28 April 1920: SP.
18. Unknown newspaper, n.d. (1924): SP.
19. *Cotton Factory Times*, 10 December 1909; *Colne & Nelson Times*, 2 October 1908.
20. Ibid., 11 July 1902.
21. Hamilton, *Arthur Henderson*, p. vii.

image. For there is no evident system in the way in which their major component, the scrapbook, has been assembled. It was clearly not put together by Shackleton himself: in that event, there would certainly have been some semblance of at least a chronological order. That leaves Margaret, his adoring daughter, and Sarah, his wife. Of the two, Margaret is most unlikely to have been content with the chaos of the scrapbook. Ernest Wilkinson and both grandchildren were clear that she was intellectually far more in tune with her father than her mother. In other words, the scrapbook's disorder suggests Sarah. So, too, does the subject of its first pages.

The way it probably happened is that at some point after Shackleton's death, Lady Shackleton, as she insists on being known, is going through his things. She comes across the drawer, or the box, into which he has for years been throwing clippings as they came to hand. They are plainly all to do with him, and sometimes with her as well. She decides not to throw them out with the other rubbish, but to preserve them. And what more obvious way of doing that than to paste them up in an album? She looks through some at the top of the pile, wondering what to start with. Then she comes across the first of a number of clippings relating to what she thinks of as the most important recent event in her own life, apart from her husband's death. The outcome is that the first pages of the scrapbook are occupied exclusively by newspaper articles, and by clippings of photographs (all identical, and by Geo. Lord of St Anne's) of Shackleton and herself – articles and photographs occasioned by the celebration of their golden wedding in 1933. After that order is not an issue until, much later, she comes to the newspaper photographs and clippings which record her daughter's wedding in 1912. Then, a fondly remembered engraving of the Antley Chapel, in Accrington, is associated and pasted alongside; and she notes beneath it, in an awkward childish hand: 'The Chapel Sir David was married' – to her.

Along with the scrapbook's lack of order, there are signs in it of a genuinely pedantic concern for detail and factual accuracy.[22] This concern was a constant throughout Shackleton's career. During the parliamentary phase, it is there in a letter to Ramsay MacDonald confirming a meeting they were to have with Richard Bell about a newspaper report concerning the latter. Shackleton anxiously tells MacDonald: 'Have the paper with you when we meet him' – and then, in a postscript, informs him that one of the titles listed in the 'order forms' for LRC leaflets is incorrect.[23] It is there, too, in the records of the civil service phase. He was both meticulous and unerring in

22. One example is a 1902 *Blackburn Weekly Telegraph* clipping of a sketched portrait with a potted biography of himself that has a number of details carefully corrected in Shackleton's hand. Another is a 1924 *Daily Graphic* cartoon with named caricatures of 17 members of the new Labour Cabinet, all in Court Dress, accompanied by the notation (again, in Shackleton's hand): 'Lord Chelmsford and General Thomson not included'. On the other hand, it was not a concern that extended more than casually to the dating and sourcing of the clippings he amassed.
23. Shackleton to MacDonald, 25 November 1903: LP Archives, LRC 11/426.

checking the accuracy of the Health Insurance Commission's minutes, and the follow-up to them – and paid equally meticulous attention to the accuracy of publications issued by organizations associated with the health insurance scheme.[24] At the Ministry of Labour, as its most senior official, there was less room for indulging this kind of finicky preoccupation. Nevertheless, it shows up in the ministry's records in a predilection to dilate on the minutiae of familiar things. Thus the 'very great detail' in which he elaborated the terms of the Treasury agreement of 1915 to an audience (apart from the minute-taker and a senior Ministry official) of two trade union shop stewards;[25] and, again, the 'very great detail' in which he explained the working of the Chief Industrial Commissioner's Department to a solicitor and an employer's representative.[26]

It is easy to denigrate such attention to detail – for instance, by thinking of it as obsessive. And that, certainly, is one way of interpreting Shackleton's comment, on returning a draft of a leaflet written by Ramsay MacDonald: 'I have read it several times.'[27] Another, however, is to see it as the mark of a thorough and, in the end, probably efficient worker – the interpretation preferred by Tom Shaw. 'Of all the men I have ever met Shackleton gave the highest "percentage of efficiency" … He never hurried, was never flurried, and apparently never tired. He worked slowly, but once a task was finished, revision was unnecessary.'[28]

This close attention to detail was associated with a generally cautious approach to things. One journalist described it as 'wariness'.[29] It dictated an early decision which later proved critical to Shackleton's selection as the LRC candidate for the Clitheroe by-election. An active Liberal until he moved to Darwen, he decided then to withdraw from 'party politics' on the ground that he was secretary of a union whose membership enclosed 'all shades of political opinion'.[30] His wariness evinced itself in frequent refusals to comment on matters of current public interest. 'Mr Shackleton', in a typical response, 'writes that he has no desire to express any opinion on the Congress publicly.'[31]

24. E.g., *Minutes*, 27 September 1912: PIN 2/20 XC/B 3441, pp. 376, 436.
25. 'Notes of an Interview…', 8 October 1917: LAB 10/399 4661, 75.
26. 'Notes of a Conference …', 12 October 1917: ibid.,78.
27. Shackleton to MacDonald, 29 May 1903: LP Archives, LRC 9/381.
28. *Manchester Guardian*, 2 August 1938.
29. Ibid., 12 November 1910.
30. *Cotton Factory Times*, 8 August 1902.
31. *Labour Leader*, 15 September 1905. Similarly, of 26 Labour and Lib-Lab leaders (mainly trade unionists) asked for their views on the registration of unions, in the light of recent judicial decisions, Shackleton's response was by far the most evasive. 'I am of the opinion that it would be unwise to discuss this matter in public at the present time. Under these circumstances you will pardon me for not giving my opinion on the question.' *Cotton Factory Times*, 13 February 1903.

Patience is a corollary of caution; and Shackleton placed a high value on it.[32] Wariness, caution also meant a nose for compromise. 'When you have knocked about in public life a little you find you cannot have your own way … you have to … compromise'.[33] And compromise meant accepting incremental gains, which in turn meant 'travelling on the lines which offered the least resistance'.[34] The 'line of least resistance', as a strategy, was a recurring theme with him.[35] He scorned the Continental textile unions' policy (as he described it) of 'asking for all they aim at at once', with the result that 'they get nothing, or at most very little indeed'. Their English counterparts, in contrast, 'ask for a little at a time, and we get it, and so we move onward by safe and easy stages'.[36]

His belief in this strategy saw him, for example, opposing a demand for an immediate eight-hour day (entailing a weekly reduction of seven hours) in the cotton industry. It was too 'severe' a claim as it stood, he said, and in any case 'some of the operatives [as piece-workers] would kick against it'. Instead, he proposed a progressive annual reduction of one hour until the desired '48 a week' was reached.[37] The same belief, too, was behind his willingness to take responsibility for the very limited private member's bill he introduced in 1910 concerning voting rights for women (see Chapter 7). 'Personally', he confessed to the House of Commons, 'I believe in a far more advanced Bill than this, but it has been one of my ideas throughout my life … to get in the thin end of the wedge … [as] the most successful way of achieving my object.'[38]

Yet, conciliatory and ready to compromise though he might be as a matter of general policy, Shackleton could still take a tough and unbending line when it suited. So, speaking for a deputation asking for legislation to prevent employers fining cotton weavers, he directly threatened (if in the milder-seeming language of an earlier age) a Liberal Home Secretary with massive strike action.

> [Y]ou ought to quite understand that our people are absolutely determined to put an end to this evil [of fining]; and we ask you to afford us relief by legislation in order to prevent us taking stronger measures … It is a big question to raise a disturbance in an industry in which something like 200,000 people are engaged; but something will have to be done if we do not get the relief we are seeking.[39]

32.   For example, his expression of thanks to two clergymen for help in an industrial dispute: 'Their extraordinary patience and perseverance was an example, even to a trade union official who has been taught by experience to cultivate these estimable traits of character.' Ibid., 16 October 1908.
33.   *Colne & Nelson Times*, 11 July 1902.
34.   *Nelson Chronicle*, 1 August 1902.
35.   See, e.g., TUC, *Report*, 1906, p. 152.
36.   *Colne & Nelson Times*, 14 July 1905. His detestation of the all-or-nothing strategy once tumbled out in a public jibe at a TUC colleague: 'Oh, yes; if our friend cannot have the stars and moon all at once, he will not have anything'. TUC, *Report*, 1907, p. 160.
37.   *Cotton Factory Times*, 18 June 1909.
38.   *Parl. Debs.*, 16 June 1910: vol. 17, col. 1203.
39.   *Cotton Factory Times*, 18 June 1909.

Similarly, there is the way he rounded on employers' representatives in a meeting about the terms of new legislation. The unions had proposed a clause enabling weavers to recover losses incurred through deliberate under-payment by employers. One employer, while accepting the clause, strongly denied that most employers were guilty in some degree of this 'habit'. Wilkinson, the unions' main spokesman, was humbly placatory, excusing his earlier remarks by saying they related 'mostly' to non-members of the employers' association. That was too much for Shackleton to swallow.

> Mr Chairman [an employer] I must give our Secretary (Mr Wilkinson) credit for trying to let you off in this matter as kindly and as pleasantly as he possibly could. I am not prepared to say all he said by a long way. But seeing that you have admit-ted the principle of our amendment, it is perhaps unnecessary to go into the ques-tion of the extent of the grievance. But I wish to impress upon you that this is a serious matter to us.[40]

★ ★ ★ ★

The two phases of Shackleton's working career involve sharply different cir-cumstances. In the politician/trade unionist phase, a major part of his work is performed in the public eye where it is open to press comment. In the civil ser-vant phase, his work is performed almost entirely beyond the public gaze, and any assessment of it depends primarily upon the files that bureaucracy creates.

The focus of press comment, in the first phase, is naturally on Shackleton as speechmaker. In addition, however, there are three occasions on which his work as chairman figured in the press: the LRC's annual conference of 1905, and the TUC's Congress in both 1908 and 1909. In 1905, a well-disposed observer thought him 'an ideal chairman' for a gathering that was not easily controlled.[41] In 1908 he again won praise from the same quarter: 'David ... knows the work and the business and everybody knows he is beyond sharp practices, and accepts his ruling with pleasure and alacrity.'[42] Less pre-dictably, the following year, he won a glowing opinion from the left: 'Mr Shackleton was a perfectly just chairman: one felt he would have been fair to the Devil if he had risen to state his case.'[43] But this time, as well, his fairness was publicly challenged. The issue was his alleged refusal of a demand from the floor for a 'card vote' (a counted vote reflecting each union's membership numbers) on a resolution supporting secular education.[44] The gravamen of the charge, levelled in an open letter from the Salford Catholic Federation,[45] was that his refusal conflicted with two other decisions he had made as

40. Conference of Textile Factory Workers' Association, cotton employers, and MPs for tex-tile districts, *Minutes*, 20 February 1901, p. 53: Tuckwell Coll., 504/94.
41. *Cotton Factory Times*, 3 February 1905.
42. Ibid., 11 September 1908.
43. *Clarion*, 17 September 1909.
44. The minutes simply record: 'The resolution was carried by a large majority'. TUC, *Report*, 1909, p. 190.
45. See *Blackburn Times*, 4 December 1909.

Congress chairman. It was alleged, first, that in 1908 he had insisted (without pressure from the floor) that a card vote was essential on a similar secular education resolution because of the importance of the matter;[46] and, second, that in 1909 he had insisted, on a resolution about a different matter, that compliance with the demand of a single delegate for a card vote was mandatory.[47] The Salford letter implied that Shackleton had refused a card vote because that would have revealed a sharp drop in support for secular education since the previous Congress, owing to divisions among the miners' and cotton unions.[48]

Public comments on Shackleton's performance as speechmaker tended to be both less glowing and less condemnatory. At the time of his retirement, Ben Turner probably got it about right: 'He was never an orator although a good speaker.'[49] It is probable that his time in the House of Commons converted him into 'a good speaker', because he seems not to have been one when his parliamentary career opened. 'Much as I esteem Mr Shackleton as a man,' an anonymous local unionist remarked in those early days, 'I cannot say ... that I admire him as a speaker. His style is too rough-and-ready, too careless ... He appears to set no store upon the expression of his ideas in clear language ... [It] is his bounden duty to the ... Labour movement ... to cultivate the art of turning a good sentence.'[50] This assessment is supported by a comment from Keir Hardie: 'Interrupted the writing of this [letter] to go & hear Shackleton speak [in the House]. I do wish our fellows would prepare better.'[51] But, evidently, he improved with experience. By 1907, it could be said of him that he had made 'remarkable ... progress' as a speaker. 'Prior to his return for Clitheroe [in 1906] his speeches were slow and uninteresting, his delivery halting and confused. Now he has the "ear of the House of Commons," and is rightly regarded as one of the finest and most vigorous speakers connected with the Labour movement.'[52]

Labour intellectuals, inevitably, were less easily impressed. His contribution to a parliamentary debate was praised as 'characteristically straightforward',

46.   The minutes record this card vote, but are silent on the point of his alleged insistence. TUC, *Report*, 1908, p. 182. On the other hand, the great importance he attached to this particular resolution is suggested by the fact that it was the one resolution to be mentioned in the brief speech with which he closed the Congress. Ibid., p. 199.
47.   But in the cited case, the circumstances were different in that the single delegate seeking a card vote was the mover of the resolution. Ibid., 1909, p. 144. The card vote (on a resolution about a Labour daily newspaper) was taken after the chairman (Shackleton) had suggested it was inadvisable, and the mover continued to insist on it.
48.   These divisions were mentioned during the Congress debate. See ibid., p. 189. The TUC's Parliamentary Committee formally replied to the Salford letter, 'pointing out in strong terms the falsity of the charges'. TUC, PC, *Minutes*, 15 December 1909.
49.   Unknown newspaper, n.d. (1925): SP.
50.   *Nelson Chronicle*, 5 February 1904.
51.   Hardie to Glasier, n.d. (1903): Glasier Papers, I.1.1903/40.
52.   Unknown newspaper, September 1907: SP.

but 'masterly' was reserved for Ramsay MacDonald's.[53] Nevertheless, they could sometimes see his style as suiting the occasion. 'There is no nonsense about Shackleton. His big, burly figure, black hair and beard, and the plain simple utterance of his words ... all give the impression of belonging to the practical man who deals in facts, and it was a straight, practical statement he had to make, and he made it.'[54] His non-Socialist supporters were readier to see virtue in his 'plain, homely, and definite statements', and his 'emphatic style', while accepting that he was 'not as eloquent as some of the [other] Labour Members'.[55]

The second, civil service, phase of Shackleton's career entailed a radical change in the context of his working life. However acute his qualms about his educational handicap in the House of Commons (see below), he always had the less daunting world of the electorate, the union and the TUC as an escape. That source of reassurance vanished after he joined the Home Office. At the same time, during the first six years of his new career, he is unlikely to have experienced really serious or continuing discomfort on this score. As Churchill's Senior Labour Adviser, he would have been on wholly familiar ground, handling industrial disputes and health and safety issues. At the National Health Insurance Commission, he was still in essentially familiar territory. Dealing with union leaders, running publicity campaigns, formulating rules, and creating administrative arrangements relating to an insurance scheme would have been grist to the mill of a man with the experience of an MP, a cotton union official, and a leading member of a major friendly society. The surviving minutes of the commission show that Shackleton took an active role in its deliberations, and was closely involved in the detailed execution of its administrative functions.[56] And he was still on familiar ground when wartime priorities diverted him into the part-time role of negotiating 'dilution' agreements between unions and employers.

All that changed, however, with his abrupt translation to the topmost level of the civil service at the new Ministry of Labour in December 1916. The uncertainty this unlooked-for promotion engendered in him is reflected in the way he buckled under the pressure of the pro-Beveridge forces, and offered Hodge his resignation (see Chapter 8). It seems that he never quite lost a sense of unease about his fitness for the post. Lack of confidence explains why he limited his contact with the Ministry of Labour staff to an extent that was so pronounced, and so exceptional, that it occasioned specific comment in an otherwise conventionally eulogistic article which a civil servants' journal published at the time of his retirement. 'His work in the

53. *Labour Leader*, 7 May 1909.
54. *Clarion*, 6 April 1906.
55. *Cotton Factory Times*, 11 September 1908; 5 February 1909. *Nelson Leader*, 1 November 1907.
56. See, e.g., PIN 2/20 XC/B 3441 (1912); PIN 2/21 XC/B 3575 (1913).

Ministry has been sound and quiet. He has not come into daily contact with the staff in the same manner as have other high officials.'[57]

A feeling of being out of his depth is also the probable explanation of two singular features of Shackleton's file minutes, the comments he appended to documents that came across his desk. One is the prevalence of marginally relevant, and sometimes quite inconsequential, comments – comments which do, however, have the effect of underlining his own effort or special knowledge.[58] The other is the relatively limited bulk of his file minutes in general and, in particular, the paucity of his comments on 'major policy decisions'.[59] To be sure, there are exceptions to these two rules. Some of Shackleton's file minutes are crisp and to the point; and he sometimes wrote firmly and at length on important policy issues.[60] But this air of confidence, uncharacteristic of his file minutes, is significantly more evident when he was talking, rather than writing.

Two cases illustrate the point. The first occurred in December 1917, when Shackleton appeared as a witness before the parliamentary Select Committee on National Expenditure, accompanied only by Harold Butler. At one point in the proceedings, he deferred to Butler ('I think as a general rule, Mr Butler knows that better than I do. He is an old Civil Servant') – but nevertheless went on to answer the question himself.[61] Otherwise, he carried the entire burden of a long cross-examination on the administration and finances of his ministry with evident command. The second case occurred a few months later, at the first meeting of a committee which was to assess the ministry's organization and consisted of all its most senior officials. Shackleton was in the chair. His opening remarks included the frank acknowledgement of personal inexperience quoted earlier (see Chapter 9) with reference to his humility. Thereafter, however, the committee's minutes portray a chairman who – while leaving the substantive issues largely to others – was plainly in command. He asks pertinent questions. He draws conclusions from the discussion about settled issues; and on occasion is prepared to express a firm opinion on unsettled ones. And he expresses particularly strong opinions on the limits imposed by the committee's terms of reference.

57. *Civil Service Argus*, n.d. (1925): SP.

58. For example, his comment before sending on to his minister a long memorandum on federalism: 'This is an interesting and instructive memorandum. It takes over two hours to read carefully' 20 May 1919: LAB 2/488/12 4000.

59. I am indebted for this impression to Rodney Lowe, the pre-eminent historian of the Ministry of Labour, and the person most comprehensively familiar with its records of the period. Letter to author, n.d. (February 1981).

60. As exemplified by a substantial and strongly argued minute in which he flatly opposed the proposal (advanced at considerable length by Humbert Wolfe, a senior colleague) that the ministry play a more active role in the wage-fixing functions of the trade boards set up under legislation relating to sweated trades. 2 February 1922: LAB 2/935/TB252 4896.

61. *Select Committee on National Expenditure*, 5 December 1917, p. 13: LAB 2/229/2837/3 4666. Butler is recorded as intervening only twice in the proceedings: once to ask for clarification of a question; and the other time to answer, 'Yes'.

However, so far as these things can be deduced from the accounts of minute-takers, Shackleton seems to have been most obviously confident when it came to discussions which involved outsiders to the ministry and were about specific industrial issues. The record, in cases of this kind, quite often conveys both a sense of mastery and forcefulness, and an impression of an acknowledging audience. The audiences, moreover, were extremely varied. There was, for example, the team of Ministry of Munitions officials whom Shackleton, confronting on his own, magisterially advised on the intricacies of wage policy in the pig-iron industry.[62] Three years later, at a meeting between the minister and senior trade union officials, Shackleton effectively reprimanded the rising Ernest Bevin, and corrected in detail his unfavourable interpretation of the ministry's earlier actions in the matter under discussion.[63] In between, there were quite different audiences. As , for example, the unofficial strike leaders of some Scottish iron moulders, whose claim to special treatment on a wage issue Shackleton firmly, patiently, and with every evidence of sympathy, rejected.[64] Or like the tramway employers whom he lectured in detail on a wage issue in a way that, towards the end, wrenched from an accepting spokesman the admission that: 'It has never been put to us in that way before.'[65]

Then there was the most distinguished audience of all, the War Cabinet. Its minutes show that Shackleton was far from backward in this august company. He made substantial contributions to discussions on many occasions, and sometimes played a notably prominent role. In July 1917, for example, he took on Neville Chamberlain, then Minister of National Service, in direct argument.[66] In October, seconded by Askwith, he led the Ministry of Labour's attack on his former patron, Winston Churchill, who as Minister of Munitions had awarded a wage increase without heeding its wider implications – and, in the course of the discussion, sharply corrected Churchill's depiction of the Ministry of Labour's position.[67] In July 1918, he led the discussion on a claim to extend a coalminers' wage increase and, in doing so, implicitly criticized the Prime Minister's handling of negotiations with the miners' leaders.[68] In October, he again had Churchill directly in his sights when he made a lengthy statement in support of legislation honouring the government's undertaking to restore the prewar work practices which the unions had conceded in the Treasury agreement of 1915.[69]

Finally, the minutes of the War Cabinet also record that Shackleton did not hold back even from contradicting his own minister in this gathering. On

62. *Conference* ..., 7 November 1917: LAB 10/399 4661.
63. *Deputation* ..., 5 October 1920: LAB 2/647 5026.
64. *Note of a Conference* ..., 21 September 1917: LAB 10/399 4661.
65. *Note of a Conference* ..., 12 February 1918, p. 9: ibid.
66. See *War Cabinet*, 185, 13 July 1917: CAB 23/3, pp. 104–5.
67. Ibid., 248, 12 October 1917: CAB 23/4, p. 93.
68. Ibid., 440, 3 July 1918: CAB 23/7, p. 7.
69. Ibid., 487, 16 October 1918: CAB 23/8, p. 35.

one occasion, it was a qualified disagreement with G. H. Roberts, of the Labour party.[70] On another, it was a flat disagreement that would scarcely have endeared him to his Conservative master, Sir Robert Horne.[71] There is thus a quite distinct difference between the style revealed in Shackleton's file minutes, which he wrote himself, and the style revealed in the minutes of meetings which others wrote. He was plainly less comfortable with the literary form of the file minute than he was with the oral form of the meeting. That is to be expected. Talking was much the more familiar medium to a man who had graduated from the factory floor to parliament, via the trade union.[72] Moreover, the nature of the audience he was addressing in each case could only have reinforced that preference, especially given his fixation about education. His audience, in the case of the file minutes, was confined (with the one, but not invariable, exception of the minister) to university graduates. In the case of the meetings, the audiences were more diverse and, in general, probably much less intimidating.

Beliefs and Policies

Shackleton's outlook on the public issues of his time exemplifies what has been called the 'ideology of labourism'.[73] In this, he was reflecting mainstream opinion in the oldest and weightiest segment of the Edwardian labour movement, which included the unions of skilled craftsmen together with those covering semi-skilled workers in cotton manufacturing and coalmining. The officials and activists of these unions tended to favour ideas and attitudes earlier identified with the more exclusive 'labour aristocracy' of skilled tradesmen.[74] Thus, while acutely conscious of class differences, they were not 'class conscious' in the Marxist sense. For their primary focus was not the oppressive bourgeoisie, but rather the rest of the working class and their own superiority to it. That sense of superiority was evinced, at a personal level, in a certain respectability of dress and behaviour, in an inclination towards temperance and religious nonconformism, and in an emphasis on the virtues of self-reliance. At an organizational level, they regarded the age, stability and wealth of their unions and friendly societies as a demonstration of their own exceptional qualities.[75] Politically, they were usually associated (up to 1902)

---

70. See ibid., 370, 22 March 1918: CAB 23/5, pp. 178–9.
71. See ibid., 523, 31 January 1919: CAB 23/9, p. 38. It is worth noting that, at a later meeting, the War Cabinet returned to the issue on which Horne and Shackleton had disagreed. Both men were again present. Horne reiterated his position at length; but this time, according to the minutes, Shackleton remained mute. Ibid., 525, 4 February 1919: CAB 23/9, p. 42.
72. On the importance of oratory to leaders of the early labour movement, see Michels, *Political Parties*, pp. 75–8.
73. Saville in Benewick et al., *Knowledge and Belief in Politics*, pp. 215–16; and see 'Introduction' above.
74. Hobsbawm, *Labouring Men*, pp. 272ff.
75. See ibid., p. 275.

with the Liberal party, particularly its 'advanced' or left wing; and they rejected Socialism.

'I am not a Socialist'.[76] Shackleton made this point publicly, in various ways, on numerous occasions. Socialism, as he saw it, involved revolution as a method, and wholesale social and economic change as a goal. Revolution he thought of as 'sudden Quixotic action' which was altogether unnecessary in England, given 'the power of the ballot'.[77] In any case, it was not a viable method, for 'English workers are not a revolutionary class.'[78] True improvement would be brought about 'by education, by constant talk with one another', by 'conversation'.[79] Not that he was altogether above action with a revolutionary tinge. In the long aftermath of the Taff Vale judgement (see Chapter 4), he publicly proclaimed his belief that if trade unions could not operate legally, in the light of judicial rulings, then they should operate illegally: 'Mr Shackleton stated that if the Government refused to re-establish the law on those ... important points ... resort would have to be made to secret combination.'[80]

He rejected the ultimate goals of Socialism not so much, it seems, because they were unworthy, but rather because they were too distant, too utopian, and because they diverted attention from lesser, more immediately achievable goals. Thus, in response to a question implying that unemployment would be solved only under Socialism, he retorted that there was 'no use thinking in the clouds' about such problems. 'We have got to deal', he said, 'with matters as we find them, the evils as they exist ... Personally I am not going to waste my time talking about things so far ahead as [Socialism]. I want to do something whilst I am alive.'[81] On the other hand, he had no hesitation in supporting Socialist proposals for the nationalization of land (which had been on the TUC and Lib-Lab agenda since the 1880s), mines, minerals, railways and canals. For he regarded these as 'a matter of pure business' and well within 'the sphere of practical politics'.[82] But the thoroughly pragmatic, down-to-earth nature of his reformism is perhaps best conveyed by his proud response to a journalist's question about the 'sanitary condition' of Darwen cotton mills:

> In Darwen we have done something which other towns ... have not done. I [am] a member of the Corporation ... and ... of the Health Committee, and during the past fifteen months a sub-committee of the latter, upon which I have also acted,

76. *Colne & Nelson Times*, 24 January 1908. He never deviated from this position, unlike Arthur Henderson, whose starting-point was the same. As early as 1906, Henderson was talking of 'an important epoch in the progress of Socialism', and he joined the Fabian Society in 1912. Leventhal, *Arthur Henderson*, pp. 28–9.
77. *Cotton Factory Times*, 2 November 1906.
78. *Labour Leader*, 18 June 1909.
79. *Cotton Factory Times*, 2 November 1906; 30 July 1909.
80. *Ibid.*, 16 October 1903.
81. *Colne & Nelson Times*, 21 September 1906.
82. *Labour Leader*, 18 June 1909.

have visited every workshop and factory in the town, and examined the conveniences both as to their sanitary condition and the number for each sex. We have made recommendations in every case where we thought it desirable ... The ... Health Committee ... will insist upon the improvements being carried into effect.[83]

Nevertheless, while Shackleton viewed public regulation of workplace health and safety issues as essential, he was in general wary of state action. In economic matters, and in industrial relations, the state's role was to keep the ring and ensure a fair balance between the contending interests. This meant, as he argued in relation to the Taff Vale judgement which disadvantaged the unions, that in some circumstances the state had to intervene in order to 'put the employer and the workpeople on equal terms'.[84] Otherwise, as Tom Shaw put it, Shackleton was 'intensely Lancashire in his pre-war outlook; and looked upon Government action as interference and as reprehensible'.[85] Thus he tended to oppose interventionist initiatives in the councils of the Ministry of Labour.[86] He thought of the ministry as an impartial government agency with minimal involvement in the relations between capital and labour. It was not that he had no ambition for it. He wanted it to be 'the centre for all Labour Intelligence'.[87] But the role he envisaged for it was primarily an informing, advising, guiding role – and certainly nothing even remotely approaching the role envisaged by his old foe, Ben Tillett, who had had in mind a Ministry of Labour that was essentially an extension of trade union organization.[88]

His general anti-interventionist position, workplace health and safety issues apart, was not unqualified. Wartime needs, he came to believe, temporarily justified quite extreme measures. More significantly, legislative intervention to protect the weak and unfortunate was essential. And so he hailed Lloyd George's momentous Budget of 1909 as 'the greatest financial reform of modern times'. By shifting the burden of taxation from the poor to the rich, he said, it would provide the means of ensuring the 'care of the aged, the feeding of necessitous school children, and the more humane treatment of the genuine unemployed workers'.[89] His compassion is unmistakable; and in explaining it to the House of Commons, he could draw on his own experience of being unemployed.

83. *Cotton Factory Times*, 16 January 1903.
84. *Parl. Debs.*, 28 March 1906, vol. 154, col. 1314. His point was that the Taff Vale decision left 'the workers absolutely at the employer's mercy' in the matter of damages arising from strikes, whereas the 'employer ought to be prepared to go into these labour wars when they occurred, and take the same risk as the trade unionists did'.
85. *Manchester Guardian*, 2 August 1938.
86. Hence his vigorous, and successful, rebuttal of Humbert Wolfe's proposal that the ministry play a more active role in the determination of wage rates subject to statutory trade boards. See Lowe, *Adjusting to Democracy*, pp. 104–5; and n. 60 above.
87. *Departmental Committee ...*, 6 June 1918: LAB 2/274/372/2 4000.
88. See Lowe, *Adjusting to Democracy*, p. 16.
89. TUC, *Report*, 1909, p. 48.

If my time [of unemployment] had been four years later than it was I should have gone to the bottom. I could not have resisted the cry of starving children, but I had no children at the time, and I was able to maintain myself through it with the help of my wife. That [unemployed, with a family] is the position of thousands of our workmen, and we should not be too hard in this matter and too hard on [them]. There should be some sympathy.[90]

Yet he never abandoned a belief in the paramountcy of individual responsibility – and in the need, therefore, to distinguish between the deserving and the undeserving poor.[91] And so, in the case of unemployment policy, he appealed for a 'scientific way' of dealing with the unemployed: 'Let the loafer be separated from the genuine worker, and let them not punish all for him.'[92] The presumption was much the same in the case of compensation for industrial accidents: the unions rightly believed in 'making a man pay for his own neglect, which would make them more careful'.[93] On the other hand, it seemed that the principle could be bent when it came to the problem of old-age. '[He] would never be a party to the State removing responsibilities from the shoulders of the individual, but he did think that .. all persons over seventy ought to have [a State] pension.'[94] In addition, he thought that the state should 'step in and prevent the present wretched state of things from going on any longer' in the case of women workers in the 'sweated' trades.[95]

The exception Shackleton made in the case of sweated women workers, as an occupational grouping, is significant. His preferred means by which working people coped with life's hazards was not the state, but rather the associations which individuals voluntarily formed in order to utilize their united strengths for protective purposes. And that, of course, was where the trade union, the friendly society, and the consumer co-operative came in. The sweated women workers were exceptional, for Shackleton, because he thought them incapable – through no failing or moral fault of their own – of maintaining such associations. 'It [is] all very well', he once remarked, 'to talk about organisation' in their case, but 'these poor people [are] too low down' for that. They could not possibly do 'what the Lancashire women [have] done in the cotton weaving and cardroom trades'.[96]

Working women, in any case, were necessarily a major concern for a union official whose membership was largely female. For a start, he thought that women who were married should not be working for wages. Their proper

90. *Parl. Debs.*, 30 April 1909, vol. IV, col. 668.
91. A widely held view at the time (though not only at that time), especially in relation to unemployment. See Bebbington, *Nonconformist Conscience*, p. 56.
92. *Cotton Factory Times*, 14 October 1904. At another time, he provided a faintly chilling elaboration: 'no man, his wife, or children should starve *if the man were willing to work*'. Ibid., 20 September 1907. Emphasis added.
93. Ibid., 3 April 1903.
94. Ibid., 15 January 1909.
95. Ibid., 8 January 1909.
96. Ibid.

place was in the home. Importantly, however, he regarded this more as their right than their obligation. 'No married woman ... ought to be at work in a mill; her domestic work was quite sufficient for her ... The men ought to take their proper places, and their womenfolk ought to demand their right to be kept out of the mill.'[97] He felt strongly enough on the issue to favour making the employment of married women altogether illegal – although he recognized the unpopularity of this position.[98] In the absence of legislation, it was initially up to husbands, individually, 'to make an effort ... and try to keep their wives at home'.[99] But as well, there was social action and the appropriate industrial goal of an adequate male wage. 'They had to ... see to it that it was possible for the man to earn such a wage as would enable him to keep his wife at home. (Loud applause.) ... They must not expect [him to do so] on ... 25s. per week ... They wanted to get 33s.'[100] Embodied in this conception of an adequate wage, as it happened, there was a even nobler goal. For, if realized, it would not only enable wives to remain in the home, it would also transform working-class living standards – a point that Shackleton intimated in a speech at Whaley Bridge:

> The workers' ideal should be that when a girl consented to wed, it was on the understanding that she did not go to any kind of work except the home; that when the young husband came home he should have everything ready for him; that the comfort of the children should be attended to; not that they should be taken out in a blanket or a cradle, first thing in the morning, to be nursed by a friendly neighbour or an old relative ... It should not be part of the wife's duty to earn wages to augment the small pittance of her husband. A man was entitled to have a reasonable return for his labour, and *conditions of living more in keeping with those of his employer*.[101]

Shackleton's perception of women, their ability and their rights, was by no means in the traditional mould.[102] He advocated that they hold the franchise on the same terms as men, and he 'spoke in terms that the radical suffragists had been using for some years' when he introduced his bill on the issue in 1910.[103] More interestingly, he thought that women cotton weavers – while

---

97.   Ibid., 12 March 1909. The opposition to wives working was also widespread on the left of the labour movement, and had strong support as well among the leadership of the Women's Trade Union League. See Lewenhak, *Women and Trade Unions*, p. 91.

98.   But 'if I voted for [such a bill] I should not be the [MP for Clitheroe] after the next election'. *Blackburn Times*, 15 February 1908.

99.   *Labour Leader*, 18 June 1909. He once cited his own case, with evident pride: 'Let me advise you to follow my example. Out of a weaver's wage, ever since and before the first child was born, I have kept my wife at home. Do it gradually yourselves.' *Blackburn Times*, 15 February 1908. His pride in being 'a sole family provider' echoed a relatively new working-class tradition. See Rose, 'Gender and Labor History', p. 154.

100.   *Cotton Factory Times*, 19 June 1908.

101.   Ibid., 27 November 1908. Emphasis added.

102.   For that, see Joyce, *Visions of the People*, p. 125.

103.   Liddington and Norris, *One Hand Tied Behind Us*, p. 246. Earlier, too, he had protested against the prison sentences imposed on militant suffragists, as 'too heavy a punishment'. *Parl. Debs.*, 22 June 1906, vol. 159, col. 463.

'quite as clever at their trade as men' and suffering no discrimination in pay rates – were in practice disadvantaged by protective legislation limiting their working hours.[104] He also believed that women who stayed home were disadvantaged, in at least one respect. 'Women's life at home was something of a drudgery, and ... the husband ought to stay in the house and take his turn one night a week while his wife went to her guild or class ... Give the women the chance of learning ... and they would not run second best.'[105] Again, the emphasis on education.

★ ★ ★ ★

The key to the problem of working wives, for Shackleton, was trade unionism. For that was the principal means by which the wages and living standards of the working class would be uplifted. 'Organisation', as he put it to the House of Commons, 'is the first condition for the improvement of the people.'[106] And years later, his experience as a Home Office official confirmed that belief: 'When we as [government] officials have to go to various parts of the country ... one finds that the standard of living is regulated by the strength of the organisation [the] people have.'[107] But, on the whole, he tended to think of unionism less as a force for change than as a defence against change. 'Advances', as he put it once, were not the main concern; unionism was 'largely [about] resisting encroachments [by employers] and preventing conditions from being worsened in times of depression'.[108]

In any case, the protection and promotion of material interests was far from the end of the matter. For Shackleton saw in the trade union a moral force as well.[109] Thus, he told one audience, the 'grandest thought' about working in unions (and friendly societies) was the 'underlying ... great spirit of helping one another, the desire to be independent and [to be] loyal to their accumulated wealth'.[110] And beyond this, he viewed unions as 'agents and advocates of thrift, and standing protests against the waste of drink and the evils of gambling'.[111] He also believed that trade unionists were becoming more altruistic, and less committed to their former 'selfishness' through a new 'regard to the general condition of people outside their own ranks'.[112]

104. *Labour Leader*, 18 June 1909. This, he argued, enabled 'the unfair competition of men [working] overtime as permitted by law', when women were 'not so allowed'.
105. *Cotton Factory Times*, 19 November 1909.
106. *Parl. Debs.*, 10 June 1903, vol. 123, col. 495.
107. Unknown newspaper, n.d. (1911): SP.
108. *Cotton Factory Times*, 18 September 1908.
109. This view of the trade union's potential was influential in both Protestant and Roman Catholic social thought at the time. See Martin, *Trade Unionism*, pp. 52–6, 63–5.
110. *Cotton Factory Times*, 9 October 1908.
111. *Colne & Nelson Times*, 11 September 1908.
112. *Cotton Factory Times*, 27 November 1908. The altruism did not, however, extend to tolerating freeloading non-unionists. As Shackleton told a Glossop audience, 'those who did not pay to trade union funds should not, in the interests of common honesty, receive the standard rate of wages' won by the union. Ibid., 15 January 1909.

Shackleton's conception of trade unionism incorporated a belief in the desirability, and feasibility, of co-operative relations with employers.[113] In his first annual report to the Darwen weavers, he expressed the hope that the union's relations with local employers would 'continue to be of a friendly character, each one endeavouring to do that which is right, one to another'.[114] And when his union career was drawing to a close, he spoke proudly of the 'good understanding' that existed between Lancashire employers and the cotton unions.[115] He went on to claim that the key to this understanding was the fact that both sides were 'well organised'. Union organization, in particular, contributed to harmony in industry by enabling industrial relationships which maximised 'the confidence ... workmen had in their employers'.[116] In the absence of 'all the good work which the unions had done' in this respect, there would be among workers a 'feeling of unrest and doubt and dissatisfaction [with] their employers'.[117]

Shackleton's belief in co-operative industrial relations was reflected in his membership of the Labour Co-partnership Association, which included employers. He once publicly expressed disappointment in the limited number of employers who had 'tried profit-sharing'.[118] On the other hand, he celebrated the joint employer–employee committees in the cotton industry as 'great bulwarks of industrial peace' because, as he put it, they provided 'the first element needed in dealing with the difficulties and intricacies of trade unions, labour, employers, and industrial peace' – and that element was 'the power of conversation with one another'.[119]

Industrial peace was a priority. It had to be, for a level-headed trade unionist. Because the alternative could be appalling, as he once explained in uncharacteristically impassioned language. 'None suffered more from industrial war than the workers themselves. It was an easy thing for the employers to fight a big battle, and see the workmen slain by the way and the suffering wives and children. It was not the man with the money bags who suffered.'[120] Nor was it simply a matter of human suffering. There was also a functional disadvantage in industrial conflict. 'Strikes', he explained to the Accrington Liberal Club at the outset of his career as a trade union professional, 'developed angry feelings, and made the possibilities of settlements more difficult.'[121] If possible, they were to be avoided; and he took pride in the the fact

113. This, too, was emphasized in contemporary Christian social thought, especially the Roman Catholic version. See Martin, *Trade Unionism*, pp. 54–5.
114. *Cotton Factory Times*, 19 October 1894.
115. Ibid., 20 May 1910.
116. Ibid., 10 April 1903.
117. Ibid.
118. Ibid., 15 May 1908.
119. Ibid., 30 July 1909.
120. Ibid.
121. *Ramsbottom Observer*, 10 March 1893.

that in his eight years as an honorary official of the Accrington weavers, the union had not had to spend even 'one week's income … in strike pay'.[122]

But there was a steel fist in the velvet glove. Although 'not one who loved strikes', Shackleton nevertheless regarded them as an utterly essential trade union weapon, and had 'given his vote for [them] where he considered [them] necessary'.[123] By the same token, he believed in preparing for them. Hence his lecture, as a fledgling full-time official, to the Ramsbottom weavers:

> How long would they be in getting a strike fund behind them if the members only contributed … at that rate? The strikes of the future would be big strikes, as shown by the cotton and coal lockouts. It was very essential, therefore, that they pay at least one penny per loom … Contributions on that scale would nicely keep the [union] on such a basis as would enable them to tide over the time of tribulation when it came.[124]

Later, as secretary of the Darwen weavers, he was again to express pride in a strike-free record, explaining that the union had been 'fortunate enough' to settle all disputes peaceably.[125] But before the settlements, there had always been the possibility of strike action. Acceptable settlements, he believed, were more readily achieved in its shadow. If workers clearly possessed 'the power to strike, they would generally get what they wanted'.[126] And it was, he believed, 'the power to strike', rather than 'the strike itself when it happened', which had proved the more effective means of increasing wages, at least in the Lancashire cotton industry.[127] On the other hand, the strike itself was often the only way to go when it came to maverick employers ('the "knobsticks" amongst the masters').[128] The two sides of Shackleton's position on the strike weapon are crisply represented in a speech he made at Marple to an audience of weavers locked out for refusing an offer beneath the rate agreed with other local employers. In the course of his opening remarks, he stated the general principle: 'Trade unions existed not to promote strikes, but to avoid them if possible.'[129] In his final comment, he dealt with the particu-

---

122. Ibid.
123. *Nelson Chronicle*, 19 September 1902.
124. *Cotton Factory Times*, 6 April 1894.
125. *Nelson Chronicle*, 19 September 1902.
126. *Cotton Factory Times*, 15 February 1907.
127. *Nelson Leader*, 10 September 1909.
128. *Cotton Factory Times*, 20 May 1910. As he explained, in defending strike action against an employer who had stood out against an agreed standard rate: 'Whatever public opinion might be in Cornholme and Todmorden, if people knew the facts they would see that the Weavers' Union had no choice; they must either strike, or concede reductions in other parts of Lancashire.' Ibid., 12 May 1905. He also drew a distinctly Hobbesian conclusion from the outcome of this strike: 'The fact they did strike, and that it was successful, proved – first, that they were powerful enough to do it, and, secondly, that they had justice on their side'. Ibid.
129. Ibid., 8 April 1910.

lar case: 'You fight here, and we [the Weavers' Amalgamation] will find the sinews of war.'[130]

★ ★ ★ ★

Basic as it was, industrial action was not the be-all and end-all in Shackleton's scheme of things. Political action, too, was important and, indeed, preferable if available – because it was, in the end, comparatively painless. He made the point in a rare piece of published writing. 'While I hold that Parliamentary action can never render Trade Union effort unnecessary, it yet seems to me a crime to force by a strike and its consequent sufferings, what can and ought to be obtained by public opinion operating through the legislature of the country.'[131] Had he not chosen to follow the star of the LRC/Labour party, his views on contemporary public policy issues would have allowed him to remain, comfortably, a Liberal. He identified himself to John Burns, at the time of the Clitheroe by-election, 'as one who has been an advanced Radical all his live [sic]'.[132] A prominent local Socialist, Dan Irving, was later reported to have doubted the 'advanced'.[133] Irving, knowingly or not, was echoing the earlier judgement of a Liberal newspaper which, after initially suggesting that Shackleton was 'far more advanced than the average Liberal politician',[134] then modified that to 'a little more advanced',[135] before concluding that, 'except in name, he is as Liberal as any of us'.[136]

Shackleton himself made no secret of his high regard for the Liberal government elected in 1906. As he explained to his Briercliffe constituents, the Liberals' accession brought 'an entirely different atmosphere' to parliament, in that Labour members found themselves generally supporting, instead of opposing, government measures.[137] He had particularly warm feelings for the Prime Minister, Campbell-Bannerman, whom he described as 'one of the straightest and most honourable men he had ever met'[138] – recalling, in particular, the Prime Minister's action on the Trade Disputes Bill when 'he came to us and said, "I voted for your measure in Opposition, and I am going to

130. Ibid.
131. 'Preface' to Tuckwell, *Women in Industry*, p. xiii.
132. Shackleton to Burns, 15 July 1902: Burns Coll., BM Add. MS 46298/82.
133. *Colne & Nelson Times*, 11 July 1907.
134. *Nelson Leader*, 24 June 1904.
135. Ibid., 27 January 1905.
136. Ibid., 29 September 1905.
137. Ibid., 11 October 1907.
138. *Cotton Factory Times*, 28 September 1906. Earlier, he had justified his decision to support the government in a division on the War Estimates (the bulk of the Labour members voted against) by expressing faith in Campbell-Bannerman's personal position on 'the war question'. *Labour Leader*, 23 March 1906.

vote for it now".'[139] Shackleton also showed respect for the Liberals by consistently refusing to campaign in local government elections on behalf of the Labour party.[140]

Nevertheless, he did choose independent political action through the LRC/Labour party. Independent action, he told a union audience in 1903, meant that the 'time had come when they must look upon their trade unions as a political agent'.[141] That, however, did not mean the new party was to be viewed as 'only a trade-union party; it was too narrow in that capacity', for it had to reach out beyond the organized working class.[142] This was a critical reason for the partnership with Socialists in 'the Labour Alliance', as he liked to describe the party.[143] It meant that 'Socialists and Trade Unionists', despite their differences, 'have common work to do'; and the outcome, he thought, was an alliance that 'wields a tremendous power'.[144] But it was a power to be exercised with restraint. It was out of the question that the alliance 'should be a revolutionary party'.[145] It had to be strictly reformist, working through parliament, 'essentially a practical party'.[146]

Most revealingly, however, Shackleton did not see the alliance as a party of government – at least for the foreseeable future. Its role was rather to use its parliamentary presence as an additional means of influencing the policies of the parties that did control government. 'Our duty in the House of Commons for years to come', he said, 'is to seize the opportunities that arise, to get hold of Liberal and Tory programmes, to smash them if they are wrong, to amend

139. *Nelson Leader*, 14 June 1907. There are no correspondingly appreciative references to Asquith, Campbell-Bannerman's successor, whom Shackleton also dealt with on a number of occasions. But two decades later, Shackleton nominated Asquith as his 'favourite statesman'. *Blackpool Gazette & Herald*, 30 June 1928. It is hard to know what to make of this, since it is inconceivable that Shackleton was unaware of (and still less, with his fierce teetotalism, condoned) Asquith's serious drinking problem: he would have seen its effects as a member of the House of Commons, and it was the subject of music-hall jokes while Asquith was still Prime Minister. See Rintala, 'Taking the Pledge: H. H. Asquith and Drink', pp. 113–14, 118. Asquith, too, strongly opposed women's suffrage (unlike Campbell-Bannerman) and spoke against Shackleton's suffrage bill in 1910. See Halévy, *Rule of Democracy*, pp. 520–3.
140. See *Colne & Nelson Times*, 30 April 1909.
141. *Cotton Factory Times*, 16 January 1903. Later on, under the spur of the Osborne judgement debarring political expenditures by trade unions, his conception of unions as 'political' agents broadened. He argued that the judgement, on a 'strict rendering', applied beyond the Labour party connection. 'All along', he said, the TUC's activities 'had been purely political work'. The Textile Factory Workers' Association, similarly, had been concerned solely with 'questions of a purely political character. It did not deal with trade matters at all'. Ibid., 21 October 1910.
142. *Labour Leader*, 11 October 1907.
143. Ibid., 18 June 1909. He also liked to stress the financial aspect of the partnership. Thus, 'the member of the I.L.P. who was not a member of his trade union was only half a Labour man, for trade unionists found over 90 per cent of the money required for the Parliamentary representation of Labour'. *Cotton Factory Times*, 1 October 1909.
144. *Labour Leader*, 18 June 1909.
145. *Nelson Leader*, 16 February 1906.
146. TUC, *Report*, 1909, p. 48.

them where necessary.'[147] Initially, this effectively meant that the 'Labour Party was going to be the left wing of the Liberal Party, pushing [the Liberals] on to work'.[148] It also meant, as he explained in his chairman's address to the LRC conference of 1905, that priority had to be given to organizational rather than policy issues:

> In regard to the question of a [policy] programme for our Party, I think we shall do well to give all our attention to strengthening our organisation in the constituencies, and in that way make our Party more powerful in the House of Commons, rather than in taking up our time discussing these matters of policy ... When we are able, by the strength of our Party in the House of Commons, to have a deciding voice in the Legislature of this country, then it will be soon enough for us to promulgate a programme.[149]

For Shackleton, as for others, the strategy of independent political action was quickly and magnificently vindicated in the passage of the Trade Disputes Act. He celebrated the strategy as well as the event. Labour was now 'recognised as a force in Parliament, and an independent policy had brought that about, and nothing else'.[150] He also emphasized the improbability of their achieving the same result had the unions relied on the old method of 'deputation to Members' of parliament.[151]

At the same time, he was wary of overvaluing the new strategy and, correspondingly, devaluing industrial action. He had encountered this tendency among Continental trade unionists, and distrusted it.[152] So, with the glory of the Trade Disputes Act fresh about him, he presciently warned against facile assumptions that 'the Labour party was going to supersede trade unionism', which would persist as 'the chief method of protecting the interests of the workers in dealing with the employers'.[153] A little later, he sharpened the comparative point: 'For many years to come employers would feel the strength of the trade [unions] more than [that of] Parliament.'[154]

Nor was it only a matter of needing unions to deal with employers. They were also needed to deal with cabinet ministers. As we have seen (Chapters 5

---

147. *Cotton Factory Times*, 1 February 1907.
148. *Dundee Courier*, 12 January 1906: quoted by Fraser in Brown (ed.), *First Labour Party*, p. 46.
149. *Labour Party Foundation Conference*, p. 219. The party did not formally adopt a comprehensive programme until 1918, at the same time as it ceased to be exclusively a federation of affiliated bodies by providing for individual membership.
150. *Labour Leader*, 21 September 1906.
151. TUC, *Report*, 1906, p. 134.
152. Reporting on an international congress of textile unions, he observed that the 'Continental delegates do not appear fully to appreciate the benefit which can be derived from trades-union effort. A dominant influence in all they do is ... political action ... The English trade unionist fully recognises the need for political action, but he realises also the further necessity of having a strong trades union.' *Colne & Nelson Times*, 14 July 1905.
153. *Labour Leader*, 7 December 1906.
154. *Cotton Factory Times*, 22 February 1907.

and 6), Shackleton repeatedly fuelled the 'overlapping' controversy between the party and the TUC by claiming an exclusive trade union role in specific dealings with government. His fullest recorded explanation of the reasoning behind this claim was given from the platform of the last Congress he attended as a union official:

> In the course of our negotiations with the Government from time to time ... the advantage has been manifested of having a Trade Union body as distinct from a political body. Our feeling is that if there is not that distinctive Trade Union element we shall always be in the position of fighting the Government of the day; and we are desirous of being able to continue our negotiations with any Government, apart from the fight that goes on in the country between the three parties.[155]

The insistence on the TUC's independence of the Labour party, in dealing with Liberal ministers, echoed the insistence on Shackleton's personal independence that was implied in his response to an interviewer immediately following his win in the Clitheroe by-election: 'I am a trade unionist before a politician.'[156] His independence in this respect was a matter of considerable public interest, especially once the LRC decided that its MPs should be required to sign a copy of its constitution ('the pledge'). Although he did not sign the pledge until October 1903, the question of whether he would act as a 'representative' or a 'delegate' (the latter conventionally identified in the press with an 'automaton' or 'machine', responsive only to the party) was there from the start. Within days of his selection as the Labour candidate for Clitheroe, he was eager to assure John Burns that 'my Committee give me an entirely free hand, on matters outside purely Labour or Trade Union questions', and equally anxious to make the same point publicly.[157] Following the by-election, he was reported as reiterating the point on a number of occasions up to the time of his re-election in January 1906.[158] Thereafter, the local press seems to have lost interest in the issue; and Shackleton never returned to it.

---

155. TUC, *Report*, 1910, p. 121.
156. *Blackburn Weekly Telegraph*, 2 August 1902.
157. Shackleton to Burns, 15 July 1902: Burns Coll., BM Add. MS 46298/81. See *Nelson Chronicle*, 25 July 1902.
158. There is one exception. In a speech to Accrington Rechabites, two months after the by-election, he is reported to have made two novel and contradictory points: first, that he was 'free to give his vote according to his convictions, on any question which came before Parliament'; and, second, that he 'was not aware of any question that was not really a labour question'. *Nelson Chronicle*, 3 October 1902. The second point is cited by Bealey and Pelling as demonstrating that 'Shackleton's attitude to parliamentary representation was rather confused.' *Labour and Politics*, p. 122. This is a questionable conclusion in the light of the probability – given the invariable reiteration of his earlier statements in his later reported speeches – that the Accrington speech was misreported in both aspects. One of the subsequent reiterations occurred at Barrowford, a year after the Accrington address and just days before Shackleton finally signed the LRC constitution – which he forwarded under cover of a letter that mentioned, without specifying, an 'objection marked' on the constitution. Shackleton to MacDonald, 22 October 1903: LP Archives, LRC 10/415. The marked objection almost certainly had to do with securing the freedom of action he claimed publicly (see Chapter 4).

Not long after his re-election, however, he took a step which did raise the question of independence – but primarily in relation to his role as a trade union official.

He chose to drop his bombshell in April 1907. In the course of a speech at Rochdale, he advocated that the minimum legal age of children working as 'half-timers' in cotton weaving sheds should be raised from 12 to 13 years (see Chapter 6). Up to that time, he had been unshakeably identified with the cotton unions' consistent opposition to any increase in the minimum age. But he denied suggestions that he had had a change of heart, saying that, personally, he had always thought 'the position of the half-timer' unsatisfactory.[159] He explained that he had publicly opposed raising the previous minimum age in the 1890s, 'the last time the question was before the country', because it was his duty as 'a humble official ... to act with his leaders'.[160] There had been a second reason as well, although he failed to mention it; a reason that had to do with the economic circumstances of weavers and their families. For in 1902, after telling a select gathering of MPs and union officials that raising the minimum age would 'in the long run be a good thing' for the weavers, he had gone on to oppose any immediate change on the ground that their current living standard depended too heavily on the half-time employment of their children.[161] His Rochdale speech, calling for change, came five years later. It followed the successful completion of the weavers' long campaign to eliminate the reduction in their wage rates which had sparked the great strike of 1878. That success, as Shackleton explained on another occasion, 'considerably improved' their financial position, and was the reason he had 'seen his way clear to give [them] a lead' on the half-time issue.[162] Subsequently, as we have seen (Chapter 6), that lead was overwhelmingly rebuffed by the rank and file of the cotton unions. But he

159. *Nelson Leader*, 16 October 1908. As early as 1898, in fact, he explicitly recommended a 'gradual increase of the [minimum] age' to his Darwen members, arguing that the half-time system was responsible for the current over-supply of weavers, and that raising the age-limit would help limit entry. DWA, *Quarterly Report*, 10 October 1898. And in 1902, while formally opposing a motion against the half-time system, he described it as 'the existing evil'. TUC, *Report*, 1902, p. 76.

160. *Nelson Leader*, 16 October 1908. He might have mentioned also the massive rank-and-file opposition to any change. In 1899, a Weavers' Amalgamation ballot of well over 70,000 members yielded majorities of 89 per cent, against raising the minimum age from 11 to 12, and 93 per cent, against raising it to 13. In the case of Shackleton's own members in Darwen, the majorities were 91 and 94 per cent, respectively. *Cotton Factory Times*, 24 February 1899.

161. *Colne & Nelson Times*, 11 July 1902. '[If] it could be done', Shackleton said, he would 'debar the children of men earning 30s. a week ... from working half-time. But the weaver who is earning [20s.] a week and has a wife and three or four children to keep is in a very different position.'

162. *Nelson Leader*, 16 October 1908. In saying this, he was seen on the far left as 'bluffing his way out of ... his [earlier] opposition to the abolition of the half-time system'. *Socialist Standard*, 1 March 1909.

continued to maintain publicly that the minimum age for half-timers should be raised to 13.[163]

* * * *

The switch on half-timers is the only radical change Shackleton ever made in his public stance on a major policy issue. His position on the great non-industrial issues of his day was not only consistent, but largely predictable. As a cotton trade unionist, concerned with an industry wholly dependent on imports for its raw material and overwhelmingly dependent on foreign markets for its finished product, he was an ardent free trader. As an advanced Liberal manqué, he was strong for Irish home rule, women's suffrage, anti-militarism, and peace.[164] In the same political vein, he was especially strong against the House of Lords. He described it as 'a marionette show' inhabited by 'mummies' after first seeing it at work,[165] and told other audiences that the Labour party should 'go in for its total abolition'.[166] When the Lords rejected the government's liquor-licensing Bill, in 1908, his public reaction was expressed in uncharacteristically passionate terms. 'It was impossible', he said, that such an institution could continue to exist 'among a free people. It was only because they were semi-slaves in this country that such a House had been allowed to survive.'[167] Nevertheless, if one tallies the references over the years, considers the language, and relates both to the circumstances of Shackleton's life, the non-industrial issues with which he was most intensely engaged were, without a doubt, temperance and education.

The liquor problem, for Shackleton, was a trade union problem. Drink he saw as 'the greatest obstacle to the progress of Labour and of trade union-ism'.[168] This was, interestingly, a conviction he shared with contemporary Russian revolutionaries.[169] But while support for temperance was strong in the parliamentary Labour party,[170] it was a highly divisive issue within the labour movement at large. On the left, there were those who believed drunk-enness was nothing more that a consequence of poverty engendered by capi-talist exploitation. Others, on the right, inclined towards the equally simple explanation that individual failing was the root of the problem – and that poverty was a consequence of drunkenness. Shackleton, on one occasion, was widely reported as having plumped for the right-wing simplification, but a

163. See *Cotton Factory Times*, 30 July 1909.
164. He thought of international trade union organization as 'making for peace between nations, and teaching workers of all countries that they are brothers'. *Labour Leader*, 4 May 1906.
165. *Nelson Chronicle*, 5 February 1904.
166. *Cotton Factory Times*, 25 October 1907.
167. Ibid., 4 December 1908.
168. *Nelson Leader*, 26 February 1909.
169. See Phillips, 'Message in a Bottle', pp. 26–7.
170. See Martin and Rubinstein, *Ideology and the Labour Movement*, pp. 132–3. Thus at the party's formal dinners, toasts were drunk in 'strictly temperance beverages'. *Labour Leader*, 13 April 1906.

letter to an editor from Edward R. Hartley, a Socialist, set the record straight.[171] Shackleton, in fact, trod a middle way. On the other hand, when it came to solutions, as distinct from causes, he was extreme, insisting that he would 'never be content until drink was placed under lock and key and labelled like any other poison'.[172] And so, despite critics like Ben Tillett,[173] he was 'determined' to devote as much time as he could to speaking on temperance platforms, in the belief that 'the success of trade unionism depended ... upon the success of the temperance movement'.[174]

If drink was the demon that had to be exorcised from the working class, education was the great gift it must be given. Shackleton, as a nonconformist, was axiomatically in favour of free and secular education, and against state aid for church schools. In addition, however, he had a personal vision of the educational opportunities open to working-class males; and perhaps the most remarkable aspect of his vision was the extent to which it changed, and expanded, in the space of barely two decades. There were three stages to this process. The first, coinciding with his early parliamentary years from 1902, involved a vision confined to secondary technical education. He expressed pride in the pioneering efforts of the working class itself to provide such education, 'through the co-operative societies of this country',[175] and urged the young men of his day to take advantage of current opportunities provided by public authorities. But he was also sensitive to the shortcomings of this form of education once one moved beyond the mill and the workshop. 'Working men who were sent to Parliament', as he put it, were not like the MPs from other classes because they alone, lacking education, had 'to hold the position by sheer intelligence and power of thought'.[176] Nonetheless, speaking to unionists, he could still make a virtue of it all – in terms echoing those employed on countless occasions by other working-class leaders, before and since. 'Parliament was all the better for having ... a few men who could speak direct from their own life's experience ... It was all very well to read others' thoughts of life, but experience was better, after all.'[177] The second stage coincided with Shackleton's later parliamentary years when he was actively

171.   'I have just read your paragraph about D. J. Shackleton's remarks about drink and poverty, and think there is a mistake somewhere. He and I spoke at the same meeting just two weeks ago ... He distinctly said: "Some people thought the one cause of poverty was drink; but he didn't. He believed they were both equal. Poverty was as much the cause of drinking, as drinking was the cause of poverty" – a very different statement to the one attributed to him, though it is no more the truth than the first.' *Clarion*, 17 June 1904.
172.   *Rechabite and Temperance Magazine*, January 1911, p. 5. His position on gambling displayed the same severity: 'the professional bookmaker ... was far better engaged serving his time in prison than in demoralising working men'. *Parl. Debs.*, 1 August 1906, vol. 162, col. 1151.
173.   See Schneer, *Ben Tillett*, p. 135.
174.   *Cotton Factory Times*, 4 December 1908.
175.   Ibid., 29 July 1904.
176.   Ibid.
177.   Ibid., 21 September 1906.

involved with Ruskin College and with the Oxford tutorial classes for indus-trial centres (see Chapter 7), both of which provided an educational experi-ence purportedly approaching university level. By this time, he was less inclined to crack hardy about the consequences of educational deprivation. Thus he admitted to members of the Royston Co-operative Society that Labour parliamentarians 'felt the need of education when they had to sit ... day after day listening to learned men, who had spent the first 25 years of their lives storing up knowledge'.[178] He enlarged on the point a week later, before the Crompton Co-operative Society: 'Practical experience of life was a good teacher, but the average working man was not equal to the man who had the opportunity of a University training.'[179] On each occasion, however, he also stressed that this imbalance was in the process of being redressed in some measure by the opportunities which Ruskin and the Oxford classes now provided for young working men.

The third stage encompassed Shackleton's time as a senior civil servant, the social watershed of the First World War, and the time when he put his nephew, Ernest Wilkinson, through Cambridge. At this stage, his vision not only extended to the possibility of a full university education but, more star-tlingly, to graduates as trade union leaders. He made the point as the author of a carefully written newspaper article:

> Conceive the Trade Union leader, the Labour Member of Parliament, who starts on his work as a young man with some years of University training behind him. It means that he has been equipped with special knowledge ... In addition to this he secures a mental perspective which is [otherwise] only available after long and weary years of experience ... I cannot sufficiently emphasise the value to the Trade Union movement of University training ... for the young men who have the abil-ity and the energy and the aptitude for work in public life.[180]

★ ★ ★ ★

Shackleton's comment on the education of trade union leaders was written while he was still a permanent secretary. Its implicit concern for the labour movement's future raises the question of how, as a civil servant, he dealt with the beliefs and loyalties he brought with him from his time in the movement.

In general, his file minutes and contributions in meetings suggest a resolve to be, and to appear, the model civil servant, acting impartially on behalf of an impersonal, disinterested state. On one occasion, however, he admitted to the possibility of something less than perfection: 'I have no interest except in the State, but if I have any bias it leans towards those with whom I have

178. Ibid., 12 November 1909.
179. Ibid., 19 November 1909.
180. *Northern Daily Telegraph*, 20 May 1920.

always worked.'[181] He made this remark as a prelude to refusing a request made by the trade unionists in his audience.[182]

This was neither the first nor the last occasion on which Shackleton might be seen as acting contrary to his self-proclaimed 'bias', in the sense of weighing in against old allegiances. In one file minute on a union recognition issue, for example, he concluded a politically-sensitive argument by strongly urging the minister 'not to let this Union of all Unions ... score against us'.[183] In another, concerning a parliamentary resolution he had negotiated with the Labour party's leaders, he recommended arranging for the government to introduce the resolution on the ground that it would be 'a mistake to let the Labour Party' take the credit for it.[184] In the War Cabinet, too, he took a notably hard line on a number of occasions when trade union interests were involved. Thus, in mid-1918 he urged rejection of a miners' wage claim, subsequently conceded by a War Cabinet fearful of strike action; and shortly afterwards he opposed, again unsuccessfully, the miners' further claim to extend their wage rise beyond the coal industry.[185]

However, there were other occasions and other issues on which his 'bias' arguably showed. Up to 1919, for instance, he was party (along with Hodge and Roberts, his first two ministers) to the highly unorthodox practice of submitting details of major legislation to the TUC prior to their parliamentary introduction.[186] Later, he strongly advocated dealing exclusively with the TUC, on the trade union side, when he advised his Minister against proposing a second 'National Industrial Conference' involving unions and employers at large.[187]

On another issue, the freedom of workers to organize, he was clearly pro-union. There is his soothing advice to a book publishers' representative confronting a union incursion for the first time: 'I know that ... you will have trouble until half is organised and after that the whole thing settles down.'[188] And, in particular, there was his behaviour in the quite different context of a War Cabinet meeting which had before it a claim from the Railway Clerks' Association to represent supervisory staff. Immediately after Horne, his own minister, had spoken strongly against the claim, Shackleton intervened to support it:

---

181. *Note of Conference* ..., 21 September 1917: LAB 10/399 4661.
182. In addition to two trade unionists (whom he might be thought to have been trying to win over with this remark), the audience included three other, more junior, civil servants and W. C. Bridgeman, then Parliamentary Secretary to the Ministry of Labour.
183. LAB 2/758/WA3509 4896: 23 July 1920. It was the Electrical Trades Union.
184. LAB 2/788 XC/B 5091: 25 March 1920.
185. *War Cabinet*, 437, 28 June 1918: CAB 23/6, p. 200; 440, 3 July 1918: CAB 23/7, p. 7.
186. See Lowe, 'Review Article', p. 120.
187. LAB 2/775 5026: 30 January 1922. The National Industrial Conference of February 1919 had been supposed to act as a kind of advisory industrial parliament. According to Lowe, 'Shackleton, concerned for the independence of the TUC, welcomed the demise of the NIC'. *Adjusting to Democracy*, p. 98.
188. LAB 10/399 4661: 24 September 1917.

Sir David Shackleton said that he had worked both in the position of a workman and a foreman, and his experience was that both grades belonging to the same Union never affected discipline, but if the Government refused to recognise this Union, it was in opposition to their avowed policy, and the Government should not try to decide who was and who was not to be in the Union. In his opinion they should trust to the honour and loyalty of the men.[189]

At another War Cabinet meeting, his sensitivity to workers' grievances was plain in the way he explained a cotton spinners' threat to strike against a Cotton Control Board agreement changing their working conditions. As he put it, 'the contention of the operatives was that, while the employers were making more money than they had ever done before, they (the operatives) would be forced by the present proposal to live on an 18 per cent increase in wages, when the increased cost of living was about 100 per cent'.[190] Again, his account of popular opinion was notably supportive when he argued against Winston Churchill on the issue of British intervention in the Russian civil war:

He himself had been surprised at the extent to which men of all classes were now coming round to supporting the Labour view that the Soviet Government ought to be given a fair chance. A further point was that we had never attempted to interfere when the Czar was in power. There was no doubt that this feeling was spreading, and he was afraid that the agitation might assume formidable proportions.[191]

And, again with Churchill in his sights, he displayed a sympathetic understanding of the problems of union officials by the terms in which he supported restoration of the prewar practices that the unions had temporarily abandoned under the Treasury agreement of 1915. If the War Cabinet accepted Churchill's advice to repudiate restoration, Shackleton said, that would only serve to strengthen the 'extremists' in the unions by discrediting their officials, 'who would be charged with having betrayed the men'.[192]

These interventions suggest that he had by no means abandoned old loyalties and old understandings.[193] As evidence of this, moreover, they carry particular weight because they involve views that were expressed in private, to strictly limited audiences and, as recorded, had a highly restricted circulation before disappearing into a mountainous filing system. In other words, Shackleton the civil servant, unlike Shackleton the trade union leader and politician, was under no pressure to weigh his words with an eye to a wider public's perception of him.

189. *War Cabinet*, 523, 31 January 1919: CAB 23/9, p. 38.
190. Ibid., 471, 10 September 1918: CAB 23/7, p. 104.
191. Quoted (from the minutes of a War Cabinet committee, 27 June 1919) in James, *Churchill*, p. 117.
192. *War Cabinet*, 487, 16 October 1918; 491, 24 October 1918: CAB 23/8, pp. 35, 48.
193. At the same time, according to Lowe, he was decidedly more conservative in policy matters than many of his senior departmental colleagues, including Harold Butler. See *Adjusting to Democracy*, p. 79.

Perceptions of Shackleton

Shackleton was quite commonly seen as a modest man, remarkably likeable, and to be respected. Shortly after becoming an MP, he was described by one journalist as 'having no side on him'.[194] A year and more later, in a letter to a local paper, 'Citizen' wrote that 'he is just the same as he was when he first became known to us. He has not "put on side", he is still cheery, unassuming, natural.'[195] And newspaper stories thereafter continued to make much the same point. One, when he was still an MP, reported a visit to investigate the complaints of workers in a Clitheroe weaving shed: 'to test matters for themselves, Mr Shackleton and Mr Cottam [the local union secretary] doffed their coats, set to work, and "ran" several looms'.[196] Another, when he was a senior civil servant, had it that he commuted by public transport rather than indulge in 'the Whitehall motor-car habit during the war';[197] and after the war he was photographed 'waiting his turn in a bus queue'.[198] Hesketh Pearson, about the time of Shackleton's retirement, confirmed this picture of an unassuming character. 'He's entirely a self-made man, though he has none of the bounce and assurance of such … He never indulges in that peculiar form of success-snobbery which likes to remind other people that they haven't been quite so successful.'[199]

He also impressed as a courteous man. One journalist referred to his 'tact and urbanity'.[200] Another, writing in a Conservative newspaper which had strongly attacked certain of Shackleton's views, was at pains to express appreciation of the way he had handled its criticism.[201] And Ernest Wilkinson, who often travelled with the Shackletons before the war, recalled that at the end of each train journey his uncle always went to the front of the train to thank the driver.

These are the marks of a likeable man. Harold Butler, the first Warden of Nuffield College, who worked at Shackleton's shoulder during the Ministry of Labour's early years, testified to this when he later wrote with open affection of 'David Shackleton with his black beard and his golden heart'.[202] Frederick Leggett, another ministry colleague, at 96 years of age recalled him as 'one of the most splendid characters I've met in my life. A lovely man …

---

194. *Cotton Factory Times*, 12 September 1902.
195. *Nelson Chronicle*, 5 February 1904.
196. *Cotton Factory Times*, 7 September 1906.
197. Unknown newspaper, n.d. (1920): SP. The temptation would have been minimal, given his intense dislike of cars. See Chapter 9.
198. *Illustrated London News*, 15 February 1919.
199. Unknown newspaper, n.d. (1925): SP.
200. *Reynolds's Weekly Newspaper*, n.d. (September 1908): SP.
201. 'We have to thank [Shackleton] for the exemplary manner in which he has dealt with our comments upon his public utterances regarding the Osborne Judgement.' *Colne & Nelson Times*, 4 October 1910.
202. Butler, *Confident Morning*, p. 116.

A lovely man ... Always the same wherever he was.'[203] But not only likeable. As Leggett added: 'Very greatly respected'. F. A. Norman, also of the ministry, similarly remembered Shackleton as a man 'who commanded respect and was not spoilt by success.'[204] And Lowe, from a greater distance, reinforces the point. 'His character certainly won him respect in Whitehall.'[205]

The reactions of middle-class, university-educated civil servants, who knew Shackleton towards the end of his career, strikingly echo reactions evident earlier – during his years as a labour leader – in the Clitheroe constituency, in the trade unions and, perhaps most remarkably, in the House of Commons.

In the case of the Clitheroe electors, likeability and respect boil down to popularity. At the general election of January 1910, there is no question of the enthusiasm surrounding Shackleton's campaign. His meetings were triumphs. In both Nelson and Colne, 'Overflow meetings were necessary ... but even these were crowded out, and many were unable to gain admission.'[206] The boisterous reaction to his win, already touched on (see Chapter 6), was summed up by the *Cotton Factory Times*: 'The enthusiasm in Clitheroe and all along the route [of Shackleton's drive with his family] will never be forgotten, and the cheering at times was almost deafening.'[207] And later that year, after it was known he was resigning his seat, the *Nelson Leader* put his popularity into comparative perspective. 'Mr Shackleton's promotion [to the Home Office] has completely altered the political situation in the Clitheroe Division ... for all time. No Labour candidate will ever command the same measure of support that Mr Shackleton did.'[208]

In the larger arena of the national trade union movement, his popularity was a matter of press comment by the time of the TUC's annual Congress in 1906. It was the thirteenth he had attended as a delegate, but only the second in which he also had the distinction of being a member of the TUC's executive body, the Parliamentary Committee. Bruce Glasier (then editor of the *Labour Leader*) remarked on the fact that a 'hearty cheer went up' when Shackleton rose to make his first speech; and he added that 'Mr Shackleton is sincerely respected in the Congress.'[209] An anonymous journalist provided harder evidence: 'No one is more popular than David ... He was right at the top of the poll for the [Parliamentary Committee], and a long way ahead of the others for the American delegation.'[210] A year later, it was not merely his

203. Interview, 25 March 1981. An anonymous civil servant wrote similarly of Shackleton's 'exceeding charm of manner'. *Civil Service Argus*, n.d. (1925): SP.
204. *From Whitehall to the West Indies*, p. 84. I am indebted to Rodney Lowe for this reference.
205. *Adjusting to Democracy*, p. 66.
206. *Nelson Leader*, 7 January 1910. One of the Nelson meetings, held in the Salem School hall, was packed with 'at least 1,500 people' more than half-an-hour before it was due to start; and afterwards Shackleton went on to a second packed gathering at the Weavers' Institute.
207. *Cotton Factory Times*, 28 January 1910.
208. *Nelson Leader*, 18 November 1910.
209. *Labour Leader*, 7 September 1906.
210. *Cotton Factory Times*, 14 September 1906.

popularity but his authority that was formally registered in his being chosen by the Parliamentary Committee as its chairman; and the point was strikingly reaffirmed in his singular re-election to the position (see Chapter 6). Observing the 1909 Congress, the second that Shackleton chaired, H. R. Stockman of the ILP reported that he 'certainly commands the respect of all the delegates ... On rising to deliver his presidential address he was received with deafening applause.'[211] And in 1910, although not in the chair, he was seen as a truly dominating figure:

> Visitors to the Congress have sighed for something dramatic, and they got what they wanted yesterday ... in the revelation of how a strong man can dominate an assembly, and turn it round from declamation to practical politics. This was what Mr Shackleton did. And in the doing of it one saw a man head and shoulders above his fellows – a kind of Parnell of the Labour movement.[212]

Following his decision to go to the Home Office, there were two particular evaluations of his influence – one friendly and one hostile – which together comprehensively summed up his extraordinary role in the labour movement of his day. The friendly comment focused on the unions and the TUC, and came from W. Brace, a Labour MP and miners' union official: 'No man,' Brace told the TUC's annual gathering, 'has wielded a greater influence in this Congress than [Shackleton] has exercised.'[213] The other comment, from the London correspondent of *Vorwärts*, the German Social Democratic party's paper, was primarily concerned with the Labour party:

> If there is one man more than another who has retarded the healthy development of the British Labour movement it is Mr Shackleton. It was he who at every Labour Conference directed himself against Socialism with all his might, and with all his weighty influence, who, to the last, threw his whole strength into the balance to prevent the Labour Party taking up that energetic stand against the Government by which alone they could have wrung any concessions from the Liberals.[214]

But of all the public arenas in which Shackleton acted, it is the House of Commons which is likely to have been the most exposed and the most testing, in his own estimation. Before 1906, as one of a tiny Labour splinter group, he was learning the trade – though, even then, he was thought to carry

---

211. *Labour Leader*, 10 September 1909.
212. *Sheffield Independent*, 16 September 1910.
213. TUC, *Report*, 1911, p. 154. Subject to the one possible exception of Henry Broadhurst, the TUC's secretary from 1875 to 1890, Brace was right. Later, Tom Shaw was later to make almost as strong a point about Shackleton's standing in the Weavers' Amalgamation: 'so long as he held the [presidency] he was, by force of character alone, almost the dictator of the organisation'. *Manchester Guardian*, 2 August 1938.
214. *Justice*, 26 November 1910. *Vorwärts*, a daily, was a widely admired and heavily used source in Socialist circles in Britain. See Hopkin in Boyce et al., *Newspaper History*, pp. 295–6, 304.

some weight.[215] It was during 1906, however, that he clearly established himself as a House of Commons man. His management of the momentous Trade Disputes Bill was primarily responsible for this: it brought him forcefully to the attention of parliament and the public, and won him general approbation (see Chapter 5). There were two other smaller, but strongly reinforcing episodes in that year as well. One was the 'Bottomley incident' (often the subject of later press comment, and still being recalled 20 years later),[216] in which Shackleton was credited with having 'killed by a single speech' a bill to legalize bookmakers and street betting.[217] The other incident excited afficionados of the parliamentary scene at the time. It concerned a committee inquiring into Post Office matters, and a Liberal minister's decision to exclude from its membership a Conservative well known as a postal workers' sympathizer. The parliamentary Labour party threw its weight behind a Conservative protest motion which was eventually withdrawn, but only after the government had accepted a compromise proposed by Shackleton.[218] 'J. H. H.' of the ILP reported the scene:

> Then Shackleton rose to speak for the party, and I have rarely seen him more effective.... He raised his figure to his full height, and spoke in a most effective, debating style. The Liberals looked on in mute astonishment, and the men on the Treasury Bench put their heads together. Every sentence in Shackleton's speech seemed to come down on them like a heavy weight, and when 'C. B.' [the Prime Minister] rose he seemed like a man who had all the spirit knocked out of him ... [and] hastened to add that if it would please the House he would adopt the Labour suggestion. No capitulation could have been more complete.[219]

Moreover, it was not simply a matter of Shackleton playing a prominent parliamentary role. For he seems, from 1906, to have had something of a special place in the House of Commons. An ILP observer described him as 'personally a favourite with the House'.[220] A Liberal journalist thought he enjoyed 'in some degree a unique position in the House'.[221] Alfred Kinnear's more restrained assessment was in much the same vein, and he emphasised Shackleton's physical presence. 'He is not quite an institution of Westminster, yet I do not think the little brown chamber would be quite the same without him. He is one of the sons of Anak[222] to be met with [in the House of Commons], and he is certainly the most imposing personality at the beck of

215.   That is the implication of a Conservative editorialist's recollection that 'Mr Shackleton was held in the highest esteem by the Conservative Prime Minister [Balfour], who consulted him on many occasions'. *Colne & Nelson Times*, 28 January 1910.

216.   See *Blackburn Times*, 30 October 1925.

217.   *Colne & Nelson Times*, 6 April 1906; and see Chapter 5.

218.   See *Parl. Debs.*, 6 March 1906, vol. 153, cols. 351–4.

219.   *Labour Leader*, 9 March 1906.

220.   Ibid., 6 September 1907.

221.   From *Daily News* (London), quoted in *Nelson Leader*, 10 January 1908.

222.   'The giants, the sons of Anak'. *Numbers* 13: 33.

Mr Arthur Henderson', chairman of the parliamentary Labour party.[223] Other observers looked beyond the physical factor and focused instead on what Shackleton said, and the way he said it. As one journalist remarked of him: 'No speaker is listened to with greater attention on both sides of the House.'[224] And a rising young Tory MP, F. E. Smith, later reinforced the point in the course of reviewing a book of Winston Churchill's speeches: 'Sir Edward Grey and Mr Shackleton are two of the most persuasive speakers in the House … There is about Mr Shackleton a rugged and honest simplicity which claims and receives sympathy.'[225] His qualities were evidently better suited to the peculiar character of the House of Commons than the greater oratorical talents of others, as an anonymous 'lobby representative of a London journal' explained in the course of discussing Victor Grayson's victory in the Colne Valley by-election:

> [Grayson] will receive a careful – even friendly – hearing when he speaks [in parliament], but it is not certain that his special gifts will capture the House of Commons, which is curiously unlike a public meeting. Both Mr Snowden and Mr Keir Hardie – who most seem to resemble Mr Grayson [as orators] – are far more powerful within the country than within these walls. Parliamentary ability is a difficult term to define, but the Labour member who in this present House has it most conspicuously is Mr Shackleton.[226]

So, although it was acknowledged that the Labour MPs of the time included men of much greater intellectual and oratorical ability, there was also a widespread perception that none could match Shackleton's parliamentary authority. This was accepted among Conservatives ('no other member of the [Labour] Party possesses a tithe of his influence over the House'),[227] among Liberals ('His influence has all along been greater than any other Labour member')[228] and, as a comment by Philip Snowden indicates, within the Labour party itself:

> No other member of the Labour Party in Parliament carried the influence which the member for Clitheroe did. There were more brilliant men in the party, but there was no one who impressed the House of Commons with such a conviction of sound judgement, common sense, reasonableness, sincerity, reliability, knowledge of technical labour questions, all combined, as did Mr Shackleton. The universal respect in which Mr Shackleton was held made him a valuable asset to the Labour Party.[229]

It was a perception, too, which in many cases involved an appreciation of him as ministerial timber. Thus Winston Churchill, while welcoming Shackleton's appointment to the Home Office, thought that he had aimed far too low:

223. *Lancashire Daily Post*, 17 June 1908.
224. From *Daily News*, quoted in *Nelson Leader*, 10 January 1908.
225. *World*, 30 November 1909.
226. Quoted in *Colne & Nelson Times*, 26 July 1907.
227. *Blackburn Times*, 11 January 1908.
228. *Nelson Leader*, 18 November 1910.
229. Ibid., 9 December 1910.

There could be no question that he is far and away the best man for the [Home Office] post ... But can he be spared from the House of Commons? I think his departure would be a very serious loss to the democratic forces and the Lib-Lab Coalition – at the same time, also a tremendous come-down for him ... I had always thought rather of Shackleton entering the Cabinet than a Public Department.[230]

★ ★ ★ ★

What is the explanation of Shackleton's exceptional standing in the two difficult, and quite distinct, arenas of parliament and the labour movement? His contemporaries also asked, and tried to answer, that question.

Physique and straightforwardness were almost always seen as important. 'His commanding presence and honest methods have been aids ... to his popularity in the House.'[231] His standing in the Labour party, some thought, depended largely on the fact that 'he is liked personally, and that ... counts'.[232] James Cornthwaite (after remarking that, while ' David Shackleton is not a brilliant man ... I question if there is any man who is more respectfully heard or more readily obeyed' in the labour movement) stressed something else: 'He rules by the force of commonsense.'[233] This, it would seem, amounts to the 'objective gravity and individual good sense' which Robert Michels thought of as characterizing major trade union leaders of the time.[234]

A critical personal quality ('his level-headedness') was similarly nominated in an article in the cotton employers' journal, but the author then went on to explain Shackleton's 'success' in purely ideological terms. 'He has not been an extremist ... but may be described ... as having taken a course between that of the Socialists in the Parliamentary Labour Alliance and that of the "old guard" of trade-union leaders.'[235] The point was well taken. It had also been made with more style (and all of three years earlier) by Philip Snowden, under the headline: 'Why He Is Popular':

230. Churchill to Masterman, 10 September 1910: Masterman Papers.
231. *Cotton Factory Times*, 28 December 1906.
232. From *Pall Mall Gazette*, quoted in *Nelson Leader*, 26 January 1906.
233. *Sunday Chronicle*, 18 September 1910.
234. *Political Parties*, p. 315. These qualities were 'often united', Michels somewhat waspishly added, 'with a lack of interest in and understanding of wider problems'. Shackleton may or may not have lacked either, but he was careful to confine his speechmaking, at least, to a limited range of topics. One London observer attributed the considerable attention his parliamentary speeches attracted to 'his refusal to speak except about subjects upon which he can speak with authority'. From *Daily News*, quoted in *Nelson Leader*, 26 January 1906. Three decades later, the point was recalled by an editorial writer: 'it was only on rare occasions that [Shackleton] ventured on to foreign or abstruse subjects'. Ibid., 5 August 1938.
235. *Textile Mercury*, 19 November 1910. Others put the non-extremist point differently, but to the same effect in the language of the times, describing Shackleton as 'not rash and violent, but acting with great discretion'; and, again, ' a staunch Labour man, but never of the violent type'. *Rechabite and Temperance Magazine*, February 1903, p. 25; *Nelson Leader*, 8 June 1917.

It is somewhat difficult to find the reasons for Mr Shackleton's success ... It is not the possession of brilliant ability, for he is ordinary and common-place. It is not oratorical powers, for he is neither orator nor polished speaker. There are two reasons one might suggest, perhaps three. He is transparently honest and sincere. He knows his own limitations and he never tries to outstep them; and he has a remarkably fine presence. But I should say the chief reason for Mr Shackleton's general popularity is that he fairly well represents what is a very large volume of public opinion today, namely, a condition of transition, a sort of half-way house between [the] Radicalism of the last generation and the Socialism of the next. He represents the state of political development of the great body of present day reformers. Such a man is always a success.[236]

While Snowden's 'always a success' may be questioned, there is little doubt that Shackleton's ideological representativeness was critical to his great success, in terms of position and influence, within the labour movement. By the same token, it was precisely the extent of that success which told most heavily against him when he opted to abandon it all for a life as a civil servant. For he stood then at the pinnacle of the movement, a leader nationally famous and widely respected – and for that reason, passionately hated on the extreme left.[237] As a result, his departure from the movement carried a symbolic weight that was entirely absent in the case of other senior union officials who made a similar transition around the same time.[238]

In friendly Socialist quarters, he had always been under suspicion of being soft on the Liberals;[239] and, from the unfriendly left, there were occasional allegations to do with base, monetary motives.[240] His acceptance of the Home Office post, with its substantial salary, inevitably gave colour to these allegations. Ernest Wilkinson, his nephew, said that Shackleton's decision left a longstanding feeling in many circles in Lancashire that he had (in Wilkin-

---

236.   *Nelson Leader*, 17 January 1908.

237.   In the journal of the Socialist Party of Great Britain (formerly the Social Democratic Federation/Party) he was referred to as 'Shackl'em', and described as a man who was 'bound to rise – like scum in a pot'. *Socialist Standard*, 1 October 1909.

238.   The most prominent of these were Isaac Mitchell, secretary of the General Federation of Trade Unions from its foundation in 1899 to 1907, when he joined the Board of Trade; and Richard Bell, general secretary of the Amalgamated Society of Railway Servants, a dyed-in-the-wool Lib-Lab MP who became Superintendant of Employment Exchanges in 1910.

239.   For example, during one four-week period, in the ILP's *Labour Leader* commentaries on parliamentary proceedings, he was taken to task for seeming 'to take too much the Government side against the Tories' (28 June 1907) and for too 'effusively thanking [the Liberal Home Secretary] for what he had done for the workers' (26 July 1907).

240.   One such charge surfaced at an election meeting in January 1910, when an interjector accused him of 'being in the Labour movement for what he could make out of it'. He was reported to have 'effectively silenced his accusers by stating that he has already refused six times the amount he is receiving from the Labour Party to-day'. *Nelson Leader*, 14 January 1910. He was certainly referring to the feelers put out in relation to his joining the Campbell-Bannerman and Asquith ministries. See Chapter 5.

son's words) 'betrayed his folk and feathered his own nest'.[241] The strength of that feeling is reflected in Arthur Henderson's swift public assurance, on the heels of Shackleton's appointment, that he himself would refuse all offers of a government post 'no matter what the remuneration was'.[242] It is reflected again a year later, when Shackleton moved to the National Health Insurance Commission, in Henderson's volunteered press statement that 'he would feel bound to decline' if invited to succeed Shackleton as Labour Adviser to the Home Office.[243] And the feeling persisted. It was there, shortly before Shackleton's retirement, in a local journalist's barbed comment on reports of his salary at the Ministry of Labour: 'There is many a "bloated capitalist" who would be glad to be in receipt of such a salary.'[244] It is detectable, too, in the whiff of envy spiralling out of a long and otherwise friendly retirement tribute written by Ben Turner, an old union colleague. 'David is doing right to [retire] and to take life more gently. I am glad he can afford to. I wish all of us at his age could do the same, but because we cannot I don't complain about those who can.'[245] And it was there still, a decade later, when Shackleton died. It was the reason why Tom Shaw, in his obituary, thought it necessary to defend Shackleton against the 'people who thought that [he] had just "gone over to the enemy"', almost thirty years earlier. 'Nothing', Shaw insisted, 'could have been less true.' But all he could add by way of confirmation was that 'Shackleton consulted the organisation [the Weavers' Amalgamation] of which he was president, and it was after this consultation that he accepted the post.'[246]

Shackleton clearly anticipated that his decision to go to the Home Office would arouse hostility in labour circles, and was plainly anxious to minimize it (see Chapter 7). He may well have been saddened by its extent. But further, and possibly greater, disappointments lay ahead. For the civil service devalued the strengths that had served him so well as a labour leader. In his new environment, with its different rules and different audiences, he not only lost the advantage of Snowden's 'half-way house', but most of the other qualities that had stood him in good stead were no longer as distinctive or as potent. Success became more problematic. His 'journey', at this time, was by no means 'all fair and pleasant sailing', as one observer blithely described it.[247]

241. Wilkinson's testimony on this point is compelling. He deeply admired his uncle, and plainly would have preferred to depict more favourable opinions.
242. Quoted in Wrigley, *Arthur Henderson*, pp. 49–50.
243. Ibid.
244. *Nelson Leader*, 11 September 1925.
245. Unknown newspaper, n.d. (1925): SP.
246. *Manchester Guardian*, 2 August 1938.
247. *Nelson Leader*, 29 December 1916.

Success, to be sure, still came in a formal sense. Indeed, in the permanent secretaryship and the knighthood, it certainly exceeded his wildest dreams.[248] And he placed a high value on formal success. But it all ended badly, and lingeringly, in a galling two-stage demotion and a forced early retirement. Not only was he ill-fitted for the upper reaches of the bureaucratic jungle, but he had the spectacularly bad luck to find himself directly in the career path of Horace Wilson, a jungle-master. In retirement, there was at least the comfort that not too much of the real ending was evident to outsiders.'

248.   Though an even wilder dream might have been implanted by a journalistic comment in 1917 that, as 'the question of Labour rising to the House of Lords is now taking shape, there is no telling where "Eawr Dave" will end. Will it be Lord Darwen, where he won his spurs as an operative leader, or Lord Clitheroe, which he represented from 1902 to 1910?' *Nelson Leader*, 9 November 1917.

Bibliography

Primary sources

Government

Departmental records, Public Record Office
  Home Office
  Ministry of Labour
  Ministry of Munitions
  National Health Insurance Commission
Hansard
War Cabinet, *Minutes*, 1917–19 (PRO)
Departmental Committee on Humidity and Ventilation in Cotton Weaving Sheds, *Report*, 1909
  (Cd. 4484, 4485)
Departmental Inquiry into the Alleged Danger of the Transmission of Certain Diseases from
  Person to Person in Weaving Sheds by means of 'Shuttle-kissing', *Report*, 1912 (Cd. 6184)

Labour Representation Committee/Labour Party

Correspondence and minutes (Labour Party Archives)
'Infancy of the Labour Party' (Coll. Misc. 196, London School of Economics)
The Labour Party Foundation Conference and Annual Conference Reports 1900–1905, Hammersmith
  Bookshop, Reprints No. 3, 1967
Minutes of Parliamentary Meetings, 1906–10 (House of Commons)

Trade Union

Darwen Weavers' Association (DWA), *Minutes* and *Reports*, 1894–1907 (Lancashire Record
  Office) (GM = General Meeting; Ctee = Committee)
Darwen Weavers' Association, *Souvenir of Celebrations*, 1924 (LRO).
Ramsbottom Weavers' Association, letter from D. J. Shackleton, 12 January 1893 (Miss Nora
  Wood, 9 Wood Road, Summerseat, Bury)
Trades Union Congress (TUC), Parliamentary Committee (PC), *Minutes*, 1904–10
Trades Union Congress, *Reports*, 1890–1911.
Weavers' Amalgamation (Northern Counties Amalgamated Weavers' Association), *Minutes*,
  1895–1911 (LRO)

Newspapers

Accrington Advertiser
Accrington Division Gazette

Accrington Observer
Accrington Observer and Times
Accrington Times
Advertiser and Northern Morning News (Accrington)
Alliance News (Manchester)
Blackburn Labour Journal
Blackburn Standard
Blackburn Times
Blackburn Weekly Telegraph
Blackpool Gazette and Herald, Fylde News & Advertiser
Burnley Express and Clitheroe Division Advertiser
Clarion (London)
Colne & Nelson Times
Co-operative News (Manchester)
Cotton Factory Times (Manchester)
Daily Chronicle (London)
Daily Graphic
Daily News (London)
Daily Post (Liverpool)
Darwen Gazette
Darwen News
Darwen Post
Darwen Weekly Advertiser
Evening News (London)
Haslingden Gazette
Haslingden Guardian
Illustrated London News
Justice (London)
Labour Advocate (Blackpool)
Labour Leader (London)
Lancashire Daily Post
Leicester Daily Mercury
Liverpool Courier
Manchester Guardian
Nelson Chronicle
Nelson Leader
New Age (London)
Newcastle Daily Leader
Northern Daily Telegraph (Blackburn)
Norwich Daylight
Pall Mall Gazette (London)
Pearson's Weekly (London)
Pioneer (Leicester)
Preston Guardian
Ramsbottom Observer
Rechabite and Temperance Magazine (Manchester)
Reynolds's Weekly Newspaper (London)
Sheffield Daily Telegraph
Sheffield Independent
Socialist and North-east Lancashire Labour News (Burnley)
Socialist Standard (London)
Sunday Chronicle (Manchester)
Textile Mercury (Manchester)
Times (London)

Times (Clitheroe)
Weekly Standard and Express (Blackburn)
Western Daily Mercury (Plymouth)
Western Evening Herald (Plymouth)
Westminster Gazette
Workers' Tribune (Blackburn)
World (London)
Yorkshire Daily Observer (York)
Yorkshire Factory Times

Personal Papers

Beveridge, Lord (LSE)
Braithwaite, William (LSE)
Broadhurst, Henry (LSE)
Burns, John (British Library)
Campbell-Bannerman, Sir Henry (BL)
Dilke, Sir Charles (BL)
Gladstone, Viscount (Herbert) (BL)
Glasier, J. Bruce (University of Liverpool)
Henderson, Arthur (LPA)
Johnson, Francis (LPA)
MacDonald, J. Ramsay (PRO)
Masterman, Charles and Lucy (University of Birmingham)
Passfield, Lord (LSE)
Scott, C. P. (BL)
Shackleton, Sir David (family)
Shuttleworth, Lord (Leck Hall, Kirkby Lonsdale)
Tuckwell, Gertrude (TUC)
Webb, Beatrice (LSE)

Works by David Shackleton

Hardie, J. Keir, Philip Snowden and David J. Shackleton, *Labour Politics: A Symposium*, ILP,
   Tracts for the Times, No. 2, London, 1903
Shackleton, D. J., 'In the Days of My Youth', *M.A.P.* (Mainly About People), 26 January 1907
Shackleton, D. J., 'Preface' to Tuckwell, Gertrude M. et al., *Women in Industry from Seven Points
   of View*, London, 1908
Shackleton, Sir David, 'Fitter to Govern: What the University Means to Labour', *Northern Daily
   Telegraph*, 20 May 1920

Secondary sources

Unless otherwise indicated, London is the place of publication.

Aaron, Daniel (ed.), *Studies in Biography*, Cambridge, Mass., 1978.
Accrington Town Council, *Accrington and its Industrial Advantages*, Cheltenham, n.d. [1917].
Adamson, John William, *English Education 1789–1902*, Cambridge, 1964.
Altick, Richard D., *The English Common Reader: A Social History of the Mass Reading Public
   1800–1900*, Chicago, 1957.
Anderson, Michael, *Family Structure in Nineteenth Century Lancashire*, Cambridge, 1971.
Arch, Joseph, *The Autobiography of Joseph Arch*, 1966.

Armytage, W. H. G., *Four Hundred Years of English Education*, Cambridge, 1965.
Arnot, R. Page, *The Miners: A History of the Miners' Federation of Great Britain 1889–1910*, 1949.
Askwith, Lord, *Industrial Problems and Disputes*, Brighton, 1974.
Aspin, Christopher, *Haslingden 1800–1900: A History of Haslingden*, 1962.
————— *Lancashire: The First Industrial Society*, Preston, 1969.
Ausubel, Herman, *In Hard Times: Reformers Among the Late Victorians*, New York, 1960.
Barnard, H. C., *A Short History of English Education: From 1760 to 1944*, 1958.
Barnes, G. N., *From Workshop to War Cabinet*, 1924.
————— *History of the International Labour Office*, 1926.
————— *Industrial Conflict*, 1924.
Baron, N. (ed.), *The Co-operative Movement in Labour Britain*, 1948.
Bartrip, Peter, '"Petticoat Pestering": the Women's Trade Union League and Lead Poisoning in the Staffordshire Potteries, 1890–1914', *Historical Studies in Industrial Relations*, vol. 1, September 1996.
Bassett, R., *1931: Political Crisis*, 1958.
Bauman, Zygmunt, *Between Class and Elite: The Evolution of the British Labour Movement: A Sociological Study*, Manchester, 1972.
Bealey, F., 'The Northern Weavers, Independent Labour Representation, and Clitheroe, 1902', *The Manchester School*, vol. 25, January 1957.
Bealey, F. and H. Pelling, *Labour and Politics 1900–1906*, 1958.
Bebbington, D. W., *The Nonconformist Conscience: Chapel and Politics 1870–1914*, 1982.
Beer, M., *A History of British Socialism*, vol. II, 1929.
Bell, S. P. (ed.), *Victorian Lancashire*, Newton Abbott, 1974.
Bellamy, Joyce M., and J. Saville (eds), *Dictionary of Labour Biography*, 1972–1993.
Benenson, Harold, 'The "Family Wage" and Working Women's Consciousness in Britain, 1880–1914', *Politics and Society*, vol. 19, March 1991.
Benn, Caroline, *Keir Hardie*, 1992.
Berlin, Edward A., *Ragtime: A Musical and Cultural History*, Berkeley, 1980.
Beveridge, Lord, *Power and Influence*, New York, 1955.
Beveridge, William H., *British Food Control*, 1928.
Blake, Robert, *The Conservative Party from Peel to Churchill*, 1970.
Blunden, Margaret, *The Countess of Warwick: A Biography*, 1967.
Bondfield, Margaret, *A Life's Work*, 1948.
Boston, Sarah, *Women Workers and the Trade Union Movement*, 1980.
Bottomley, Horatio, *Bottomley's Book*, 1909.
Boyce, George, J. Curran and P. Wingate (eds.), *Newspaper History from the Seventeenth Century to the Present Day*, 1978.
Braithwaite, William J., *Lloyd George's Ambulance Wagon*, 1957.
Brett, Judith, *Robert Menzies' Forgotten People*, Sydney, 1992.
Briggs, Asa, and J. Saville (eds.), *Essays in Labour History 1886–1923*, 1971.
Broad, Lewis, *Winston Churchill: The Years of Preparation*, New York, 1958.
Brown, D., *Labour and Unemployment 1900–1914*, Newton Abbott, 1971.
Brown, E. H. Phelps, *The Growth of British Industrial Relations: A Study from the Standpoint of 1906–14*, 1965.
Brown, K. D. (ed.), *The First Labour Party 1906–1914*, 1985.
————— *John Burns*, 1977.
————— *Labour and Unemployment 1906–14*, Newton Abbott, 1971.
————— 'Nonconformity and the British labour movement', *Journal of Social History*, vol. 8, Winter 1975.
Bullen, Andrew, *The Lancashire Weavers' Union: A Commemorative History*, Manchester, 1984.
Bullock, Alan, *Hitler and Stalin: Parallel Lives*, 1992.
————— *The Life and Times of Ernest Bevin*, vol. I, 1960.
Burn, W. L., *The Age of Equipoise: A Study of the Mid-Victorian Generation*, 1968.

Busbey, Katherine Graves, 'The Women's Trade Union Movement in Great Britain', *Bulletin of the Bureau of Labor*, no. 83, July 1909.

Butler, David and J. Freeman, *British Political Facts 1900–1965*, 2nd ed., 1968.

Butler, H. B., *The Confident Morning*, 1950.

Butt, Ronald, *The Power of Parliament*, 1967.

Chapman, Sydney J., *The Lancashire Cotton Industry: A Study in Economic Development*, Clifton, NJ, 1973.

Cherulnik, Paul D., L. C. Turns and S. K. Wilderman, 'Physical Appearance and Leadership: Exploring the Role of Appearance-Based Attribution in Leader Emergence', *Journal of Applied Psychology*, vol. 20, October 1980.

Church, Richard, *The Golden Sovereign*, 1957.

———— *The Voyage Home*, 1964.

Churchill, Randolph, *Winston Churchill*, vol. II, 1967.

Churchill, Winston, *Liberalism and the Social Problem*, 1909.

Clarke, Peter F., *Lancashire and the New Liberalism*, Cambridge, 1971.

Clegg, Hugh Armstrong, *A History of British Trade Unions Since 1889*, vol. II, Oxford, 1985.

Clegg, H. A., Alan Fox and A. F. Thompson, *The History of British Trade Unions Since 1889*, vol. 1, Oxford, 1964.

Cliff, Tony, and D. Gluckstein, *The Labour Party – A Marxist History*, 1988.

Clynes, J. R., *Memoirs: 1869–1924*, vol. 1, 1937.

Coates, Ken and T. Topham, *The History of the Transport and General Workers' Union*, vol. I, Oxford, 1991.

Cobbett, William, *Advice to Young Men, and (incidentally) to Young Women, in the Middle and Higher Ranks of Life*, 1842.

Cole, G. D. H., *James Keir Hardie*, 1941.

Cole, G. D. H. and R. Postgate, *The Common People 1746–1946*, 1961.

Cole, Margaret, *Makers of the Labour Movement*, 1948.

Connolly, Joseph, *Jerome K. Jerome: A Critical Biography*, 1982.

Craik, William W., *The Central Labour College 1909–29*, 1964.

Cranfield, G. A., *The Development of the Provincial Newspaper 1700–1760*, 1962.

Cruickshank, Marjorie, *Church and State in English Education: 1870 to the Present Day*, 1963.

Cupples, Anne Jane, *Hugh Wellwood's Success; or, Where There's a Will There's a Way*, 1869.

Daalder, Hans, *Cabinet Reform in Britain 1914–1963*, Stanford, 1963.

Dangerfield, George, *The Strange Death of Liberal England*, 1966.

Davies, A. F., *Essays in Political Sociology*, Melbourne, 1972.

———— *Skills, Outlooks and Passions: A Psychoanalytic Contribution to the Study of Politics*, Cambridge, 1980.

Davies, Clarice S., *North Country Bred: A Working-class Family Chronicle*, 1963.

Dibblee, George Binney, *The Newspaper*, 1913.

Druker, Janet, 'Women's History and Trade Union Records', *Bulletin*, Society for the Study of Labour History, no. 36, Spring 1978.

Dunleavy, John, 'Debates and Dancing', *Pennine Magazine*, vol. 4, February 1983.

———— 'Decline and Fall', *Pennine Magazine*, vol. 4, March 1983.

Edwards, George, *From Crow-Scaring to Westminster: An Autobiography*, 1922.

Edwards, Maldwyn, *Methodism and England: A Study of Methodism in its Social and Political Aspects during the Period 1850–1932*, 1943.

Ehrman, John, *Cabinet Government and War 1890–1940*, Cambridge, 1958.

Elliott, Gregory, *Labourism and the English Genius: The Strange Death of Labour England?* 1993.

Ellison, Mary, *Support for Secession: Lancashire and the American Civil War*, Chicago, 1972.

Elton, Lord, *The Life of James Ramsay MacDonald (1866–1919)*, 1939.

Eyre, Kathleen, *Lancashire Landmarks*, Clapham, North Yorkshire, 1976.

Finer, Herman, *The British Civil Service*, 1937.

Flanders, Allan, *Management and Unions: The Theory and Reform of Industrial Relations*, 1975.

Foote, Geoffrey, *The Labour Party's Political Thought: A History*, 1985.

Fowler, Alan and Lesley, *The History of the Nelson Weavers' Association*, Nelson, Lancs., n.d.

Fulcher, James, *Labour Movements, Employers and the State: Conflict and Cooperation in Britain and Sweden*, Oxford, 1991.

Geary, Dick (ed.), *Labour and Socialist Movements in Europe before 1914*, Oxford, 1989.

Geipel, John, *The Cartoon: A Short History of Graphic Comedy and Satire*, Newton Abbott, 1972.

Gilbert, Bentley B., *The Evolution of National Insurance in Great Britain: The Origins of the Welfare State*, 1966.

Gilbert, Martin, *Churchill: A Life*, 1991.

Golby, J. M. and A. W. Purdue, *The Civilisation of the Crowd: Popular Culture in England 1750–1900*, 1984.

Graetz, Heinrich, *History of the Jews*, vol. 1, Philadephia, 1974.

Grainger, J. H., *Character and Style in English Politics*, Cambridge, 1969.

Green, Martin (ed.), *The Other Jerome K. Jerome*, 1984.

Greene, Julia, '"The Strike at the Ballot Box": The American Federation of Labor's Entrance into Election Politics, 1906–1909', *Labor History*, vol. 32, Spring 1991.

Greenslade, S. L., *The Church and the Social Order*, 1948.

Halévy, Elie, *Imperialism and the Rise of Labour*, 1961.

————— *The Rule of Democracy, 1905–1914* (Books I and II), 1961.

Halsey, A. H., *Change in British Society*, Oxford, 1986.

Hamilton, Mary Agnes, *Arthur Henderson: A Biography*, 1938.

————— *Margaret Bondfield*, 1924.

Hammond, J. L., *C. P. Scott of the Manchester Guardian*, 1934.

Hankey, Lord, *Government Control in War*, Cambridge, 1945.

Harris, José, *William Beveridge: A Biography*, Oxford, 1977.

Harrison, Royden, 'Labour Party History: Approaches and Interpretations', *Labour History Review*, vol. 56, Spring 1991.

Haw, George, *From Workhouse to Westminster: The Life Story of Will Crooks, M.P.*, 1911.

Henderson, W. O., *The Lancashire Cotton Famine 1861–1865*, New York, 1969.

Hewitt, Margaret, *Wives and Mothers in Victorian Industry*, Westport, Conn., 1958.

Hikins, H. R., 'The Liverpool General Transport Strike, 1911', *Transactions of the Historic Society of Lancashire and Cheshire*, vol. 113, September 1961.

Hinton, James, *Labour and Socialism: A History of the British Labour Movement, 1867–1974*, Brighton, 1983.

History of the Ministry of Munitions, 12 vols., 1920–22.

Hobsbawm, E. J., *Labouring Men: Studies in the History of Labour*, 1964.

————— *Uncommon People: Resistance, Rebellion and Jazz*, 1998

————— *Worlds of Labour: Further Studies in the History of Labour*, 1984.

Hobson, S. G. (ed. A. R. Orage), *National Guilds*, 1914.

————— *National Guilds and the State*, 1920.

Hodge, John, *Workman's Cottage to Windsor Castle*, n.d.

Hoggart, Richard, *The Uses of Literacy*, 1957.

Hopwood, Edwin, *A History of the Lancashire Cotton Industry and the Amalgamated Weavers' Association*, Manchester, 1969.

Howell, David, *British Workers and the Independent Labour Party, 1888–1906*, Manchester, 1983.

————— *The Politics of the NUM: A Lancashire View*, Manchester, 1989.

Howell, George, *Labour Legislation, Labour Movements, and Labour Leaders*, 1902.

Hughes, Emrys, *Keir Hardie*, 1956.

————— *Keir Hardie's Speeches and Writings*, Glasgow [1927?].

Hyndman, Henry Mayers, *Further Reminiscences*, 1912.

Inglis, K. S., *Churches and the Working Classes in Victorian England*, 1963.

Irving, Terry, 'Labourism: A Political Genealogy', *Labour History*, no. 66, May 1994.

James, David, Tony Jowitt and Keith Laybourn (eds.), *The Centennial History of the Independent Labour Party*, Halifax, 1992.

James, Robert Rhodes, *Churchill: A Study in Failure 1900–1939*, 1970.

Jenkins, Edwin A., *From Foundry to Foreign Office: The Romantic Life-Story of the Rt. Hon. Arthur Henderson*, 1933.
Jenkins, Roy, *Asquith*, 1964.
———— *Sir Charles Dilke: A Victorian Tragedy*, 1968.
Jessop, Bob, *Traditionalism, Conservatism and British Political Culture*, 1974.
Jones, Peter d'A., *The Christian Socialist Revival 1877–1914*, Princeton, 1968.
Jones, Thomas, *Whitehall Diary*, vol. II, 1969.
Jowitt, J. A. and A. J. McIvor (eds.), *Employers and Labour in the English Textile Industries, 1850–1939*, 1988.
Joyce, Patrick, *Visions of the People: Industrial England and the Question of Class 1848–1914*, 1991.
———— *Work, Society and Politics: The Culture of the Factory in Later Victorian England*, Brighton, 1980.
Kent, William, *John Burns: Labour's Lost Leader*, 1950.
Keynes, J. M., *Essays in Biography*, 1961.
King, J. E., '"We Could Eat the Police!": Popular Violence in the North Lancashire Cotton Strike of 1878', *Victorian Studies*, vol. 28, Spring 1985.
Kirk, Neville, 'Cotton Workers and Deference', *Bulletin*, Society for the Study of Labour History, No. 42, Spring 1981.
Laybourn, Keith, *Philip Snowden: A Biography 1864–1937*, Aldershot, 1988.
———— 'The Rise of Labour and the Decline of Liberalism: the State of the Debate', *History*, vol. 80, June 1995.
Laybourn, Keith and Jack Reynolds, *Liberalism and the Rise of Labour, 1890–1918*, 1984.
Leventhal, F. M., *Arthur Henderson*, Manchester, 1989.
———— *Respectable Radical*, 1971.
Lewenhak, Sheila, *Women and Trade Unions: An Outline History of Women in the British Trade Union Movement*, 1977.
Liddington, Jill and Jill Norris, *One Hand Tied Behind Us: The Rise of the Women's Suffrage Movement*, 1978.
Lloyd, Trevor, *The General Election of 1880*, Oxford, 1968.
Lowe, Rodney, *Adjusting to Democracy: The Role of the Ministry of Labour in British Politics 1916–1939*, Oxford, 1986.
———— 'The Erosion of State Intervention in Britain, 1917–24', *Economic History Review*, vol. 31, May 1978.
———— 'The Failure of Consensus in Britain: The National Industrial Conference, 1919–1921', *Historical Journal*, vol. 21, no. 3, 1978.
———— 'The Government and Industrial Relations, 1919–39', in Chris Wrigley (ed.), *A History of British Industrial Relations, 1914–1939*, vol. II, Brighton, 1987.
———— 'The Ministry of Labour, 1916–1924: A Graveyard of Social Reform?', *Public Administration*, vol. 52, Winter 1974.
———— 'The Ministry of Labour, 1916–19: A Still, Small Voice', in Burk, K. (ed.), *War and the State: The Transformation of British Government 1914–1919*, 1982.
———— 'Review Article', *British Journal of Industrial Relations*, vol. 13, no. 1, 1975.
Maccoby, S., *English Radicalism, 1853–1886*, 1938.
McCord, Norman, 'Taff Vale Revisited', *History*, vol. 78, June 1993.
McKenzie, R. T., *British Political Parties: The Distribution of Power within the Conservative and Labour Parties*, 1955.
McKenzie, Robert and A. Silver, *Angels in Marble: Working Class Conservatives in Urban England*, 1968.
McKibbin, R. I., 'Arthur Henderson as Labour Leader', *International Review of Social History*, vol. 23 (Pt.1), 1978.
———— *The Evolution of the Labour Party 1910–1924*, Oxford, 1974.
———— *The Ideologies of Class: Social Relations in Britain 1880–1950*, Oxford, 1990.
———— 'James Ramsay MacDonald and the Problem of the Independence of the Labour Party', *Journal of Modern History*, vol. 42, June 1970.

Mackintosh, John P., *The British Cabinet*, 1962.

McLean, Iain, *Keir Hardie*, New York, 1975.

Mann, Tom, *Tom Mann's Memoirs*, 1923.

Mansbridge, Albert, *An Adventure in Working-Class Education: Being the Story of the Workers' Educational Association 1903–1915*, 1920.

———— *University Tutorial Classes*, 1913.

Marquand, David, *Ramsay MacDonald*, 1977.

Marshall, J. D., *Lancashire*, Newton Abbot, 1974.

Martin, David E., 'Shackleton, Sir David James', in Joyce M. Bellamy and John Saville (eds.), *Dictionary of Labour Biography*, vol. II, 1974.

Martin, David E. and D. Rubenstein (eds.), *Ideology and the Labour Movement: Essays Presented to John Saville*, 1979.

Martin, Ross M., *Trade Unionism: Purposes and Forms*, Oxford, 1989.

———— *TUC: The Growth of a Pressure Group, 1868–1976*, Oxford, 1980.

Michels, Robert, *Political Parties: A Sociological Study of the Oligarchical Tendencies of Modern Democracy*, Glencoe, Ill., 1958.

Miliband, Ralph, *Parliamentary Socialism: A Study in the Politics of Labour*, 1961.

Miller, Harold, *Growing Up with Primitive Methodism*, Sheffield, Methodist Chapel Aid Lecture, No. 5, 1995.

Minkin, Lewis, *The Contentious Alliance: Trade Unions and the Labour Party*, Edinburgh, 1991.

Mitchell, W. R., *Life in the Lancashire Mill Towns*, Clapham, North Yorkshire, 1982.

Mommsen, Wolfgang J. and H. G. Husung (eds.), *The Development of Trade Unionism in Great Britain and Germany 1880–1914*, 1985.

Moody, T. W., *Davitt and the Irish Revolution 1846–82*, Oxford, 1981.

Moore, Roger, *The Emergence of the Labour Party, 1880–1924*, 1978.

Morgan, Austen, *J. Ramsay MacDonald*, Manchester, 1987.

Morgan, Kenneth O., *Keir Hardie: Radical and Socialist*, 1975.

———— *Labour People: Leaders and Lieutenants, Hardie to Kinnock*, Oxford, 1987.

Morison, S., *The English Newspaper, 1622–1932*, Cambridge, 1932.

Muller, William, *The 'Kept Men'? The First Century of Trade Union Representation in the British House of Commons, 1874–1975*, Hassocks, Sussex, 1977.

Murphy, J. T., *Modern Trade Unionism: A Study of the Present Tendencies and the Future of Trade Unions in Britain*, 1935.

Nordlinger, Eric A., *The Working-Class Tories*, 1967.

Norman, F. A., *From Whitehall to the West Indies*, 1952.

Nowell-Smith, S. (ed.), *Edwardian England, 1901–1914*, 1964.

O'Connor, T. P., *Sir Henry Campbell-Bannerman*, 1908.

O'Neil, John, *The Journals of a Lancashire Weaver: 1856–60, 1860–64, 1872–5* (ed. Mary Brigg), The Record Society of Lancashire and Cheshire, vol. CXXII, 1982.

Oxford and Asquith, Earl of, *Memories and Reflections, 1852–1927*, 2 vols., 1928.

Parry, Keith, *Resorts of the Lancashire Coast*, Newton Abbott, 1982.

Payne, Elizabeth Anne, *Reform, Labor, and Feminism: Margaret Draier Robins and the Women's Trade Union League*, Urbana, Ill., 1988.

Pelling, Henry, *A History of British Trade Unionism*, 1963.

———— *The Origins of the Labour Party 1880–1900*, 1954.

———— *Popular Politics and Society in Late Victorian Britain*, 1968.

———— *A Short History of the Labour Party*, 1962.

———— *Winston Churchill*, 1974.

Penn, Roger, *Skilled Workers in the Class Structure*, Cambridge, 1984.

Perkin, Harold, *The Origins of Modern English Society, 1780–1880*, 1969.

———— *The Rise of Professional Society: England since 1880*, 1989.

Pevsner, Nikolaus, *The Buildings of England: Lancashire: The Rural North*, Harmondsworth, 1969.

Phillips, Laura L., 'Message in a Bottle: Working-Class Culture and the Struggle for Revolutionary Legitimacy, 1900–1929', *Russian Review*, vol. 56, January 1997.

Poirier, Philip P., *The Advent of the Labour Party*, 1958.

Pomfret, Joseph, *Borough of Darwen 1878–1928, The Fiftieth Anniversary of the Incorporation of the Borough: Official Souvenir*, Darwen, 1928.

Price, Richard, 'The Future of British Labour History', *International Review of Social History*, vol. 36, 1991.

————— *Labour in British Society: An Interpretative History*, 1986.

Radice, Giles and Lisanne Radice, *Will Thorne, Constructive Militant: A Study in New Unionism and New Politics*, 1974.

Read, Donald (ed.), *Edwardian England*, 1982.

Reed, Michael, *The Landscape of Britain: From the Beginnings to 1914*, 1990.

Rintala, Marvin, 'Taking the Pledge: H. H. Asquith and Drink', *Biography*, vol. 16, Spring 1993.

Roberts, B. C., *The Trades Union Congress, 1868–1921*, 1958.

Roberts, Robert, *The Classic Slum: Salford Life in the First Quarter of the Century*, Manchester, 1971.

Rose, Jonathan, 'Willingly to School: The Working-class Response to Elementary Education in Britain, 1875–1918', *Journal of British Studies*, vol. 32, April 1993.

————— 'The Workers in the Workers' Educational Association', *Albion*, vol. 21, Winter 1989.

Rose, Sonya O., 'Gender and Labor History: The Nineteenth Century Legacy', *International Review of Social History*, vol. 38 (Supp.), 1993.

Roskill, Stephen, *Hankey: Man of Secrets*, vol. I (1877–1918), 1970.

Ross, Stephen, *Asquith*, 1976.

Routh, Guy, *Occupation and Pay in Great Britain 1906–79*, 1980.

Rowell, George, *The Victorian Theatre 1792–1914: A Survey*, Cambridge, 1978.

Rule, John, *The Labouring Classes in Early Industrial England, 1750–1850*, 1986.

St Joseph's Catholic Church, Ramsbottom, *History of the Parish 1862–1962*, Bury, 1963.

Saville, John, 'The Ideology of Labourism', in Robert Benewick et al. (eds.), *Knowledge and Belief in Politics: The Problem of Ideology*, 1973.

————— 'Notes on Ideology and the Miners before World War I', *Bulletin*, Society for the Study of Labour History, no. 23, Autumn 1971.

————— 'The Trade Disputes Act of 1906', *Historical Studies in Industrial Relations*, vol. 1, March 1996.

Schafer, William J. and J. Riedel, *The Art of Ragtime: Form and Meaning of an Original Black American Art*, Baton Rouge, 1973.

Schneer, Jonathan, *Ben Tillett: Portrait of a Labour Leader*, 1982.

Sellers, Ian, *Nineteenth-Century Nonconformity*, 1977.

Sexton, James, *Sir James Sexton Agitator: The Life of the Dockers' M.P.: An Autobiography*, 1936.

Sheldrake, John, *Industrial Relations and Politics in Britain 1880–1989*, 1991.

Sigsworth, Eric M. (ed.), *In Search of Victorian Values: Aspects of Nineteenth-century Thought and Society*, Manchester, 1988.

Simon, Brian, *Education and the Labour Movement, 1870–1920*, 1974.

Singleton, John, *Lancashire on the Scrapheap: The Cotton Industry 1945–1970*, Oxford, 1991.

Skidelsky, Robert, *John Maynard Keynes*, vol. I, 1992.

Snell, Lord, *Men, Movements and Myself*, 1936.

Snowden, Viscount, *An Autobiography*, vol. I, 1934.

Soldon, Norbert C., *Women in British Trade Unions 1874–1976*, Dublin, 1978.

————— (ed.), *The World of Women's Trade Unionism: Comparative Historical Essays*, Westport, Conn., 1985.

Spender, J. A. and C. Asquith, *Life of Herbert Henry Asquith, Lord Oxford and Asquith*, vol. I, 1932.

Stead, W. T., 'The Labour Party and the Books that Helped to Make It', *Review of Reviews*, vol. 33, June 1906.

Stocks, Mary D. B., *The Workers' Educational Association: The First Fifty Years*, 1953.

Stogdill, Ralph M., 'Personal Factors Associated with Leadership: A Survey of the Literature', *Journal of Psychology*, vol. 25, 1948.

Symons, Julian, *Horatio Bottomley*, 1955.

Tanner, Duncan, *Political Change and the Labour Party, 1900–1918*, Cambridge, 1990.

Tax, Meredith, *The Rising of the Women: Feminist Solidarity and Class Conflict, 1880–1917*, New York, 1980.

Taylor, H. (ed.), *Ramsbottom, Lancashire: The Official Guide*, Cheltenham, n.d. [1934].

Thomas, J. H., *My Story*, 1937.

Thompson, F. M. L. (ed.), *The Cambridge Social History of Britain 1750–1950*, vols. 1 and 3, Cambridge, 1990.

Thompson, Lawrence, *The Enthusiasts: A Biography of John and Katherine Bruce Glasier*, 1971.

———— *Robert Blatchford: Portrait of an Englishman*, 1951.

Thorne, Will, *My Life's Battles*, 1989.

Tracey, Herbert (ed.), *The Book of the Labour Party*, 3 vols., 1925.

Tsuzuki, Chushichi, *Tom Mann, 1856–1941: The Challenges of Labour*, Oxford, 1991.

Tuchman, Barbara W., *Practising History*, 1983.

———— *The Proud Tower: A Portrait of the World Before the War 1890–1914*, New York, 1962.

Turner, Ben, *About Myself, 1863–1930*, 1930.

Turner, H. A, *Trade Union Growth, Structure and Policy: A Comparative Study of the Cotton Unions in England*, 1962.

Tyler, Paul, 'The Origins of Labour Representation in Woolwich', *Labour History Review*, vol. 59, Spring 1994.

Vincent, David, *Bread, Knowledge and Freedom: A Study of Nineteenth-Century Working Class Autobiography*, 1981.

———— *Literacy and Popular Culture*, Cambridge, 1989.

Waites, Bernard, *A Class Society at War: England 1914–1918*, Oxford, 1987.

———— 'Popular Culture in Late Nineteenth and Early Twentieth Century Lancashire', in Open University, *The Historical Development of Popular Culture in Britain (1)*, Milton Keynes, 1981.

Walter, James, *The Leader: A Political Biography of Gough Whitlam*, St Lucia, Queensland, 1980.

Walton, John K., *Lancashire: A Social History, 1558–1939*, Manchester, 1987.

Ward, Stephen R., *James Ramsay MacDonald: Low Born Among the High Brows*, New York, 1990.

Warwick, Countess of, *Afterthoughts*, 1931.

———— *Life's Ebb and Flow*, 1929.

Waterhouse, Richard, *From Minstrel Show to Vaudeville: The Australian Popular Stage 1788–1914*, Kensington, NSW, 1990.

Watson, Aaron, *A Great Labour Leader: Thomas Burt, M.P.*, 1908.

Watts, John, *The Facts of the Cotton Famine*, 1866.

Wearmouth, R. F., *Methodism and the Struggle of the Working Classes 1850–1900*, Leicester, 1954.

Webb, Sidney and Beatrice, *The History of Trade Unionism*, 1920.

———— *Industrial Democracy*, 1902.

Weiler, Peter, *Ernest Bevin*, Manchester, 1993.

Wertheimer, Egon, *Portrait of the Labour Party*, 1929.

White, Joseph L., 'Lancashire Cotton Textiles', in Chris Wrigley (ed.), *A History of British Industrial Relations 1875–1914*, Brighton, 1982.

———— *The Limits of Trade Union Militancy: The Lancashire Textile Workers, 1910–1914*, Westport, Conn., 1978.

Williams, Keith, *The English Newspaper*, 1977.

Williams, Philip, *Hugh Gaitskell: A Political Biography*, 1979.

Williams, Raymond, *The Long Revolution*, New York, 1961.

Wilson, Horace, 'Shackleton, Sir David James', in *Dictionary of National Biography: 1931–1940*, 1949.

Wilson, John, *CB: A Life of Sir Henry Campbell-Bannerman*, 1973.

Wilson, Trevor, *The Downfall of the Liberal Party 1914–1935*, 1966.

———— (ed.), *The Political Diaries of C.P. Scott 1911–1928*, 1970.

Winter, Jay (ed.), *The Working Class in Modern British History: Essays in Honour of Henry Pelling*, Cambridge, 1983.

Wrigley, C. J., *Arthur Henderson*, Cardiff, 1990.
———— *David Lloyd George and the British Labour Movement: Peace and War*, Hassocks, 1976.
———— *A History of British Industrial Relations*, Brighton, 1982.
Yorke, Paul, *Ruskin College, 1899–1909*, Oxford, 1977.

Index

National Health Insurance Commission
119–21, 125, 166, 170, 198
see also social insurance
National Industrial Conference 189
nationalization *see* socialization
National Patriotic Fund Committee 52
Neil, T. 120n.
Nelson, A. 97
Nelson Leader 70n., 73, 96, 108, 110n.,
132, 159n., 192
Nelson Overlookers' Association 44n.
Nelson Textile Trades Federation 35
Nelson Town Council 97
Nelson Weavers' Association 23n., 25n.,
28, 30n., 35, 41, 49n.
Newall, A. B. 33–5, 37n., 41, 43, 45n.,
50n., 53
'Newcastle Resolution', the 52, 57
non-conformism 173, 187
see also Methodism
Norman, F. A. 192
North-east Lancashire Amalgamated
Weavers' Association 22
Northern Counties Amalgamated
Associations of Weavers *see*
Weavers' Amalgamation
Northern Counties Amalgamated
Weavers' Association *see* Weavers'
Amalgamation
Northern Counties Central Weavers'
Committee *see* Weavers'
Amalgamation
Northern Daily Telegraph 70n., 108
Northern Education League 66
Northrup loom 24, 89n.
Nuffield College 191

O'Connor, T. P. 119n.
old-age pensions 42, 80, 84–5, 92n., 104,
176
Oldham weavers 114n.
Ormerod, D. 45n.
Osborne judgement 100n., 102–4, 107n.,
112, 153, 154n., 182n., 191n.
'overlapping' 85–6, 90, 99, 184
Oxford University 115–16, 188

Padiham Trades Council 35
Padiham Weavers' Association 35

Pall Mall Gazette 60, 101
Palmer, Absalom 141
Pankhurst, Emmeline 42–3, 100
Parker, D. 51
Parkington, John 48
Parliament *see* House of Commons;
House of Lords
Parliamentary Committee *see* Trades
Union Congress
parliamentary Labour party *see* Labour
party
payment of MPs 42, 111n., 112n.
see also salary
peace 179, 186
Pearson, Hesketh 164, 191
Pease, Edward 70n.
Pelling, H. 62n., 70n., 184n.
permanent secretary *see* civil service,
appointments
Phillips, Morgan 58n.
Pickard, Ben 50n.
'pledge', the 53–4, 57, 184
political action 3, 41n., 102–3, 181–4
direct representation 24–7, 29, 30n.,
35, 36n., 43–4, 47, 49
independence
of the Conservative and Liberal
parties 36n., 43–4, 52–6, 61, 183
of the Labour party 184
see also industrial action
Pretoria pit explosion 118
Primitive Methodism *see* Methodism
profit–sharing 179
protection *see* free trade
Protestants 42n.
see also Christian social thought

Quelch, Harry 153

Radicals *see* Liberal party/Liberals
Radio Times 145
Railways Clerks' Association 189
Railway Executive 124
Ramsbottom Trades Council 25
Ramsbottom Weavers' Association 16,
19, 21–3, 49n., 129, 180
Rechabites, Independent Order of 14,
64, 133, 139, 143–4, 159, 184n.
see also friendly societies